"A knowledgeable and whony absorbing elegy."—*Time*

"A somber and moving account . . . Matthiessen's passionate concern for these ordinary lives renders them extraordinary and universal."—*Dallas Morning News*

"Matthiessen . . . has written about the fishermen of New England with the same reverence for human dignity and capacity to capture the cadence of spoken language that was James Agee's gift."—*Atlanta Journal-Constitution*

"Peter Matthiessen has an uncanny ability to capture the moods of nature, the essence of place, and the everyday drama of human life."—*Philadelphia Inquirer*

"Matthiessen has brilliantly recorded a way of life that is unlikely to survive much longer."—*Atlantic Monthly*

"This is a book that makes you first pity the victims of human shortsightedness and then rage against the arrogance of those who are responsible. Still, if these sturdy and self-reliant men had to pass on, it is good that they had Peter Matthiessen to write their elegy."—*Playboy*

"A stirring human drama unfolds in this latest book by one of the most important writers of our age."—*Houston Post*

"Passionate, descriptive, moving."—*Milwaukee Journal*

"Excellently done."—*Chattanooga Times*

"Matthiessen writes with evocative lyricism about a vanishing breed of fisherfolk who cling steadfastly to the hardscrabble ways of their forefathers."—*San Francisco Examiner*

# PETER MATTHIESSEN

# MEN'S LIVES

VINTAGE BOOKS

A DIVISION OF RANDOM HOUSE     NEW YORK

*It's not fish ye're buyin, it's men's lives.*
Sir Walter Scott

All rights reserved under International and Pan-American Copyright Conventions. Published in the United States by Random House, Inc., New York, and simultaneously in Canada by Random House of Canada Limited, Toronto. Originally published, in hardcover, by Random House, Inc., in 1986.

Library of Congress Cataloging-in-Publication Data
Matthiessen, Peter.
Men's lives.
1. Fishers—New York (State)—Long Island—History. 2. Seining—New York (State)—Long Island—History. 3. Long Island (N.Y.)—History. I. Title.
[HD8039.F66U5   1988]
338.3'72709747'21   87-40095
ISBN 0-394-75560-X (pbk.)

Book design by Marysarah Quinn

Manufactured in the United States of America

# CONTENTS

# ACKNOWLEDGMENTS

This book owes its existence to Adelaide de Menil, whose friendship with the fishermen brought to life an idea put forward by fisherman-photographer Doug Kuntz.

Quotations from Elisha Ammon, Carol Havens, Robert Vetault, Jenny Syvertsen, Sally Lafoe, Ruth Lester, and John Wood come from interviews (now part of the archives of the East Hampton Town Marine Museum) by John Eilertsen. These voluminous transcripts, indexed and annotated by Hortense Carpentier, are now accessible to future generations. Fishing and historical articles in the *East Hampton Star* by Susan Pollack and others (see Notes) proved extremely valuable. Researcher Anne Witty, librarian Dorothy King, and the staff of the *East Hampton Star* suggested and furnished useful documents. Baymen's Association Secretary Arnold Leo supplied data on striped bass legislation, and Carleton Kelsey furnished certain points of historical information.

My warm thanks to such friends and old fishing associates as Bill Lester, Milt Miller, William Havens, Stewart Lester, and Richard Lester for patient, generous help in putting together this account of the lives and history of the baymen. Thanks are due also to Brent, Walter, and Wally

Bennett; Donnie Eames; Jack Edwards; Johnnie Erickson; Ann, Ben, and Billy Havens; Lindy Havens; Danny King; Doug Kuntz; Calvin Lester; Francis and Jens Lester; Jimmy Lester; Lottie Lester; Gail and Madge Lester; Tom and Cathy Lester; Mickey Miller; Stuart Vorpahl, Jr.; Sandy Vorpahl; and Jarvis Wood. All made significant contributions; most checked the text for accuracy; none is responsible for any errors that may remain.

The book's emphasis upon ocean haul-seining and the haul-seining families inevitably excluded some of the best fishermen on the East End. I extend sincere regrets to the many baymen, past and present, whose names do not appear. Like a good boat or a good net, a story that works must be well made, and a confusing number of names and characters would only do damage to a book intended to honor every bayman, whether his name appears in the text or not.

SAGAPONACK, NEW YORK
*May 1985*

# PREFACE

T wo humpback whales, the first I have seen in a decade, roll softly on the surface, like black shining rocks in the silver ocean. Great whales were once so common off the coast at this far east end of Long Island that shore whaling was an industry, but I have seen them from the shore only a few times in my life, and, feeling elated, walk with them along the beach a little way. They move slowly to the east, off the narrow strip of sand that separates Georgica Pond from the Atlantic.

The wind is out of the northwest, and the day is cold, but already the sea breathes its sweet stink of regeneration. The great animals spout thinly in the cold clear light, and the wind fans the spume to mist on the huge horizon.

A few years ago, on another day of spring, a Sagaponack neighbor brought a fish into my yard that had turned up in the nets early that morning. For several years I had hauled seine with the beach crews, and this farmer-fisherman had done so for much longer, and neither of us had ever seen this beautiful silver fish, ten pounds or better, that he held before him with both hands in instinctive ceremony.

I turned toward the house to fetch my book of fishes,[1] then turned back, grinning. It was not the arrangement of the fins that told me what it was but a pang of intuition. Perhaps this rare fish from the cold Atlantic was on its way to the ancient mouth of the Connecticut River, which fifteen thousand years ago (before the melting glaciers raised the level of the seas, separating Long Island from the southern New England coast) was located at what is now Plum Gut, off the North Fork of this great fish-tailed island. Like the great whales, the Atlantic salmon—once so abundant in the fresh clear rivers that the Massachusetts colonists were forbidden to feed it to indentured servants more than once a week—had been reduced to these wandering survivors, to be wondered at in the cold spring sun like emblems of a New World prematurely old.

This book is witness to the lives of the commercial fishermen of the South Fork of Long Island. The inshore fisheries with which it will concern itself fall into five divisions—netting, trapping, dragging, shellfishing, and setting pots. A full-time fisherman, or bayman, might participate in most of these activities in a single year. Those with large work boats of thirty-foot or better may devote themselves to dragging all year long, adapting their boats in certain seasons to lobstering, or setting cod trawls, or long-lining for tilefish, swordfish, tuna. Because a big boat with high fuel costs and overhead must be kept working, such men rarely fish inshore, and are not baymen. However, many baymen crew on draggers in the wintertime, and many draggermen return to the bay as they grow older.

Full-time baymen—there are scarcely one hundred left on the South Fork—must also be competent boatmen, net men, carpenters, and mechanics, and most could make good money at a trade, but they value independence over security, preferring to work on their own schedule, responsible only to their own families. Protective of their freedom to the point of stubbornness, wishing only to be left alone, they have never asked for and never received direct subsidies from town or county, state or federal government.[2]

Being self-employed, they receive none of the modern social supports such as unemployment insurance and sickness compensation, and because their income is uncertain and irregular, they can rarely obtain bank loans and mortgages. Yet every year they find themselves taxed harder for boats and trailers, trucks and gasoline, shellfish digging and fish shipping licenses, docking license, scallop opening license, permits to take certain species (shellfish, lobster, striped bass). Nearly a dozen taxes, permits, and licenses plague every bayman ready to engage in the various fisheries according to seasonal availability and market demand, as the inshore fisherman must do if he is to earn his living all year round.

Meanwhile his livelihood is threatened by powerful sportsmen's organizations seeking to limit the commercial harvest of so-called game fish, in particular the striped bass, a species that, for most commercial men of the South Fork, represents the difference between bare survival and a decent living. For the past half century, the sportsmen's crusades to reserve this fish for their own use were defeated by the bass itself, which seemed to grow more plentiful each year. Then, in the seventies, the species suffered a serious decline, apparently the result of cumulative pollution of its main spawning grounds in the tributaries of the Chesapeake Bay. In New York State in 1983 the angler's organizations, supported by federal agencies, succeeded in promoting legislation that drastically curtailed the striped bass harvest by commercial fishermen and threatened the very survival of their way of life.

Among South Fork fisheries, the one most imperiled by bass legislation is ocean haul-seining, which no longer exists anywhere else in the United States except on the Outer Banks of North Carolina. Because their fishery will be the first to disappear, Long Island's ocean haul-seiners are the main subject of this book. In haul-seining, a net-filled dory is launched through the open surf, an enterprise that, on a rough Atlantic day, demands nerve and experience as well as skill. Without the striped bass, haul-seining is unlikely to survive, and the end of this fishery will mean the end of a surfboat tradition that began when the Atlantic coast was still the American frontier.

Most of the surfmen come from the main fishing clans, which descend from the farmer-fishermen and the offshore whalers of centuries ago. In recent decades, most fishing families have been forced to sell off land that had been in the family for generations. Those who are left subsist in the last poor corners of a community in which they were once the leading citizens. Meanwhile their townsmen, prospering on the bland resort economy, have mainly lost a historical sense of the ocean character of the South Fork that attracted so many wealthy visitors in the first place. Few of the few who are even aware that a fishing community still exists enjoy the continuity with the past represented by boat-filled backyards in the oak woods of Amagansett and the Springs, by sharpies and scallop dredges, flag buoys and fish traps, by a dory in black silhouette on the huge empty sky off the ocean beach.

Here within sight of the blue shadow of New England's industrial seaboard ten miles to the north, moving at daybreak on back roads, the fishermen go their traditional way down to the sea. They are tough, resourceful, self-respecting, and also (some say) hidebound and cranky, too independent to organize for their own survival. Yet even their critics must acknowledge a gritty spirit that was once more highly valued in this country than it is today. Because their children can no longer afford to live where their families have harvested the sea and land for three hundred years, these South Fork baymen—old-time Americans who still speak with the Kentish and Dorset inflections of Elizabethan England—may soon become rare relics from the past, like the Atlantic right whales, a cow and calf, that in the winter of 1984–1985 have been appearing here and there off the ocean beach.

On December 4, 1984, finishing the first draft of these journals, I walked down to the ocean for a breath of air. The day was cold, with a northwest wind shivering the rainwater where ice was broken in the puddles. Rising and falling in flight along the dunes, a flock of gulls picked up the last ambient light from the red embers in the west. The silent birds, undulating on the wind, shone bone white against massed somber grays, low over the ocean; the cloud bank looked ominous, like waiting winter.

From the beach landing, in this moody sky and twilight, I saw something awash in the white foam, perhaps a quarter mile down to the eastward. The low heavy thing, curved round upon itself, did not look like driftwood; I thought at first that it must be a human body. Uneasy, I walked east a little way, then hurried ahead; the thing was not driftwood, not a body, but the great clean skull of a finback whale,[3] dark bronze with sea water and minerals. The beautiful form, crouched like some ancient armored creature in the wash, seemed to await me. No one else was on the beach, which was clean of tracks. There was only the last cold fire of dusk, the white birds fleeing toward the darkness, the frosty foam whirling around the skull, seeking to regather it into the deeps.

By the time I returned with a truck and chain, it was nearly night. The sea was higher, and the skull was settling like some enormous crab into the wash; I could not get close enough without sinking the truck down to the axles. I took careful bearings on the skull's location, and a good thing, too, because four hours later, when the tide had turned, the massive skull had sunk away into the sands, all but what looked like a small dark rock in the moon-white shallows. I dug this out enough to secure a hawser, then ran this rope above the tide line, as a lead to the skull's location the next morning. But fearing that an onshore wind or storm might bury it forever, I went down at dead low tide that night, under the moon, and dug the skull clear and worked it up out of its pit, using truck and chain. Nearly six feet across, the skull was waterlogged and heavy, five hundred pounds or better. Not until one in the morning—spending more time digging out my truck than freeing the bone—did I hitch it high enough onto the beach to feel confident that the tide already coming in would not rebury it. By morning there was onshore wind, with a chop already making up from the southwest, but the whale skull was still waiting at the water's edge. Bud Topping came down with his tractor and we took it home. When Milt Miller, who was raised by the old whalers, had a look at it a few weeks later, he said it was the biggest skull he ever saw.

SAGAPONACK, NEW YORK
*May 1985*

# THE
# OLD
# DAYS

# 1.
# Indians, Whalers, Farmer-Fishermen

I n 1633 the bark *Blessing of the Bay* was sent forth by Governor John Winthrop of Connecticut to explore the fisheries of what Dutch navigator Adriaen Block, in 1614, had named Lange Eylandt. Marine fisheries were the main support of the New England colonies, and the voyage affirmed the abundance of marine life, but Winthrop noted in his report that Long Island's Indians were "very treacherous."

These local bands of coastal Algonkians grew beans and squash and corn, preserving the corn for winter use in a farina or porridge known as samp; with arrowheads fashioned from beach pebbles of chert and quartz, they hunted the bountiful game. But the foundation of their diet was food from the sea, in particular the myriad shellfish—clams, oysters, scallops, mussels, whelks—that were available all year. Like most coastal Indians, they used fiber nets and basket traps and made weirs of branches on the mud flats that trapped fish moving into deeper water on the falling tide. They also towed branch traps, fashioned hooks from bone and antler (weighting their lines with grooved-stone sinkers) and hurled deer-bone harpoons. Their midden heaps contained shells, scales, and bones of sea turtles, sturgeon, and a variety of bony fishes, which were dried on scaffoldings or smoked for winter provender. The Shinacuts, or Shinnecocks, who fished originally from the Pehick Konuk or Peconic River all the way east to Accabonac Creek, in what is now East Hampton, and the Meantecuts, or Munnataukets, who were concentrated in the vicinity of Montauk Great Pond, were skilled boatmen who traveled to the mainland in big dugout "cannows." Because they made offerings to the fierce Pequots of Connecticut, the east end of Long Island was known as Pommanocc, or "place of tribute."

The year after the voyage of *The Blessing of the Bay*, the Pequots were slaughtered by British troops at Mystic, an event deplored by an engineer named Lion Gardiner, who had constructed a fort at Saybrook on the Connecticut shore. Gardiner was friendly with the Montauk sachem Wyandank, his ally in the Pequot Wars in the Connecticut River Valley, and in 1639 he paid Wyandank for a fair island, seven miles long and three across, where the north and south forks of Long Island opened eastward to the sea. The Englishman named it Isle of Wight, but later it became plain Gardiners Island.[1]

The Indians prized fine seawan, or wampum, made from the purple-white shell of the quahog clam and the pink shell of the channeled and knobbed whelks called "winkles." Competing with the French for Indian furs, the English had developed a steel drill for fashioning wampum from these large "winkles" that were so common in Long Island's shallows. Since the fisheries looked promising, and since Gardiner had been so well received, a band of venturesome settlers from the Massachusetts Bay Colony debarked in 1640 at what is now North Sea, in Southampton, going ashore from the Great River, the name given by the *Blessing of the Bay* to the drowned valley between the high glacial moraines of the north and south forks of this great fish-tailed island. The Great River is now Peconic Bay. A few years later, some Southampton settlers joined newcomers from Massachusetts in the founding of Maidstone,[2] a name that was changed within the decade to East Hampton Town.[3]

For assisting the British in the Pequot Wars the warlike Montauks were repaid with the blessings of Christianity, to judge from the fact that "Cockenoe de Long Island," counselor to Wyandank, was helping a reverend Mr. Eliot translate the Bible into the Montauk tongue within a few years of the first settlements. The pioneer settlers were so few that they avoided disagreements with the Indians, all the more so since the much-diminished Indians served as unpaid labor, and were more serviceable alive than dead. When, in 1649, some local Indians killed Mrs. Thomas Halsey of Southampton while out burning houses in protest against the coerced sale of their lands for rum and trinkets, it was agreed that they must have been put up to it by agitators from the New England tribes, which had earlier plotted to slaughter the East Hampton settlers.[4]

In the early years, the South Fork towns had little contact with Dutch New Amsterdam, and East Hampton allied itself with the Connecticut Colony in 1647. When the British took over New Amsterdam seventeen years later, the towns were forced to join the new state of New York. Nonetheless—and for three centuries thereafter—the local people maintained kinship with New England, or the Main, which on a clear day was visible as a blue shadow rising beyond the North Fork and its islands. Fishermen from Narragansett, in Rhode Island, worked Gardiners Bay as early as 1665, and Massachusetts settlers continued to arrive, including those Quakers who fled Puritan persecution toward the end of the century, taking refuge on the peaceful and protected place in the mouth of the Great River known as Shelter Island.

In the year of Mrs. Halsey's death, the bewildered sachems of the Montauk, Shinnecock, and Shelter Island
bands had deeded East Hampton to the settlers for twenty
coats, twenty-four knives, hoes, hatchets, and mirrors, and
one hundred muxes, or steel wampum drills. The covenant
specified that the Indians would receive the "fynnes and
tales of all such whales as shall be cast up [for religious
offerings] and desire that they may be friendly dealt with
in the other partes [which they liked to eat]." Because the
settlers were still few, the town dealt respectfully with Wyandank; when Gardiner bought ocean-front property in
Southampton, Wyandank could still demand that "whales
cast up shall belong to me and to other Indians within these
bounds." But Wyandank died the following year, when two-
thirds of the remaining Montauks fell in epidemic, after
which respectful treatment of the Indians came to an end.

The drift whales stranded on the ocean beach were
highly valued, and in the early days these dead leviathans
were the common property of the community. Every able-
bodied man except Mr. Gardiner and the minister took his
part in the hard, dirty work of flensing the blubber and
"trying out" the "oyle." But as the demand for oil increased,
the settlers negotiated with the Indians to hunt right whales
as they passed along the coast. Unlike most whales, this
baleen species floated after it was killed and could be towed
ashore; therefore it was "the right whale" to pursue.

While Indian invention of shore whaling is disputed,
there is no doubt that Indian canoes of twenty-five to thirty
feet, rigged with harpoons and wood floats, went offshore
after whales seen from the beach, and the slim, swift whaleboats of the Europeans may have derived from them. Certainly it seems unlikely that these Englishmen from Kent
and Dorset knew how to manage the rude Atlantic surf, not
to speak of the perilous techniques of harpooning immense,
inscrutable dark creatures of such strength and speed. In

1643 the blacksmith at Southampton had been forbidden to make "harping irons" for the Indians, lest they be used to harpoon English yeomen, but Indian whale crews were conscripted from the start.

According to the earliest account of Long Island, in 1670,[5] "Upon the South Side . . . in the winter lie store of whales . . . which the inhabitants begin with small boats to make a trade catching to their no small benefit . . ." The leaders in this "whale design" were Jacobus Schellinger and his stepson James Loper, two Dutchmen who, with the family Van Scoy, had removed to the East End when New Amsterdam became a British colony in 1664, and were paying Indians three shillings a day to go off after whales on their behalf. In 1672 Loper was invited by the new settlement on Nantucket to go there to teach those islanders the shore-whaling industry, but the following year he married Lion Gardiner's granddaughter and decided to remain in East Hampton Town. By 1675, when he and Schellinger acquired a second whaleboat—the two boats were crewed by twelve Indians from Montauk and Shelter Island—there were seven whaling companies in the two townships, with potworks for trying rendered blubber into whale oil as far west as Wuno'hke, or "good ground" (now Hampton Bay) and at Ketchaponac (now Westhampton).[6] Competition for whalemen was already so fierce that young settlers were joining the Indians in the boats; the history of the surfmen had begun.

As late as 1702, a young woman on horseback riding the ocean beach from East Hampton to Mecox counted thirteen whales drifted on shore, in addition to the great herds of leviathans spouting out beyond the bar. Shore whaling reached its peak about 1707, when four thousand barrels of oil were tried on Long Island. Soon thereafter it gave way to ocean whaling in pursuit of sperm whales, as voyages of several weeks were extended for months and years; the era of the Nantucket and New Bedford whalers had begun. By mid-century, when the first wharves were built at Sag Harbor, shore whaling was dying, and young Montauks and Shinnecocks went off as harpooneers on whaling voyages, throughout the great oceans of the world. The more numerous Shinnecocks became first mates, captains, and in one case[7] the entire crew of Sag Harbor vessels.

Even before the English settlements, the Indians had been woefully afflicted by white men's diseases, and encroachment on Indian land and rights had intensified as the settlers expanded and the Indians waned. After Wyandank's death, little realizing what sale of their ancestral lands might mean—how does one own or sell air, earth, and water?—the band accepted payment for its Montauk lands from the first of this region's still prosperous line of commercial developers, the so-called Proprietors of Montauk. Thereafter harsh limits were imposed on the people's seasonal movements from place to place in search of food. By the end of the eighteenth century, they had lost their language and were all but gone,[8] together with the forest and wild creatures. In the frenzy of land-clearing that characterized the settlement of the New World, the settlers had obliterated most of the native hardwoods and destroyed much of the wild game; bear, wolf, and bobcat soon disappeared. And yet it seemed that the ocean and creeks and bays were inexhaustible, that the great multitudes of whales and fishes would always return.

Although cattle-raising was the main industry of the early settlements, and meat, hides, and tallow the bases of trade, the abundant fisheries were essential to the economy, with important benefits to local agriculture in the form of fertilizer. As a rule, striped bass, cod, salmon, and other species were taken for human consumption and salted or smoked for winter use, while lesser fish were used for hog food or plowed into the fields. Like the Indians, the colonists gained much of their sustenance from the sea, and fishing was ever a winter occupation of the farmers, who used trawl lines[9] of baited hooks (strung between two anchors marked by buoys) for the big cod that moved southward and inshore in the cold weather.

Within a few years of the first settlement of East Hampton, a community of fifteen or twenty houses had arisen at Northwest Harbor, facing the New England shore, and from Northwest, after 1700, salt cod were shipped commercially from a wharf built by Abraham Schellinger, master of the sloop *Endeavor,* which carried furs, whale oil, timber, turpentine, and grain to Boston, returning with European goods as well as West Indian hardwoods and other products. Schellinger, a founder of the community at Amagansett ("place of good water") and first supervisor of East Hampton Town, was a business associate of Samuel Mulford, who established a second warehouse at Northwest in 1702. Although Schellinger also used Abraham's Landing,[10] which was closer to Amagansett, Northwest remained the main port of East Hampton until the mid-1700s. From this anchorage, well protected from northers and easterly winds, the whaling companies of Sagaponack and Mecox shipped their oil. The casks were carted across to the bay side on a wooded road known as Merchant's Path, which wanders the scrub oak pitch pine woods to the present day.

The Sag Harbor seaport was constructed in 1730 at the head of Northwest Harbor, and in 1786 a Sag Harbor vessel, the *America,* Captain Daniel Havens, put into New London with three hundred barrels of oil from the South Atlantic; a century of Sag Harbor whaling had begun. A few years later the first British and American vessels rounded Cape Horn into the Pacific, and the first local whaleman to make this voyage was Captain Jonathan Osborn of Wainscott,[11] master of the *Union.* Osborn was "Long Tom Coffin" in a whaling novel by James Fenimore Cooper, a sometime Sag Harbor resident who was part owner of his vessel. In the next seven decades, more than one hundred ships were fitted out in the port of Sag Harbor, which served both East Hampton and Southampton townships, and many men from local families—Havens, Bennett,[12] Lester, Loper, Miller, King—served on the crews.

In 1790 Sag Harbor became New York State's first customs port; its original Long Wharf, built in 1808, served the main commerce in salt cod and whale oil. The Havens family, which had settled on Shelter Island before 1700, developed one of the many shipbuilding enterprises on the East End, using timber from the remnant forests of Montauk and Hither Hills, and ships from the East End fished cod and halibut on Georges Bank and the Nantucket Shoals, carrying the picturesque ricks of stacked-up dories; the banks dory was later adapted to the haul-seine fishery off the ocean beach. From 1815 to 1825, Sag Harbor was a principal port of the Atlantic coast, with a fleet of sixty whale ships, many of them carrying Indian harpooneers, and a lighthouse to guide the ships to port was constructed in 1839 at Cedar Point, at the mouth of Northwest Harbor.

But already the whales were much diminished, and the California Gold Rush, then the Civil War, disrupted the commerce, as petroleum found in Pennsylvania replaced whale oil with kerosene as fuel. By now, the last forests had been stripped from the hills (a 250-acre tract on Gardiners Island is the last stand of ancient white oak forest on the East End), the Peconic shipbuilding industry had died, and much of the eroded land—bare poor pasture for more than one hundred years—had returned to wood lots.

With the decline of whaling, the shipping tonnage declined, too. The last whale ship, the *Myra*, sailed in 1871, and never returned. Ten years later the old Customs House (to this day one of the loveliest buildings on the South Fork) was closed. Where the Long Wharf stands today, at the end of Main Street, was a graveyard of stranded and derelict hulks called Rotten Row.

In the second half of the nineteenth century, Greenport Village, on the North Fork, where the railroad arrived in 1844, was the fishing, packing, and shipping port for the East End, and the steamer *Shinnecock* carried salt cod and smoked eels from nearby Orient to New York City. Additionally, Greenport had prospered from an early decision to transfer its investment from the dying whaling industry to a new fishery for the deep-bellied bony member of the herring family called the menhaden, the bountiful "bony fish" or mossbunker first reported by the *Blessing of the Bay*. Since the end of the eighteenth century, menhaden had been taken with community haul seines and used as fertilizer in the fields; now they were sought primarily for "bunker oil," as large ocean-going steamers, using purse seines, harvested this fish in immense amounts to be processed in factories ashore. The menhaden haul seines now fell into disuse, but a few of the seine gangs persisted, using smaller seines to catch striped bass, shad, bluefish, sturgeon, and other species in the great longshore migrations off the ocean beach.

In the winter of 1880–1881, the Norwegian gill net, or set net, was used to good effect for cod off the ocean beach and later came into year-round use throughout the bays. Amagansett men "set fykes [portable basket traps] and they occasionally fish with seines for striped bass and other species on the Atlantic side"[13] or "Backside," as the early boatmen named Long Island's rough Atlantic shore, a hundred miles of ocean coast, from Montauk to the Hudson, without a navigable inlet, much less safe harbor. In spring and summer fykes might be set for the diamondback terrapin (or torpin) of the saltwater estuaries and the snapping turtle (or torp or torrop) of freshwater ponds. But most of the farmer-fishermen harvested menhaden and other scrap fish for the fields; food fish were for home consumption and local barter. Although small quantities of fish (packed in ice blocks cut from winter ponds) were shipped to Greenport, commercial fishing was negligible on the South Fork until the railhead at Bridgehampton was extended to Montauk; the year was 1895, more than a half century after the train had come to Greenport. Sturgeon and sturgeon roe, or caviar, were among the first products shipped directly from the South Fork to New York; another popular export was the black sea bass, which remains today the preferred fish in Chinese restaurants.

In 1882, ocean whaling by bunker steamer was attempted by Captain Joshua Edwards on the *Amagansett;* the one whale caught was towed to New York for exhibition. Subsequently, shore whaling was resumed as an incidental occupation by the farmer-fishermen, led by the Wainscott Osborns, the East Hampton Dominys—better known as clockmakers and woodworkers—and "Cap'n Josh," now a white-bearded patriarch who "went off" for the last time on February 22, 1907, in the whaleboat of his son, Cap'n Sam. The right whale taken on that date was the huge creature later suspended from the roof of the great hall in the American Museum of Natural History; another killed by Oliver Osborn the same day was the last whale taken by that Wainscott family.[14]

The inshore whales were already uncommon, and the round-bottomed whaleboats, narrow, elegant, and swift, dried out and rotted in the sheds back of the beach. The last whale killed, in August 1918, off Napeague Coast Guard Station, by an Edwards and Dominy crew that included descendants of James Loper, was towed fifteen hours around Montauk Point to Promised Land and tried out at the menhaden factory, producing some thirty barrels of oil that found no market.

In December 1921, a small right whale sighted off

Southampton Coast Guard Station was unsuccessfully pursued by a whaleboat crew under Captains Sam and Everett Edwards and a dory crew under Felix Dominy (both crews were towed west by power launch), but the cry "Whale Off!" had brought such small response from the local villagers that Cap'n Evvie wondered later "what the matter was. Am I growing old or are times changing?"

# 2.

# The Early Surfmen

A lifelong fisherman whose family came here more than three centuries ago is Milton Miller, born in 1915 in a small cottage back of the Amagansett dunes at the ocean end of Atlantic Avenue, where several whale houses and fish shanties once stood. The Millers were the earliest settlers on Accabonac Creek, also called the Springs. Though the several Miller clans claim an English origin, Milt believes that the first Millers, or Mullers, were Dutch, and that they were here before the English colonists from Massachusetts; their descendants include that Captain Sylvester Miller of Amagansett who sailed around the Horn in pursuit of whales between 1829 and 1845 and recorded in his log that this life was "rugid." On his mother's side, Milt's great-grandparents were Lopers, descendants of that first James Loper who made a local industry of shore whaling.

In a Puritan community that at first feared and later despised the Indians, Milt Miller's ancestors on both sides claimed a long tradition of friendship with the native people, who had aided the first Millers to survive in a sod-roofed dwelling built into the steep slope south of Louse

Point until a simple farmhouse could be completed; traces
of that "soddie" were still present in Milt's boyhood. The
Loper clan, too, welcomed Indian friends at their tables and
under their roofs. A descendant of one of the last sachems
of the Montauks, Stephen Pharaoh, or Talkhouse, and his
wife would stay at the Loper house at the east end of Amagansett when they came off Montauk. One day he found
Milt's Great-Grandmother Loper dying of the dropsy—her
sister had died the day before—and saved her life with an
herbal medicine made from a red-berried ground plant
known as deerfeed.[1] The recovered child was subsequently
befriended by the sachem's daughter, whom Milt knew as
Aunt Maria (Mo-RYE-ah), and Milt himself was "a grown
boy before I knew that she was no relative to the family.
But it didn't make any difference as we all showed her the
greatest respect and love as we did Granny." Milt still recalls
the two old ladies in their shawls, sitting in rockers and
taking snuff as they talked happily of days gone by. At the
age of about eighty-five, the two friends "went to the happy
hunting ground together, and I'm sure they wanted it that
way." Aunt Maria's second husband was a black man named
Banks, and her children "married into the black people in
Freetown in East Hampton, because they got an awful raw
deal off of these Englishmen around here."

"The English were very aggressive," Milt Miller explains.
"They stole most all their land off the Indians, called them
savages; in my family, the home land was *bought* off of the
Indians, who were treated as people. My grandparents on
my father's side had a large farm and the Indians would
help plantin and harvestin the crops. They would butcher
the pigs and cattle for meat, take clothin and food for pay.
People them days fished and farmed to survive; money
didn't mean but very little. More important was to make it
through the winter months, and they worked like beavers
to do that." In the 1890s, when Milt's mother, Nettie Payne,

had come to work on his Grandfather Miller's farm in Accabonac, the Indian people were still helping with the harvest.

"My mother used to can stuff all summer, put stuff up, and the kids, we all got our little pans and went together to get cranberries, we'd gather beach plums, blueberries, huckleberries, and elderberries, and that was all preserved. The women would keep the house and make the butter and cheese, salt and smoke the fish and meat, prepare the vegetables and fruit for the winter months. They had a very large table, and all the family, including the Indians, sat to eat. There were times that the Indians stayed overnight, and there was plenty of room made for them. The Indian was treated as any other guest would be treated. It's a hell of a good feelin to know that you come from a family that never had no discrimination against nobody."

Because of the view of the ocean distance from the high bluff back of the beach, the Edwards clan had built houses "up on the hill"; their boat sheds and bait shanties were near the lifesaving station on the beach below, where whale crews could be mustered quickly. Living so close to the fish shacks on the beach, Milt Miller was more or less raised among the Edwardses, and his father, Russell Miller, had worked on the Edwards crews. Russell's brother Wilbur, also a fisherman, drowned in 1902 when a sharpie overturned in rough weather while lifting fish traps for Captain Frank Parsons in Fort Pond Bay. (The Edwardses and Parsonses were the most successful fishing families on the South Fork, expanding their operation into fishing boats, docks, and packing houses; most of the Parsonses, who later succeeded in engineering enterprises, fished out of Montauk.) Like many fishermen in those days, Russ Miller helped man the surfboats at the old lifesaving station—later the Amagansett Coast Guard—which had a cupola on the roof, where a watch was kept day and night for ships in distress. The stations were spaced every four miles along the beach. In late autumn, with the onset of cold weather, the great whales would appear in the silver sea; the man on watch at the lifesaving station was often the first to cry "Whale off!"[2] and the crew at the station was always on hand to go off in the first boat that could be mustered.

"In the winter months, in severe weather, they really had some bad wrecks," Milt remembers, "and they had to have real good men that knew how to go through the surf and rescue people off these ships that come ashore. The captain had a special knowledge of the surf, and the crew were also good surfmen, good oarsmen, actin on the captain's command without hesitation. It's probably unbelievable today that men could even row a boat out through the surf in this type of weather. . . . They never talked too much about what they did. It was nothin to be a hero about, it was their job, helpin out in shipwrecks, saving lives, ready at all times to help each other. It gave me a sense of pride to be around a bunch of men like them, even with all the teasin that I had."

In later years, Cap'n Russ was in charge of Coast Guard beach stations farther west, but he still had a local reputation as a surfman. Milt recalls with pride the day of the great hurricane of 1938, when he was getting a ride home with Captain Bert Edwards, at that time supervisor of East Hampton Town. After the storm had passed, "the water was way up over our knees and we had to stop the car and walk the rest of the way." During the walk, Cap'n Bert spoke of Russ Miller's quiet competence many years before when a storm came up on a winter day while the two were cod-fishing. Those were the days when small boat engines had first appeared, and Cap'n Bert had put one in his whaleboat. "I didn't know anything about engines," he told Milt, "and it wouldn't start, water pump froze up. But your father knew that engine and bypassed that pump somehow; otherwise we would have never made it, never would have got in. I owe my life to him."

Milt's mother worked in the household of Captain Gabe Edwards, younger brother of the patriarch, Cap'n Josh. "My mother was a servant for them people, but not the way you would think of a servant now; she was part of the family, and I was, too. My mother worked for Cap'n Gabe's wife at the time, and she used to tell me about how they cooked doughnuts and chickens and stuff in the whale fat while the men was working. Cook big meals right in the whale oil, that's why it got the name 'whale rally,' a big rally, because the whole town would participate, come to the beach, women with children, with babies in their arms, children running all over the place. Up in that lot across from Cap'n Gabe's house, that's where the whale works was; all the Edwards lived along that area."

Milt Miller believes that fishing is in his blood. Even before his birth, he says, his mother would carry him down to the ocean when fishing boats came in. The Miller cottage near the lifesaving station was the only house down in the dunes that was occupied year-round, and young "Freckles" Miller, as he was known to the rough surfmen, spent most of his early years in adult company. He still regrets having been too young to take part in the whaling adventure, but he has a vague memory of Cap'n Josh, then a very old man in a long white beard, and also of helping to shove off the boats "although I was probably in the way in more ways than not. Sometimes I would get knocked down only to be helped up again with a friendly pat on the head and the words, 'take hold,' which meant to help. I went out through the surf when I was a small boy, probably six years old. The men picked me up and put me in the boat, I couldn't hardly see out over the top of the boat, settin in the bottom, that's how small I was."

From his earliest years Milt would hang around the fish

shanties and listen to stories, "the times when after hours
of bein towed at tremendous speed many miles from home,
the harpoon pulled out, and sailin and rowin back all night
empty-handed." His father told him how he once was towed
all the way west some twenty miles to Shinnecock, and having to tow the dead whale back as other boats came with
food and coffee for the crew. "Couldn't beach it at Shinnecock because there was no try works; might take all day
and all night before they got that whale rowed back to Amagansett. Other times the whale would smash one of the boats
and the other boat would pull men from the water and
continue the chase. These were the bravest and boldest men
that ever went whalin.

"Even in them days whaleboats cost a good deal of
money, and the whales didn't show up very regular. The
Dominys in East Hampton had their own captains and
boats, but the main whaling captains was the Edwardses;
they owned the boats, and they must've had money at the
time that they came here to settle, because they always had
men workin for 'em." Besides bunker fishing and haul-
seining, the Edwardses tended big ocean barrel traps, set
off Napeague, which were very profitable for six to eight
weeks of the spring run, and Milt Miller and other boys
would gather snow in winter and pack it down for storage
into a deep cistern, for icing the fish.

"Them Edwardses was a hard bunch of men; they was
some fishermen, I'll tell you that, they owned just about all
the fishin equipment around here. Nevertheless they was
down-to-earth people. The captains was generally the outstanding men, the elders, let's say, in the church. Those
captains used to make me go to Sunday School; Cap'n
Gabe'd treat you to a sermon if you didn't go. Cap'n Gabe,
Cap'n Clint, and the sons of Cap'n Josh—the Edwards boys,
what they called the Edwards Brothers, Cap'n Sam, Cap'n
Bert, Cap'n Evvie, and their sons, too—I fished with quite
a few of 'em and they was really fine men, outstanding men

in the town; there was never nothin you could hold or say against 'em.

"The crews was always a rugged bunch. I don't think many of 'em attended church or done anything else outside o' drink and raise hell, and this is so even today. I have seen these same captains and crews standin on the beach lookin offshore at a whale and countin how long it took between the time the whale sounded and the time it blowed; they would predict the length and how many barrels it would yield. To hear them yell, *Thar she blows!* with a gleam in their eyes and hearty laughter! The urge to put chase and capture the whale was still there although whalin had stopped several years before . . .

"Never a day would go by without a walk along the ocean beach. The smell of the fresh salt air would awaken my whole body, and a walk at sunrise, watching the sun climb up out of the ocean would sometimes reveal a large arctic owl, all kinds of seabirds, geese, and ducks. It was not unusual to try to see how close I could crawl up on a seal that lay asleep. One time I found a drownded man who had washed ashore, and it didn't take me long to return home and tell my story, cause this was the first dead person I'd ever seen.

"The whaleboat house was only a short distance from my house. With no other boy my age to play with, I spent many hours in an imaginary world of my own. The whaleboats were ready to go and all equipment in them—the sails, the oars, the harpoons, water kegs, everything in place where it should be, just the way the boats were made ready after the last whale chase. They had not been used for several years. These whaleboat houses were never locked and never a thing out of place or taken, until with age they decayed and collapsed, as their time had ended."[3]

Before the coming of the railroad, commercial fishing on the South Fork was largely confined to salt or smoked fish and menhaden products, which could be processed and shipped without refrigeration. The railroad to Montauk, completed in 1895—three decades after rails had crossed the continent—ran right out onto a fish dock constructed at Fort Pond Bay, and a special fish train left Montauk every evening, stopping to pick up big "sugar boxes"[4] of fresh fish carted up to depot platforms at Napeague and Amagansett, and arriving at the Fulton Fish Market early next morning.

In the first decades of this century the leading local fishery was cod. "In them days cod took care of the town all winter," Milt Miller recalls. The fishery supported not only fishermen but also men laid off from summer building jobs or other work. These men dug the big skimmer clams[5] used for bait, opened clams and baited cod trawls, tended the fish shanties and the horses used to drag the heavy boats above the tide line, and boxed and iced the fish when the boats came in. Forty or fifty bushels of skimmers might be required for a single crew, and each man was paid by the bushel or trawl according to what he did; only the regular fishing crew worked on shares. Codfishing also gave off-season work to farmers, who carted the boxes to the railroad station and took away the heads and guts, piling the offal under hay or seaweed in mounds perhaps one hundred feet long, to dress their gardens in the spring.

One of the men who dug for clams was Milton's uncle, Elisha Ammon, Sr., who lived at that time in Accabonac. "When I was a kid," says Elisha Jr., who was born in that Springs community in 1911, "my father'd get up in the mornin early, walk to Amagansett beach, help put the boat in the water, and the gang would go fishin, and he'd come back with the horse and wagon, drive all the way to Springs and clam, drive all the way back again to the bait house, open bait and bait trawls until the gang come ashore, ship the fish, and then they sat there till about ten at night baitin trawls for the next day, then he'd walk home to Springs. *That* was something! *That* was hard money."

Usually, two men fished as partners, and sometimes a

third man served as shore crew. Where there was no shore crew, the fishermen themselves would gut and dress the fish, open the bait clams (perhaps two bushels of skimmers to a tub of gear) and rebait and load the hooks for the next day. Often they worked until late at night, only to rise at four in the morning of what was often another eighteen-hour day.

Since the fish bit hardest at first light, great pains were taken to prepare tubs carefully so that the trawls could be set quickly even in darkness. Ordinarily four tubs or trawls, depending on conditions, were set out end to end, in a line nearly two miles long that extended seaward from behind the offshore bar. The cod trawl was a heavy tarred cotton runner rigged every six feet with a lighter "snood" line about thirty inches long, that carried the baited hook: each trawl was about five hundred fathoms (or three thousand feet) long. The five hundred-odd snoods were coiled carefully in a butter tub or a square wooden box, tapered so that it was wider at the top than at the bottom, with the baits hooked around the rim. In the early days cod were so plentiful that the boats would lay to offshore for an hour or so while the big fish found the baits; then the crew picked up the trawls and rowed ashore into the northwest wind, through the cold salt spray and ice-caked water. In later years, the crews would rise at 4 A.M., run the trawls out in the winter dark, and return to shore lifting trawls from the previous day before braving the surf with the heavy cargo.

In Amagansett there were four fish shanties on the beach, with large brass kerosene lamps hung from the ceiling, and also a line for drying the wool mittens. On hooks along the wall hung sticky oilskins—heavy cotton garments painted with an evil-smelling mix of linseed oil and paint dryer to make them waterproof. The shacks were warmed by pot-bellied stoves on which big pots of coffee were always ready; there were built-in bunks where fishermen could sleep for a few hours, and work tables where the shore crew baited trawls for the next day.

"When there was an extra big catch," Milt says, "the boat crew would start gutting the cod on the way in, to lighten up the boat. If the captain didn't think it was safe to go over the surf, he would string the fish on a line to lighten the boat even more and tow the fish in." But even the best fishermen took chances coming ashore. One day Milt saw Captain Frank Lester's boat, laden with cod, swamp in the surf, and codfish and trawl tubs washing down the whole length of the beach.

"The men at the shanty had now seen the hundreds of gulls followin the boat, and there was a joy of laughter. The bets were on of how many fish the boats would have, and a bottle of rum was passed around; the men would squirt their tobacco juice out and hold a cud of tobacco in their hand while taking a good long snort. The skids and rollers, the horse team, was ready, and as soon as the boat hit the beach, the men were in action. The team was hooked on and the rollers and skids in place and the boat was hauled up out of the surf to safety. The fish would be frozen stiff. The cap'n and crew, with icicles hangin off their sou'westers, saltwater ice glistenin on their oilskins, and the steam comin from their warm mittens, would head for the shanty and hot coffee when the boat was made secure, and the rest of the men would use hayforks to unload the fish into the wagons alongside." The fish were carted to the bait shanties and forked out onto a fish-cleaning table; next to this gutting bench was a big tub of fresh water for rinsing the cleaned fish, and a stack of fish boxes. The heads and guts were slung into big wagon boxes for the farmers. Not far off, a doorless privy faced the ocean, so that its occupant might keep an eye out for returning boats.

In early spring the ocean crews would set gill nets for sturgeon. One calm morning—because the boy claimed he had permission from his mother—Captain Clint Edwards took Freckles Miller in the boat. "We left the beach by sunup and I was feelin fine until I lost sight of the land and then I was as seasick as I ever was or has been since. The whole world seemed to tumble around, and I can only remember Cap'n Clint had me lay across a seat and took a rope and tied it around me so I would not fall overboard while they were tendin net. I can only remember the first net and seein them roll in two large sturgeon; I was so seasick I passed out and only came to on the way back as soon as I could see the land. There must have been at least a half dozen more of these big sturgeon in the boat, over two hundred pounds each. The mate called the cap'n to show him that one of 'em had a ripe roe, cause his fingers when he pulled 'em out was covered with black eggs; this was caviar and was worth more than the fish.

"Upon arrivin at the beach the first thing I saw was my mother standin there with her arms folded, and a hair-brush, and as I tried to walk on the beach after bein so sick, I couldn't get my footin and was sick all over again. My mother was sayin 'Where have you been, young man?' havin the hairbrush ready to lay it on me, but Cap'n Clint took hold of her arm, sayin 'Nettie, he's been punished enough,' and made her promise not to lick me when we got home. I can imagine now how upset she must've been when she got up in the mornin and I wasn't home and she made several trips to the beach and couldn't find me. Talkin later, the Cap'n and me, I knew it was important to tell the truth if I was ever to go fishin with him again.

"I was always underfoot down on the beach; learned how to cuss before I learned how to talk, and probably drank some liquor, too." By the time he was six, Milt was opening clams, with a nickel or a dime for pay; later he learned how to scavenge from cod heads and guts the valuable livers and tasty tonguelike palates which he would ship off to the Fulton Fish Market by the quart. ("Ten, twelve above zero, bare-handed, down there in the guts, pulling them livers off, cutting them tongues out; I only lived a short ways from the fish shanty, but I used to come home cryin, my hands ached me so bad.") His hard work won him a new nickname, Fishtongue, as well as a new mail-order bicycle, the Hawthorne Flyer, which was the envy of every kid in town.

The men teased him hard, tossing fish guts at him, or giving him a big cod to lug home by the gills, a thirty-pound fish that would cause him to step on the tail and trip and fall in the snow, making them laugh. The big fish and its roe fed his family for days; his mother would make codfish cakes, and cut the jowls from the cod head for fish chowder. They also ate beef-like pieces of red meat from the heads of the big sturgeon that were caught in spring. "In them days, money was real scarce and food was cheap; fish, clams, scallops, farm crops, and always plenty of potatoes, cabbage, left over in the fields, and homemade canned fruits, pies, nothing but the finest. You lived better then than you do now because there was no preservatives, the stuff was good for you. The men used to go on Montauk two–three days grapin, the women would take what they wanted for grape jelly and the men would barrel up the rest and make their wine. This was the life, and time and money didn't seem to matter as much as livin close together and bein friendly with everybody, not dog-eat-dog like it is today."

For a number of years, such fishermen as Captain Elisha Osborn in Wainscott had been using small cedar-wood Jersey boats with one-cylinder engines to go through the surf, but many of the surfmen preferred dories.[6] In 1929, when Captain Clint Edwards took Milt Miller with him on his dory crew, Milt was just fourteen years old. "I suppose no one could have had a happier moment in their lives than to be asked to be one of the boat crew with a captain you had always admired and re-

spected . . . The honor soon became reality after the first
day of rowin and pullin the large oars with every muscle
put into use to make a good impression on the captain,
the large blisters beginnin to appear in the palm of my
hands, the achin, achin of every muscle, many that I
didn't even know I had, that I must endure without a
word." But endure he did, fishing all summer, helping lift
the gillnets in the early autumn mornings before going to
school, and running back to help out again at evening. "I
don't think that boys today have the opportunity I had to
work around somebody who would help him out, try to
give him some knowledge; and a kid can pick up a lot of
knowledge by just watching. Today the grown people
chase the kid away, sayin he might get hurt. I used to
work right around with these grown men, and the Lester
boys and others that come up in a fishing family in
Amagansett was raised the same way."

The following April, when spring fishing began, Cap'n
Clint made Milt stroke oarsman, and Milt also tended Cap'n
Gabe's gill nets on a share basis: the old man, feeble and
nearly blind, was over eighty. "Sometimes I'd go to see him,
and there he'd be, mendin net in his yard, and he'd know
me by my footsteps comin across the grass and call my name
without even turnin around. Cap'n Gabe was like a father
to me, and in the early thirties, when I was seventeen, I took
over his rig for him."

Cap'n Gabe still came down to the beach in his horse-
drawn wagon, anxious as ever to go off in the boat. He
would help shove off, then hang onto the stern, and once
the dory was safely beyond the breakers, Milt would jump
back aft and haul him aboard. Then one day Cap'n Gabe's
son Nat, a prosperous trap fisherman in Montauk, said,
"Milt, I don't want Father on that boat any more, but he
wants to go, so you'll have to try to get off before he gets
to the beach. Don't take him off." But Cap'n Nat had not

said this to his father, and the first time the old man came down with his horse and wagon to find Milt and another boy already out lifting his nets, he was very upset. The old whaler had not realized until then that his days of going off in a small boat through the ocean surf were at an end.

# 3.
# The Edwards Brothers
# and the Lester Boys

"The Lesters and Edwardses done most of the fishing around here," according to Francis Ray Lester, Cap'n Frank, born in Amagansett in 1890. The Lesters were originally Leicesters from northern England, according to an East Hampton genealogy prepared by Cap'n Josh's granddaughter,[1] and John Lester came to Connecticut from England in 1654. At some time in the next century, certain Lesters settled at Northwest and became fishermen-farmers, and in the nineteenth century one Lester clan moved to the west end of Amagansett, a community handy to both the ocean and the bay, known today as Poseyville. Though still farmers, the 'Gansett Lesters followed the sea, and eventually became full-time commercial fishermen. "They were newcomers two hundred years ago," Milt Miller says, "but the Lesters have carried on the tradition of ocean beach fishing more than any family around. Cap'n Frank, well, I remember, he used to be some fisherman, that guy!"

Frank Lester's father, Nathan Talmage Lester ("a big kind of burly man, a lot of light hair, close to six foot four," according to his grandson Francis, "a very very gentle man who loved children") said he'd once helped catch a dozen whales a year, and he owned two whaleboats that were used for haul-seining–mostly for "scrap for the land"—and cod-fishing. Like all six sons of Cap'n Nathan, Frank was a surf-man at an early age, and in 1907 he rowed on the Edwards crew that took the huge right whale that went to the American Museum. The Edwardses, whose frugal ways were commonly held accountable for their success, withheld his share, saying he did not count as crew, being too young, although for several years—ever since his father had been laid up with Bright's disease—Frank and his brother Harry, two years older, had been providing for the family. With the breakup of the ice in the February thaw—traditionally, February 10— they set "a gang o' fykes" (two men might tend one hundred fykes between them) as far away as Gardiners Island, rowing them all the way across the channel; these flatfish fykes caught three- or four-pound flounders, now long gone. In warmer weather, when crabs and horse-foots snarled the fykes, they tended two big fish traps at Barnes Hole that were frequently damaged, Frank recalled, by the coal-burning wooden bunker steamers of the Edwards Brothers. They netted weakfish "up Peconic Bay," and sometimes in summer Frank went dragging out of Fort Pond Bay in Montauk, going as far east as Block Island in small open boats with one- or two-cylinder engines that were overhauled only every few years. These boats, rarely more than twenty feet in length, lacked winches and net reels; the heavy nets were hauled from the deep water by hand.

Frank Lester was anxious to tow in the last whaleboat that went offshore from Amagansett in 1918. "He was so sore they wouldn't take him," says his brother Bill, "that Pop said, 'Well, I'll let you have my share.' Frank went up and bought himself some boots and oilers, but that whale was a small one, with no oil to speak of, what they called a dry skin, and Frank's share never paid for that new gear."

Frank Lester had two dollars to his name, he said, when

in 1908 he married Sadie Eames, whose grandfather came over from Connecticut in the nineteenth century. Sadie was born down at Napeague in a community of about fifteen houses known at that time as Squatters Land. Later it was called Lazy Point, after a local tradition that most of the inhabitants were easy-going clam diggers who did little besides drink from November to May. All winter the Eames family worked supplying bait clams for the cod trawls, and Sadie helped dig clams and open scallops for her husband. She also bore him three daughters and five sons, and all five sons are fishermen today.

For two weeks each year Frank moved down to Napeague to shoot ducks and geese for the winter larder, and during the Depression, when the Lesters—and many other fishermen—lost most of their Amagansett land to unpaid taxes, Frank and Sadie returned to her family's house at Lazy Point. They had no car, only a horse and wagon, and they used old-time kerosene lamps, but they had chickens, a garden, and a root cellar, and canned all sorts of vegetables and wild berries—blackberries, blueberries, cranberries—and smoked a lot of deer, rabbit, and squirrel. Frank Lester was a cheerful, optimistic man, and in his recollection, they lived "happy and good." In their spare time, such as it was, they were apt to go fishing for fun, or go sit on the beach in a sociable way while mending net. As his eldest son Francis recalls, "In them days there wasn't too much to do outside of that, so they spent quite a lot of time down around the beach. In the winter we'd all go down there and take a little somethin to eat and drink, a little tea or lemonade. In them days there wasn't many people on the beach."

Like his father ("All he done was fish"), Frank Lester worked for others only when there was no other way to feed his family. One summer he cut cauliflower for a dollar fifty cents a day; another year he raised vegetables for a small store run by his wife. Both times he saw a fish truck go by with a good catch and went back fishing. "He wasn't afraid of paid work, it wasn't that; he didn't *like* it," Francis says. "Every time he went to work, somebody caught a lot of fish, so he decided he wouldn't work any more for anybody." For a time, Frank Lester wore glasses, but he never discovered a way to keep them clear, especially in the winter spray; he got so disgusted with the last pair he ever wore that he threw them overboard.

"In Pop's time," recalls Frank's brother Bill, born in 1900, "they used a 660-foot net for haulin seine, and a horse cart, dump cart, with wide wheels, carried less than a pickup truck today. In them days Edwardses hauled seine some, too, but they were into bigger stuff, made a lot of money, had ocean traps out here tended by steamers. Anyway, a dump cart full was a good haul in them days. Took what they needed to eat, I guess, and spread the rest of 'em— evil fish and food fish, too—out on the fields. Sold some to the workers in the watchcase factory over Sag Harbor—no way of shippin 'em before the railroad come." In those days menhaden, or mossbunkers, were eaten with as much enthusiasm as the incidental catch of striped bass, bluefish, weakfish, summer flounder (fluke), flounder, and shad. "We got some of them old people yet likes to eat bunkers. Feller come around just the other day, said his mother wanted bunker, took a mess home to eat."

When Bill Lester married Sadie Spicer in 1918, he moved from Cap'n Nathan's house north of Montauk Highway to his present house a hundred yards away. The wedding took place not long after the ship *Kershaw* went aground on the outer bar "off the bath house" at Main Beach, and flour from the salvaged cargo came in handy for the wedding cake. "People liked to say that our weddin cake was kind of sandy but of course it weren't. That ship must have been three–four hundred foot, and they had to unload her to haul her off the bar, and the only thing they saved off her was the liquor. She were carryin *everything*, liquor, cigarettes, tobacco, hides, bolts of cloth, salt peanuts; we had peanuts around here by the tons, just went aboard and loaded up what we wanted. That 'Kershaw cloth' was around these parts for years. And one time after that, when Cap'n Josh's son there, Doctor Dave, cut somethin out of me, he give me a glass of whiskey off the *Kershaw* to straighten me up."

During Prohibition, local fishermen helped unload the contraband liquor all the way from Montauk to Westhampton, in a part-time profession known as bottle-fishing. "Had a Jersey skiff and a dory in them days, and used 'em both; we done very good with it," Bill recalls. "Supposed to get five dollars a case for every one deliverd to the beach, but some of them cases never made it. One or two off every boatload might fall overboard behind the surf, y'know, and somebody might throw out a flag buoy in the middle of 'em, come along that way before daybreak 'n set around 'em. One of them hauls got thirty-five cases, from what I heard. Anyways, one night west of Main Beach we took off one thousand cases and one hundred barrels of malt before one of them rum-runners hollered 'Finish up, there's a boat a-comin out the east'rd!' Well, *next* night a boat come, sure enough, government destroyer or somethin, and they was caught, but all they was seein that first night was the eastern star, low in the winter sky."

Not all of the skirmishes were so peaceful. A state trooper was killed in a shoot-out at Montauk and an unlucky fisherman of Greenport "had his guts shot out," according to Elisha Ammon. But most fishermen remember Prohibition with affection: Jarvis Wood of Springs, one of many who chanced upon jettisoned cargo, bought a new Ford in 1930 for $620. In those days, Jarvie says, there were liquor joints on Lily Hill, "beyond the bridge," at the village end of Accabonac Road, and liquor was served at home square dances, or hoedowns, with accordion tunes by a man named Toonie Allen.

"Every week they had a dance somewhere, or a party somewhere, somebody's house. Throw out the couch and the chairs and the stove sometimes, if it's warm weather, take up the oilcloth and go dancin; have a keg of beer, probably, and most people had somethin to drink. We had square dancin, round dancin, someone played a fiddle or their accordion, dance all night, then put the stuff back in and go on home."

With his older brothers Harry, Frank, and Charlie, Bill Lester set gill nets for sturgeon, which were sometimes as large as five hundred pounds. Sixteen nets, anchored at each end, were set out in a line extending from a half mile to two miles offshore. "Long about 1918, there was an abundance of 'em." Bill recalls. "We skun them sturgeon off, got sixty cents a pound, which is near twice what we get for 'em today. Lots of trouble with sharks messin up the nets, but we done real good. Pop had his shack out there across Further Lane, and I guess there's a pile of sturgeon scales in them dunes yet." A thousand-pounder, caught by Nathan Lester around the turn of the century, is the largest sturgeon in local memory, and the only reason it did not bust through the net, Cap'n Nathan said, was because he had been short of good net anchors; where he had hitched on an old mower wheel, the net was slack and had entangled the huge fish.

Sometimes in rough weather, the sturgeon nets would be left untended for three days at a time, and would come up loaded with dead sharks and big barn-door skates of such violent odor that some of the fishermen actually got seasick. The rotting fish would attract huge lobsters, ten to twenty pounds, that were often worth more than the sturgeon. ("They used to get plenty of 'em," says Frank Lester's grandson, Walter Bennett. "Sometimes three or four hundred pounds. Used to break 'em open with a mallet cause they would tangle the nets up. Can you imagine that? If I ever saw a twenty-pound lobster now, I don't think I'd break him with a mallet!") A five-hundred-pound fish might have four and a half pounds of roe, and Nathan Lester taught his sons to make sturgeon caviar for the buyers who came down from New York, rolling the roe through a mesh screen to separate the eggs, then mixing them thoroughly with small-grained salt.

"Once we caught a small whale in them nets," Bill says. "Went to lift, y'know, and we felt this awful heft down there, and next thing we knew that net was ripped right out of the boat! Could've ripped us right over with it! So we went and lifted them other nets, come back, tried her again, and that whale had drowned; had so much net wrapped around his fluke, couldn't get to the surface. So we towed him down to Main Beach bathhouse, anchored him off. Our idea was to bring him ashore next mornin, throw a tent over him, y'know, charge ten–fifteen cents admission. But them anchors dragged, and he come ashore high and dry durin the night, so there wasn't too much that we could charge for."

When the spring sturgeon run came to an end, at the end of June, Nathan Lester's sons went hand-lining for black sea bass on the wreck of the *Panther* off Shinnecock, taking as many as two thousand pounds a day, and usually they would harpoon one or two swordfish on the way up and down the coast, for in those days the swordfish came in close to shore. They also set gill nets in the bay and ocean. In windy weather, and in winter, they went "baitin" in the salt ponds, netting spearing or silverside minnows (called whitebait on the market) and white perch (a small bronzy relative of the striped bass) in Georgica or Montauk Great Pond. Sometimes they trot-lined for blue crabs, using one hundred baits on a long line and harvesting them by the barrel.[2] They also set eelpots, and in certain years, speared eels through the ice. In fall and early winter they went scalloping, and raked or tonged clams when nothing else was handy.

Codfishing began right after Thanksgiving, when the ocean was still warm enough for the cod to approach shore; in the winter the fish moved off to deeper water. At least twenty crews kept gear in shacks along the beach, all the way from Napeague to Southampton. Among the cod fishermen were Captains Clint and Sam Edwards, both of them captains of big bunker steamers in the summer. The Edwardses had no need to do this rough cold work, the Lesters knew, because their family had acquired a lot of good land in the early days and had already made a lot of money, but it was recognized that they were fishermen and must act accordingly.

The steep-sided Nova Scotia dory, a good surfboat, was used for codfishing as well as haul-seining, but increasingly the crews used Jersey skiffs, lapstrake "clinker-built" boats with one-cylinder inboard engines. "Steered awful hard, heavy, and cumbersome," recalls Bill Lester, "but they were good sea boats, and they carried a good load. Moved 'em into the surf on planks and rollers and hauled 'em back up with capstans. Feller named Oscar Birg had one of the first ones. His shack was down there where that big motel is now, closest point to Napeague Harbor, so's to have them piss clams handy for his baits. Went off one day and just never come back. Must have broke down, and the northwest wind blew him offshore, froze him to death. Never found a trace of him, nor that Jersey boat neither.

"That's some empty place out there in winter. Them New England cod boats used to come down here, put out eight–ten dories. If a fog come in, they might find all their men or they might not—not hard to lose one."

The trawls were run every winter day that a boat could go off safely in the surf. It was said that cod bit best in a nor'wester ("The bigger the bait, the bigger the fish," Nathan Lester said). The best fishing could be had in a hard winter, with plenty of northwest blows to knock the surf down, so that the boats could go off safely and get back in. But that offshore wind bit hard on the long trip back, especially in later years when the cod moved farther and farther off the coast. The men piled on plenty of wool clothes and used big loose-knit wool mitts that, wet, kept the hands workable, especially when the mitts were caked with ice. In those days, the swift channel between Fireplace and Gardiners Island often froze over, permitting wagons to cross over the ice, and the air was so cold, it was said, that a big codfish, hauled aboard, would stiffen right out before it struck the bilges.

East winds made the sea unruly, but usually the seas took time to build; what was feared most was a sou'wester, which could come up suddenly and be blowing a whole gale before slow fish-laden boats out of sight of land could return to shore. Or sometimes there would be a heavy ground swell from an offshore storm, the men would feel its ominous lift under the boat. By the time they neared shore, these heavy swells would be breaking on the bar, a rise in the bottom about four hundred feet off the beach formed by the scouring action of longshore currents. (The bar may be eight feet below the surface, while the water inshore of it is eighteen or twenty feet deep.) Bill Lester and his father once got caught in a bad blow that nearly sank their boat when sea after sea broke over the stern as they slid down the faces of the waves.

"The main thing was to get across that bar and through the surf," Francis Lester says. "You had to cross both, as the outer bar was breakin pret' near constantly. When you got in the surf, you was a little bit nearer shore and you wasn't quite as worried. If anything happened out there on the bar, you'd be in trouble because it would be hard for anybody to help you . . . But they used pretty good judgment most of the time—they had to, if they wanted to survive."

"Surf fishin is a dangerous job," Bill Lester says. "You take chances, and you have to know what you are doin. When there is bad weather and rough sea, the boat might turn over or she might fill up. You might get hit with the boat or the net might wash on top of you.

"One morning my brother Frank and I, we went down codfishing. There was quite a lot of sea out there, and we didn't go because we had a gang of fykes in Montauk Lake, so we went down and lifted fykes. Young Nat Edwards and his cousin Kenneth hauled down, but it didn't look too good, and they hauled back. For some reason they decided to haul down again, and they went off, took a bad sea, and filled the boat. That water was awful cold, and young Nat drownded. We set a codfish trawl around that spot, but the people on the beach pulled it in too quick and we never hooked him. Sometime later, Frank and I were settin trawl up here, maybe a mile west of where Nat drownded, and we seen somethin strange-lookin come up in a poose,[3] just come up, y'know, and went down again; we rowed over there but we never saw nothin more. But a little later, another feller seen it again and pulled it out, and it was Nat. Wasn't much left to him—all the top was gone, nothin left but his legs and up to his backbone a little bit. Funny thing was, still had his white socks on and no boots. We thought some way them boots must have come off him just a little while before we seen him in that poose."

Kenneth Edwards told his younger brother Joshua, called Jack, that as they pushed off he had hollered to Nat, "Pull!" Kenny was standing in the stern of the small dory, pushing as Nat pulled on the same oars. When they cleared the first wave, Nat slacked up, getting his breath, and Kenny was turning to sit down beside him on the thwart (they would each take an oar) when they were struck by what the surfmen know as a freak sea—a big wave, out of the pattern of the others, that looms up quite suddenly out of nowhere. The boys swam back to the overturned dory, and this time

Nat found footing on the false bar (a shallow bar that some-times forms close to the beach) and stood up laughing. Kenny was yelling at him to kick his boots off when another sea struck him and he disappeared.

On one of the search parties along the beach, Jack Ed-wards found Kenny's oilskin jacket at Ditch Plains, faraway east in the opposite direction. He speculates that his cousin Nat, unacquainted with the character of the false bar and the channel inshore of it, had attempted to wade in, and had sunk his boots in the soft sand on the false bar's inner slope—"always quicksand on the inside of it," Bill Lester says—and been dragged under. He must have been numbed by immersion in the icy water, and apparently he had no time to kick his boots off.

According to Milt Miller, who was close to the Edwards clan, the whole community was shaken by Nat's death. "Cap'n Gabe's son Cap'n Nat was a big trap fisherman down Montauk, and his son, young Nat, was my age. Young Nat hadn't been brought up on the ocean, but worked the bay with his father; his cousin Kenny was the son of Cap'n Sam, and Kenny knew more about the bay than the ocean, too. There was quite a swell on, and we told 'em not to go. Why, we helped pull that boat back up to the dunes, and I went over Napeague to get some skimmer clams for cod bait."

Francis Lester also recalls that the Edwards boys were inexperienced in the surf. That day Francis decided to "take off for Montauk and go oysterin, had a lot of oysters after Montauk Lake was opened up. But before I went, I went over there and told 'em, 'Boys, that's not very good weather, and if I was you, I wouldn't try it.' Well, they said they'd wait a while; sometimes it'll calm down on a change of tide, y'know. And I said, 'You better forget about it today.' I took off and went oysterin, and they hung around, and the more they hung around, the more they thought it was gettin bet-ter. But it was still pretty rough, and they went forth, and they took a big sea. It threw the boat up and turned it over, and Kenneth got ashore, but the other boy, it was a long while before they found him."

"We did everything we could to try to recover the body," Milt Miller remembers. "The Lester Boys was there, too, draggin with cod hooks, but we couldn't come up with him. I remember Cap'n Nat walking that beach every day, until finally parts of him come ashore, the head, one shoulder, all chewed up by crabs and sand fleas. Kenny Edwards was messed up in his head for quite a while after that, and I myself never went fishin for two or three weeks, because people were close-knitted in them times, and we took it hard."

# 4.

# The Return of
# the Striped Bass

D uring the twenties, as oil-fueled ships replaced the old coal-burning steamers, the shore codfishery had declined, like shore whaling before it. The beam trawl had been replaced by the more efficient otter trawl,[1] and huge draggers sent out by a Boston syndicate would take hundreds of tons of cod from a single area. Eventually ships were sailing all the way to Greenland to find cod in adequate numbers to support this new technology, until finally the cod syndicate went bankrupt.

With increasing pressure, the bunker hordes had also diminished, and one by one the fish factories closed down, from Hicks Island all the way around the bay to Greenport. The sturgeon grew smaller, then all but disappeared, and bluefish were extremely scarce, as they had been periodically since the eighteenth century. In 1908 they all but vanished, only to come back strong again in 1909.

No bluefish have been caught on the fishing grounds in Gardiners Bay this summer. Probably the oldest inhabitant does not recall a summer during his lifetime when some bluefish were not caught in the waters about the east end. It is told, however, as a fact, that over a century

ago there was a period of fifty years in which not a bluefish was seen in these parts.

East Hampton *Star*, August 28, 1908

It is many years since there has been such fine bluefishing at the tide rip off Gardiners Point. The fish are there
in great schools, acres of them, as far as the eye can see.
Fluke are also extremely plentiful. There is scarcely a
fishing boat that goes out but returns with a good load.

East Hampton *Star*, August 13, 1909

Bluefish were abundant once again in 1920–1921 but must
have declined shortly thereafter, since Bill Lester says that
"in the twenties, Harry, Frank, and Charles and me set gill
nets in the ocean—that's all we done. And bluefish was so
scarce, you know, everybody was lined up for 'em. We got
fifty cents a pound, sold every one, cause we only got
one–two bushels a day. Then some years they disappeared
altogether, couldn't find a one." Frank Lester recalled that
no bluefish were caught for seven years.

As for striped bass, "When I was a boy, for a long long
time, there wasn't any," Bill remembers. "Round about
1920, I guess, we made one haul and got sixty bass and that
was big news all over the Island! First bass seen in a good
while, and the last ones, too. So most of our fishing was set-
netting in them days. Used to set about six gill nets in maybe
sixteen foot of water, between the outer bar and shore, each
net forty-five fathom long. Set some in deeper water, too,
back of the bar, cause that was safer. If you set between the
surf and the outer bar, and you got a bad storm, might lose
your nets or get 'em tore to pieces; no anchor'd hold 'em
with that sea washing along. We would catch a lot of fish by
setting off-and-on—one net straight off and then a wing
along the beach, west in the spring, east in the fall. Could
rig it different ways, y'know, with anchors to hold it against
the set, maybe a hook in it to hold the fish in a kind of pen.

Fish comin along would strike that net, turn offshore and hit the wing, or stay in the pocket till you come along and hauled. But settin off-and-on that way was dangerous, too, and we lost a lot of gear. One summer me and my youngest brother, Ted, lost eighteen nets, kept borrowin money at East Hampton Bank, come back with new nets, but the only one to make money was the twine company. So to get out of debt we went down Montauk to go dragging. We went about a year, done very good, and paid the bills off.

"Once I tried a month of plumbin with George Schellinger; he was my brother-in-law. Fishin was poor probably, had no money, I was probably forced to it. If I had any money, I wouldn't have went, and that's for sure. I like to go fishin and just as long as I can crawl, I am goin down there.

"My brother Ted was ten years younger—he was the baby of the family. Ted got married at seventeen or eighteen, same as me, but he never had no place to live, so I give him a piece of land up near the tracks and he got enough lumber some place or other to build two little rooms for him and Jenny. Ted started fishin about 1925, and it was me kept him a-goin in the Depression. When there was no weather to go fishin, we'd try somethin else. We'd go down Montauk in the mornin, go blueberryin all afternoon, sleep with the wood ticks in the old haybarn used to be down behind Third House, berry in the mornin, come back home, and sell them berries off ten cents a quart."

In the late twenties, young Ted had gone off swordfishing with Punk Beckwith, one of the Nova Scotia men who had come south to work in the Montauk fishery; sometimes they took Punk's small boat all the way down off Fire Island. (On one trip, Ted recalled, they saw sixteen or seventeen swordfish the first day, and Punk missed every one of them; the next day Punk struck and boated five out of six.)

Most of the swordfish boats, Bill Lester says, were twenty-one-foot Jersey skiffs launched from the beach. "In the early thirties," he remembers, "Ted and me caught an abundance of swordfish, as high as six a day. We had a big box built out here in back, packed 'em with ice until the price came up, because the Fulton Fish Market was only given us ten–twelve cents a pound. If the market give us a penny, you know, we had to take it, and it's the same today. So my wife, Sadie, who was a Spicer girl, and Ted's wife, who was Jenny Bennett, would take a swordfish around from house to house, sellin it off for thirty-five cents, bring home maybe a hundred dollars. That way we was able to pay the gas for the next day.

"Ted was a good swordfisherman, you know—too good! Tried to do every damn thing himself! So nervous, you remember how he was, had to holler at him all the time to calm him down. One time there back in the thirties, Ted and me was out with our brother-in-law John Erickson, and I seen this big fish finnin an awful distance off, a mile and maybe more, the way you do sometimes. Ted was up on the tower, but some way he couldn't pick up that fin, even when he was only two–three hundred yards away. So I hollered at him to take his time, I would come up easy, put him right on it, but no, Ted couldn't wait, you know, couldn't waste time goin down the ladder, just grabbed the cable from the tower and slid right down onto the pulpit! Struck that fish with them burnt hands and thought about it later, that's the way Ted was—a real piss-cutter![2]

"I guess Ted harpooned the biggest shark was ever landed around here, shipped seven boxes of meat out of it, as I recall. Don't know whether it was a white shark, or a black or a pink; we paid no attention to that stuff in them days, had to fish too hard. We caught all kinds and thousands of 'em, wore out four–five baseball bats, tendin them sharks. Used to get ten–twelve cents for mako when ten–twelve cents was still worth somethin, cause there's people will eat shark. I never et a piece of shark meat in my life, and don't guess I'll ever get around to it, no, no.

"Here and there across the years there'd be a run of bass," Bill says "and we'd go seinin. Hauled by hand, you know, and sometimes we had a slow old horse." In the twenties and thirties the farmers had converted from horse-drawn wagons to narrow-tired trucks that could not travel on the beach, and until the early beach vehicles were developed, the fish had to be lugged up to the road in hand carts and barrels. "Long about 1930, when we done good draggin, I got hold of a DeSoto, nearly new, that was hit by a fallen tree and smashed the roof in; got her real cheap, and she worked good in the sand. Her clutch slipped just enough so she didn't dig down, and every two weeks or so we just slapped a new clutch into her, cost about two dollars and a half. Well, we carried that little dory on a platform in back, and we hauled seine with her. Back her down, hook up to the net, go forward—back and forth like that. I guess that was the first car on the beach.

"Frank had his own crew, and Harry and Charlie jumped around between us; they didn't do so much fishin as the rest of us. Charlie done some fishin all along, but he was always more interested in farmin. Frank and Harry always set fykes in spring, y'know, but when summer come, Harry went over to housepaintin. He had moved away from us, over to the other end of town.

"I believe I had Henry Havens with me in my first crew—big tall man, very slow and strong. When Henry put them oars into the water, that boat *went* somewhere!" In the summer, Henry sometimes set nets in the ocean with Charlie and Happy Lester; their catch was sold in Charlie Lester's small fresh food shop, and those who were broke might trade eggs or vegetables for a fish.

"My younger brothers Ted and Harold, the one they called Happy, fished with me a good number of years. Then Ted split off from me, took Harold with him, put together his own crew. Ted was a feller always wanted to overdo somethin; never had enough. We was fishin all the way west to Wainscott, weren't no beach trucks then, and had to cart them fish over the beach banks to the landins, and *still* he'd want to keep a-goin further west!"

Henry Havens's young son Billy was a close friend of young Billy Lester, and spent much of his youth in the house of Cap'n Bill. "My pop was some strong, I guess; seemed like he made one pull on them oars every half hour. Happy Lester—he was the youngest next to Ted—rowed with my pop, and that looked kind of funny, cause Happy always had them short quick strokes." In his first years on the beach, in the late thirties, Billy Havens fished on Bill Lester's crew, together with Ted, Bill's older son Kenny, Ding Schellinger, and Stuart Vorpahl, Sr. "Because we was young, me and Kenny Lester was paid one dollar a haul! Course we used to make a lot of hauls with them little nets, even haulin by hand, and one day us two made thirteen–fourteen dollars when the regular crew gettin full shares didn't make nothin. I don't believe that Bill and Ted forgot *that* one for a while, do you?"

Even in those days, Ted Lester was notorious as a hard driver, and Billy Havens—who came to be called Will, or William, to avoid confusion with Billy Lester, and later with his own son—remembers a time when "Ted had me goin east along the bar, he was up in the bow peerin down, lookin for bass, and before he spotted one little bunch 'bout as big as the boat, I'd rowed that dory all the way from Georgica to Gurney's Inn. Course that boat wasn't but sixteen-foot long, and for a seine we never had nothin but three gill nets run together with a bunt. Anyway, we set around them fish, got twelve–sixteen, which wasn't a bad haul back in the thirties.

"Bill couldn't take Ted's nervousness; he was nervous enough himself. Ted never meant no harm, y'know, but he never let up. Must have been long about the time of the hurricane of '38, Bill just got disgusted with Ted for pushin so hard, all that hurryin and jumpin, and he told us, 'That's the last time I ever fish with *him!*' Bill strung a few gill nets together, went off on his own, took me and his boy Kenny with him, but it was another year, I guess, before Kenny and me were gettin a full share. Happy went with Ted, and I guess he drove Ted kind of crazy, because soon's he got off the beach, y'know, he'd go right to the bars. Stuttered, y'know, and had terrible piles, and all that beer never helped them piles too much. But he was a bachelor, didn't have no family to support or nothin, lived with his mother across the way in the old homestead."

By the late thirties, striped bass had resumed their place as a local sport fish, to judge from the fact that a 1936 "Long Island Fishing Guide" put out by the East End Surf Fishing Club includes an enthusiastic article on this species. "I guess it was 'long about the late thirties, early forties, when them bass started to come back strong," Bill Lester says. Sometimes the Lesters would set gill nets by anchoring one end on the beach and letting the other be carried offshore in a "run-out," where the surf pouring off the beach formed a sort of current straight offshore. Then a day came when a gill net was hauled in solid full of bass. "One day I went down with Ted, and the ocean was full of striped bass, everywhere you looked! Acres and acres, just boilin with 'em, and nothin but small bass. Ted tried 'em anyway, got seven or eight truckloads, but by the time he got them undersize fish sorted away—they was already a limit then of sixteen inches—he had saved out about three. But later we got thirty-seven chunks of 'em, all legal fish, in just one haul.

"Course everything changes, y'know. Was thinkin just the other day about chunks. A chunk was a heavy box, loaded around 350 pounds. Back before then we used sugar boxes, carry five–six hundred pounds, used to cart 'em up to the railroad and h'ist 'em up onto the cars. But the men could throw 'em around by hand, and the railroad men, too. Men these days gettin awful weak, seems like, because the boxes are gettin smaller all the time. After the chunks we had them shad boxes, with partitions, carried maybe 280; then there was a 200-pound box; then the 125-pound crate that we used in them years you was fishin with us. Now the wood boxes are all gone, they use them cardboard cartons, hold about 60–70 pounds apiece."

During World War II, most of the few vehicles on the beach were Model A's; the dories were still hauled down to the water on rollers. There was a night curfew on the beach, and because the "A's" could carry no more than fifteen boxes, the Amagansett Coast Guardsmen sometimes helped with a late haul, to get the fishermen off the beach by dark.

"We never had no winch," Bill says, "until right after World War II; Briggs and Stratton with 3:1 reduction gear, turnin a niggerhead on the bed of an old Army truck. That ain't much different than what we got today." After the war, converted weapons carriers and other vehicles with four-wheel drive rapidly replaced the tough old Model A's and makeshift beach cars.

Even in the late forties, the bass runs were sporadic, and haul-seining was confined to six weeks in spring, six in the fall; in other seasons, the men set gill nets or went over to the bay. For eight or nine years in the 1940s, Bill Lester went beam-trawling for yellowtail flounder on the *William D,* from Montauk Point east to Noman's Land, off Martha's Vineyard, where a colony of Japanese fishermen was harvesting shark livers and fins for sharkfin soup; he recalls the colors of the rocks in the light of sunset at Gay Head, when the *William D* laid over in Menemsha, and the tepees of an Indian powwow on the shore. "We was rigged for swordfish, and one time we struck this one had a white scar on it, an old harpoon scar by the look of it, and Cap'n Bill Parsons sent me off in the dory to tend the keg. Well, this

fish was some green, y'know, and damn if he don't bang
that sword up through the bottom of the boat, broke her
off right into the coil of line between my boots! Next time
he come up, I got a strap around his tail and just hung on.
Wasn't a dry spot on me but I held him—he never went
down again." One day Bill went out with Elisha Ammon,
whose boat had vibrations that scared swordfish, but the
*William D* "let you get fast to a fish; one year we seen just
eighteen swordfish and we got 'em all.

"Back then somewheres, Frank bought the whole corner
over here on the highway for $450, put gas pumps in there,
called it the Amagansett Service Station. His wife had a little
restaurant, made clam chowder, clam pies, sold a few cigars
and knickknacks. Then she got sick and another feller had
it; then Frank's son-in-law took over, Brentford M. Bennett,
called it Brent's Store. And along there some time, Ted
went into business, too."

After World War II, Ted Lester had worked out of
Montauk as captain of a private boat, the *Pumpkin Seed,* with
his brother-in-law Vern Bennett as his mate. The owner
gave him all the swordfish he could harpoon, and in the
summer of 1945 Ted took fifty fish. In the same period, he
invested in his own boat, a twenty-eight-foot Jersey skiff,
the *Sand Eel,* which was run mostly by his brother Harry,
assisted by another brother-in-law named Elmer Fenelon.
Harry Lester, oldest of the "Posey Boys," was already close
to sixty, a small quiet man who made his living as a carpenter and house painter, but went back to the water whenever
he could.

"End of the war," says his brother Bill, "Ted got in with
a rich feller down Montauk, ran his yacht for him, he did,
and this man bought him that house down street there.
Never could see yachtin myself, too much cleanin up after
other people; come them little dewy nights, you had to wear
tennis shoes and mop your decks up. But Ted done good
with it. They was taking thirty-five–forty swordfish every

summer, and Ted sold everything them people couldn't eat. Took that money, y'know, and went in with Frank Tillotson, built that freezer under his house, 1947–48, called it Montauk Seafood.

"Frank Tillotson was from over Southampton way, and him and my brother Frank's boys Harry and Robert, and Brent Bennett, them fellers was hand-linin sea bass off the wreck of the old *Panther* down off Shinnecock, and a big run o'striped bass come in, and they rigged a net, made a big haul—had to use town trucks to cart 'em all away! So we went west, got some of them fish, too. Why, in them days, we used to take our old cars all the way west to Tiana! [Hampton Bays–Quogue] Nowadays we got good trucks, but there's too many people on the beach and not enough fish, so we don't go nowheres."

# 5.

# In Bonac:
# Clammers and Scallopers

I n 1684 the East Hampton Town Trustees sent sixteen men to Meantecut to help the Indians open
the tidal creek from the bay into Montauk Great
Pond, apparently to revive its oyster beds with more salt
water. Big local oysters, often a foot long, were a basic food
of both Indians and settlers, and because—unlike fish—they
could survive the sea voyage to market in New England and
New York, oysters, like clams, were harvested for export as
well as for extensive local use.

In the 1700s an immense oyster bed was located to the
west, off Blue Point, on the Great South Bay, attracting an
ever-increasing group of men "who depended for their subsistence upon the products of the waters of the bay. They
were called baymen. For nine months the baymen lived on
the profits derived from the oyster beds, and depended
upon the other three for clamming and fishing. They were
poor for the most part, but independent."[1] Working from
small catboats, sloops, and the flat-bottomed sharp-prowed
work skiff called the sharpie, the baymen harvested these
beds with tongs, and by the early nineteenth century had
all but exhausted the Blue Point field. But oyster packing
houses in Patchogue continued to buy oysters taken else-

where on Great South Bay, which were shipped in kegs to New York's Fulton Fish Market. In the 1860s, when oyster tongs were replaced by the dredge, the last beds were already overfished, and soon the independent baymen were put out of business by large companies that planted oysters on prepared grounds and saw to it that the use of dredges was outlawed elsewhere.

On the South Fork, where the salt ponds and harbors were once crusted with wild oysters, this fishery had been domesticated, too. In 1831 Isaac Van Scoy of Northwest received permission from the East Hampton Town trustees to plant an oyster bed in Northwest Creek, and by century's end large oyster operations based in Greenport were laying beds in Peconic and Gardiners Bays; the "Gardiners Bay salt" challenged the Blue Point as a celebrated oyster in the city markets. By 1900, the last wild oysters were old lone "coonfoots" on rocky bottoms avoided by the scallopers and clammers. All that remained of this great public fishery was the name "baymen," which had spread eastward with the refugee fishing families from Great South Bay. The heretofore independent baymen were reduced to dredging jingle shell cultch[2] for the privately owned oyster beds, and even today, the few oysters taken by the baymen are mostly sold as seed stock to the corporations.

One of the best oyster grounds in the whole township was Accabonac Creek, a few miles northeast of East Hampton village. In the early fifties, when I first came there to live, the Springs, or Bonac, was mostly farmland owned by Bennetts, Talmages, and Millers, sloping down across the tidewater to Bonac Creek; at the head of the creek was a community building and a gas pump and general store. Originally the main source for salt hay for the settlers' stock, Bonac Creek was a peaceful and very pretty place of meadowland and cedar fields and a quiet lead of water, widening out eastward past Tick Island to the sand spit at Louse Point and Gardiners Bay.

This backwater had changed very little in the long slow decades since the turn of the century, when the Wood family arrived here from the Great South Bay, one of the first fishing families (they are still coming) to be driven eastward by the destruction of the fisheries farther west. "They were clam and oystermen, they had sloops, and they went clammin in the ocean, and flounder fishin, eelin," says Jarvis Wood, born in the Springs in 1908, and they were baymen (although Jarvie says that this name did not come into general use out here until recent decades). "My grandfather, he fished all the time, he was a fisherman all his life. And my father was a fisherman, only thing he ever done. So naturally I started, I come fishin, too."

At the creek head (still called Pussy's Pond after an old Miss Pussy Parsons) the Parsons oyster house, used for opening scallops "after the oysters run out," later became Smith's general store, where storytelling took place every Sunday evening. In the twenties, dances were held there once a week. The two churches were Episcopal and Presbyterian, divorce and unwed couples were still scandalous, and old people without furnaces or relatives went to the poorhouse thirty or forty miles "up-Island" (Jarvie's father-in-law was Overseer of the Poor). For many years his mother took in laundry for the summer people in East Hampton, which had turned from a farming-fishing town to a resort by the turn of the century.

"Nobody was in a real rush to do anything, they didn't need all this money, all this stuff to go to, all they wanted was to make a livin. Everybody was fishin or farmers; s'all there was. Either go fishin or farmin, and a lot of the farmers went fishin. In the summertime, when they had their crops in, they'd go down clammin; in the wintertime, when their crops are gone, they go scallopin, oysterin. Everybody got along, y'know, they had taters in the cellar, maybe a barrel of pork, something like that; no one went hungry.

"In them days, fishin wasn't so easy as it is today. Today

you got trucks and motors, you got everything to do all your work with; them days, you done all your work with your hands. If you wanted to go somewhere you took a pair of oars and you rowed your boat; you didn't just steer a boat, go down where you wanted to fish! But flounders, used to be so many in the bay, if you set a fyke out you couldn't even get 'em in, there was too much in the fyke. Then all of a sudden they disappeared, couldn't get no flounders, everybody went out of business. Then they come back again, though there ain't as many as there used to be cause of the draggers."

As a small boy, Jarvie lived at Lazy Point in Napeague, where his family were clammers and dug skimmers for the cod trawls in the ocean; he remembers that eels were collected in a barrel until some "backer" (tobacco) was tossed in to stun the slippery creatures before attempting to "skun 'em out." (Some baymen put ashes on their hands for "sloimin," others use burlap bags to grasp the eel, which is fixed by the head on a nail stuck through a wall; the throat is then cut through the bone, and a slit made down the length of the belly, after which the head and skin are stripped away.) For a time he worked on "Old Man Schellinger's" farm, one of many in the neighborhood that raised chickens and corn and wheat. But Jarvie quit high school after a year to become a fisherman.

"If we wanted eels or clams or fish, we always got 'em fresh, cause there was no problems gettin stuff to eat. In the wintertime we used to shoot ducks. Them days people didn't kill themselves like they do t'day, cause there was no problems. Whatever you want'd to catch, there was plenty of it. You go out and catch a couple bushel clams, if you was ambitious three bushel; man had a big family, he had to work harder. Any time you didn't have nothin to do, you'd go out clammin."

Quahogs, or hard clams (in market terms—in ascending size—littlenecks, cherrystones, and chowders) have been a

Long Island subsistence food since prehistoric times. The Indians used the purple and white interior for wampum, and the strong valves served very well as hoe blades. Even today the hard clam is the most dependable of all the fisheries, between seasons, in winter, and when times are poor. (Soft clams, or steamers—known to the commercial men as piss clams because of the jets of water they emit in times of stress—are dug from soft mud flats with a clam hook, like a short forked hoe, or "grinded" in shallow water by an outboard propeller that spins the clams up to the surface. Like the long clam (surf clam or skimmer)—the big clam cast up on the ocean beach in storms and used as ashtrays in the summer cottages that began to turn up on the dunes in the 1880s—soft clams were considered unworthy of human consumption in the early days, and were mainly harvested for cod bait, hog and poultry food, or fertilizer. The common blue mussel and the whelk, or winkle, once so sought after for wampum, were ignored. Today steamers, winkles, and mussels are much in demand, and the fried clam served in summer restaurants is usually the lowly skimmer.)

Hard clams are mostly taken with a scratch rake fitted out with an iron basket. A longer and larger rake with back strap and crossbar pull handle, called the bull rake, is often used by the commercial men in deeper water.[3] In winter the bayman may resort to long-poled double-basket rakes in the form of pincers, worked from a small boat and known as tongs. Whatever the implement, even when hard clams were common, the average bayman rarely took more than five bushels on a tide (although Bill Lester, in his days on Montauk Lake, took six or seven). Now the clams have been overharvested. The three-bushel limit is hard to achieve, and its value varies: chowder clams may be worth just five dollars a bushel, whereas cherrystones—five for a penny at the turn of the century—may sell for fifty dollars a bushel, sometimes more. Especially on rocky bottoms (and also in winter, when the sand is hard and dense, and the clams are deeper) clams are much more work for a lot less money than the free-swimming scallops, which in most years support a very profitable local fishery.

In the Depression, as Captain Nathan Lester told the *Island News* in 1933, it was "pretty hard to make a decent living fishing." Like many baymen, Jarvie Wood tried work at regular jobs, returning to fishing about 1940. In the early fifties, when I lived in the Springs, he had opened a small store near his Neck Path house, on the road to Amagansett, but in 1964 he sold the store and returned to fishing once again. "Was makin some good money, too," he told me twenty years later. "But I said to my wife, 'What we ever goin to do with all that money? Get to be old, y'know, ain't nothin much you want to do anyway.' She didn't want to sell but she agreed to it, just to go along with me."

In the early fifties the Springs was still back in the woods, and rents were very inexpensive. My friend John Cole lived in the old Parsons house across from the old school and Pete Scott lived in a small cottage on the salt marsh. (During World War II, on visits to East Hampton, I had become friends with John's family, and sometimes, as a friend of Pete Scott's brother, I had stayed in the Scott cottage, called the Box, a very old house near "Home Sweet Home" on East Hampton's Main Street.) With my wife and infant son, I found a cottage on Fireplace Road just west of the horse and cattle farm of George Sid Miller. In those days there were few writers in the region, and apart from the Coles and Scotts, most of the people that we saw were painters. Francile and Sherry Lord, Lee and Jackson Pollock, Charlotte and Jim Brooks were neighbors as well as friends, and many other painters lived not far away, with more still coming. To the local people, all of us were "people from away," the forerunners of many still to come. (As Milt Miller says, "I always thought of all outsiders as foreigners—still do, I guess.")

The fall of 1953 was my first season clamming and scalloping in Three Mile and Northwest Harbors. My fishing partner was John Cole (who like myself was unsuited to urban work and had sought a leaner way of life outdoors) and our scallop boat was a nineteen-foot double-ended Quebec codfish boat with a short mast and a one-cylinder engine (hence her name, *Vop-Vop*) which, in size and sound, if not in her appearance, must have reminded the old-timers of the first Jersey boats launched through the surf. Rigged out with culling board and scallop dredges, the *Vop* was moored in a small anchorage just north of Emerson Taber's lobster dock in Three Mile Harbor—the Town Commercial Dock site, given to East Hampton by the Gardiner family back in the thirties. On the still warm Indian summer days of mid-September, no dredges or culling board were necessary; we drifted the broad harbor flats south of the long neck called Sammis Beach,[4] pouring a little bunker oil upwind to smooth and clear the surface of the water and using the rim of long-poled dip nets to tap the edges of somnolent scallops in their sand nests in the eelgrass, causing them to somersault backward into the mesh.

The delicious inshore pecten, or bay scallop, was regarded with suspicion by the early settlers. Scallop shells abound in the Indian middens, but the creature's lurid interior design, set off by a mantle of phosphorescent turquoise, was apparently not approved by local Puritans, especially when plainer shellfish were so plentiful. Even a cat, it was related, might discover that its tail had fallen off after eating a scallop. This peculiar species was a free-swimmer, not easily confined to domestic beds; unlike more stick-in-the-mud mollusks, it was able and ready to rise up from the bottom and jet through the water by opening and shutting its valves, and might gallivant "down bay" for a considerable distance before this errant impulse had subsided.

But if the settlers were conservative, they were also practical. Local opinion of the scallop changed in the middle of the nineteenth century—or so it is said—when an enterprising fisherman from Connecticut did very well with a cargo of scallops from Peconic Bay, inspiring a beached whaleman of Sag Harbor to develop a small market for this seafood in New York City. With the appropriation of the oyster industry by private interests, the desperate baymen flocked to the new fishery, and by 1873, five thousand bushels were taken in one season from Peconic. Old discarded oyster dredges worked well with scallops, which would flip upward in a backward somersault into the wide mouth of the oncoming dredge, and almost any small craft, rowed or sailed, would suit the purpose. By the turn of the century, two hundred small boats were engaged in scalloping.

In those days, eelgrass was widespread in Gardiners Bay, and the scallops so thick, according to Jarvie Wood, that a sloop could bail a boatload in a half day. In 1928 the eelgrass died off in a mysterious plague, and the bay scallop (and also the small coastal goose known as the brant) all but died with it. For some reason, the soft clam vanished, too. Eelgrass, scallops, and soft clams returned to the harbors in the early thirties, but the grass has yet to take hold again out in the bay. Decades later, juvenile scallops still appear as thick as ever on Jarvie's trap stakes, but without the shelter of the grass, most seem to wash ashore or are otherwise lost.

Already in the thirties it was realized that there might be a limit to scallop numbers, which fluctuated a good deal from year to year, and in 1934 the town set a daily limit of five bushels. At present a daily limit of ten bushels per licensed bayman, fifteen per boat, is still in force in East Hampton Town waters.[5]

Not all baymen haul seine or lift gill nets and traps; these days, because "the clams are down," there are probably a few who do not clam. But almost every able-bodied bayman will go scalloping, at least in the early weeks of a good season, when the daily limit may be harvested in two hours' work. In most years the scallop is the major resource of the bayman, who pursues it from the soft days of Indian summer until the hard windy days of early spring, when the adult scallops begin to die. Usually his income is increased by his own family; his wife may sort scallops on the culling board, and many women in the fishing community are expert openers, or shuckers, separating the firm white "eye" (the adductor muscle that closes the two scallop-edged valves) from the colorful but unacceptable mantle and guts.

Most commercial men use the traditional fourteen-foot sharpie, which is the bayman's all-purpose skiff (the so-called trap sharpie, used for lifting traps, is longer and wider). Until the mid-sixties, when the use of power was permitted, the scalloper anchored, drifted downwind perhaps two hundred feet, then hauled, or kedged, back up the running line, dragging a dredge and sometimes two behind. The scallop dredge, thirty inches across and weighing more than twenty pounds, is the same "Greenport sloop dredge" used at the turn of the century. Pronounced "drudge" (as in "hung new twoine on thim drudges, did ye?"), it may scrape up over fifty pounds of eelgrass, mud, water, rock, and shell that must be heaved onto a culling board before the scallops can be sorted.

Unlike more sedentary bivalves, the scallop lives only about eighteen months, and scallop seasons vary considerably, depending on weather conditions at the time of spawning as well as survival of the small "bug" scallops over their first winter. In 1953 the bugs had prospered, and in the first weeks of September the scallops were so thick that, using dip nets, we harvested our boat limit in a few hours' pleasant work. Loading the crunching burlap sacks into John's old greenish truck, we would cart them across Abra-

ham's Path (named for that Abraham Schellinger who built
the first wharf out at Northwest in 1700) through the warm
September woods of pitch pine and scrub oak to the scallop
openers in Amagansett.

With windy weather, as Indian summer turned to fall, the
scallops became scarce in shallow water. We turned to heavy
labor with the dredges, dumping the wet loads of eelgrass
and codium, or Sputnik weed,[6] onto the culling board. The
load was never twice the same. The elegant scallops, snapping their shells, were occasionally accompanied by an un-
wary flounder, together with an indiscriminate assortment
of crabs, horsefoots, sand worms, glass shrimp, sea horses,
sponges, whelks, stones, bottles, sneakers, dead shells, and—
not uncommonly—a small clump of wild oysters.

Later that autumn, when the scallops thinned out inside
the harbors, we went prospecting for virgin scallop beds as
far away as Napeague, Montauk Lake, and Gardiners Island, putting in at Promised Land for our supplies. One
day of late October, as we scalloped off the western shore
of Gardiners Island, a cold front came in toward midday,
with a stiff wind out of the northwest. Though heavily
crusted with quarterdecks, or boat shells, the scallops on
this rocky bottom were plentiful, and we were hurrying to
complete our twenty-bushel boat limit and head home when
the one-cylinder motor on my old boat conked out and
would not revive. Hoisting the *Vop*'s patched gaff-rigged
sail, we beat upwind toward the mainland.

Already a hard gale was blowing; despite her deep keel,
the boat was banging into white-capped waves. Halfway
across the channel the pine mast broke off at the deck, and
mast, boom, and canvas crashed upon our heads. Not saying
much, we sorted out the mess as the wind carried us back
toward Gardiners Island. (Years ago, an old-timer named
Puff Dominy broke down off Lion Head Rock and drifted
back east to Gardiners on this same course. Told to throw

over the anchor, his retarded crewman cried, "No twing! No twing!" Impatient and uncomprehending, Puff hollered, "Let 'er go, goddamn it, 'twing' or no 'twing'!" Thrown overboard with no "string" attached, Puff's anchor disappeared forever, but "twing or no twing" has survived in local lore.)

Nearing the island, we threw over an anchor, but by the time the grapnel finally took hold, the *Vop* was scarcely two hundred yards offshore in Bostwick Bay, buffeted by wind and seas in the growing weather. It was midafternoon of a swift day of late autumn, and a cold sun was sinking fast, with no boat in sight, nothing but whitecaps and wind-blown gulls and long black ragged strings of cormorants beating across the wind toward the southwest. Not only was the boat wide open, but the hatch covers of the fish holds forming her deck were only three inches lower than the gunwales, which provided no shelter from the wind. On this north end of Gardiners Island, never inhabited, the view from the sea was as wild as it was three centuries before when the Algonkian people known as Montauks escorted Lion Gardiner to his New World home.

In 1676, by the Dongan Patent, Gardiners Island— roughly seven by three miles, or about 3,300 acres—had been deemed a manor, and it is, in fact, the last of the old English manors to remain in the same New World family to the present day. In the 1690s, Captain William Kidd, a minister's son and retired sea captain pressed into service as a privateer by a syndicate that included the English governor of Massachusetts, was arrested in Boston and sent to England. There he was hanged for disputed reasons, among them, it is said, the protection of the reputations of those who had benefitted from his voyages, including the hard-living "Lord John" Gardiner, son of the incumbent Lord of the Manor, David Lion Gardiner, who had first welcomed Kidd to Gardiners Island. Captain Kidd's only known treasure of gold dust, gold coin, jewelry and the like, retrieved from the pond behind the beach in Cherry Harbor off which we had been scalloping when the boat broke down, was turned over to the authorities by Lord John, who escaped unpunished. In 1728 the manor was commandeered for three days by real pirates, causing the family to look for safer lodgings in East Hampton Village. Since then, Gardiners Island has been occupied intermittently by the Gardiner family, which has often leased it to other people.

In the 1950s the island was still inhabited by an estimated five hundred pairs of ospreys, by far the largest colony of these striking fish hawks in North America and perhaps the world. High cliffs to the eastward (a source of clay for the early settlers) slope gradually to low fields in the west, with broad lowlands, salt marsh, ponds, and sand spits, north and south. Where we were anchored was the windward shore of the northern sand spit, in Bostwick ("Bostic" to the fishermen) Bay, where a bad August storm of 1879 had overturned a lobster boat out of New London, drowning two crewmen. Another storm in 1892 parted this sand spit, creating an islet out at the north point where a lighthouse had been built in 1855;[7] the shoddily constructed building, weakened by storms, collapsed two years later, and the light was abandoned. During the Spanish-American War, a round structure called Fort Tyler was built upon this shored-up islet, part of a whole string of forts on Plum, Gull, and Fishers Islands designed to protect Long Island Sound from unfriendly gunboats.[8] Since its abandonment in 1924, Fort Tyler has been much diminished by erosion and bombing practice, and is usually referred to as "the ruin."

Twilight had come, and a sharp autumn cold. To the north the old fort, in dark and gloomy silhouette on a cold sunset, rode like a ship in the running silver tide against the lightless islands and the far black line of the New England hills where the last light faded in the sky. Our young wives would not worry about us until after nightfall, so no help could be expected until next day.

Eight miles to the northeast lay Fishers Island, the easternmost point of Suffolk County, where I had spent most of my first fifteen summers;[9] five miles to the southwest lay Three Mile Harbor in East Hampton, where I visited first in 1942. Now it was 1953, I was in my mid-twenties, and had moved permanently to the South Fork. Thus I had lived in Suffolk County all my life, on or about the edges of these waters; this wild and lonely place where our small boat washed up and down on the high chop lay at the very heart of my home country.

On this cold rough October evening, hunched knee to knee in a cramped anchor cuddy, we ate raw scallops from the upright burlap bags that hunched like refugees on deck, and listened to the waves slap on the hull; if the anchor dragged during the night, our small wood boat would wash ashore on Gardiners Island. It was already gunning season, and we wanted no night dealings with Charlie Raynor, the caretaker and dangerous enemy of enterprising young gunners such as ourselves who would sneak ashore at the south end while out coot shooting around Cartwright Shoals and be reasonably sure of snagging a few pheasants along the airstrip. Raynor's reputation as a man who would shoot first and talk afterward saved him a lot of trouble on the job. Especially in the hunting season, he made no distinctions between castaways and trespassers, and anyway he lived too far off to be of help.

At daylight the cold wind from the northwest had not diminished, and there were no signs of boats or sail. All Gardiners Bay was tossed in a white chop, crossed by the strings of cormorants, the hurrying scoters and solitary loons, the wind-tilted gulls, hard wings reflecting a wild light that pierced the metallic clouds.

Toward midmorning a Coast Guard plane came over;

when we waved our arms, the plane went away, and still there were no boats on the rough horizons.

In early afternoon a black fishing boat appeared. Its hardy skipper was Fanny Gardiner Collins of Three Mile Harbor, a member of the island clan and avid fisherwoman who knew much more about Gardiners Island and its waters than her wealthy kinsmen. Fanny took us in tow and hauled us back to Three Mile Harbor.

In November, when the scallops became scarce, I helped out now and then on a small haul-seine rig led by Jimmy Reutershan, who came from a local "up-street" family of nonfishermen, and had John Cole and Pete Scott as his steady crew. The rig consisted of Jimmy's Land Rover, small dory, and small seine, and it stuck pretty close to a stretch of beach near the old Georgica Coast Guard Station.[10] On those bright cold autumn days, with sharp sand blowing, the silver ocean, sparkling and clear, seemed empty; we were beginners, and we made one dry haul after another, standing around the limp and forlorn bag as if puzzling out an oracle. On one such morning Jimmy drew an ancient black banana from the seat box on the Land Rover and offered it upright, with his wry tough smile, to his weary crew. "Have a banana," Jimmy said, "lightly flecked with brown."

# THE
# FIFTIES

# 6.

# Poseyville
# and Captain Ted

In the spring of 1954, I joined the ocean haul-seine crew led by Ted Lester who lived in Amagansett on a short street through the scrub oak woods known as Cross Highway. The obscure street was an extension of Abraham's Path, connecting the Montauk Highway with the old Indian trails back of the dunes that are now called Further Lane and Skimhampton Road. This community of small houses and big work yards full of dories and beach vehicles and nets spread out to dry was known locally as Poseyville, or Fish Gut Alley, and most of its inhabitants were known as Poseys. It is the Posey Lester clan in Amagansett that Milt Miller has called "the backbone of what fishin is still left today."

Of the original six sons of Nathan Lester, the eldest, Harry, and the second youngest, Harold, or Happy, had died in recent years, while Charlie (who liked to recall the fresh swordfish he once found on the beach in front of the fashionable Maidstone Club) had retired from the water and was raising vegetables and chickens for his small store near Ted's house; the other three, Frank, Bill, and Ted, each ran a haul-seine crew.

In 1954, bony-faced Frank Lester, calm and smiling, was

already in his mid-sixties, and shared the leadership of his family crew with his son Francis; because of his ever-present pipe, he was known affectionately as Cap'n Smoker. His brother Bill, a decade younger and still strong and vigorous (I remember him as a big silver-haired handsome man in black shirt and black waders), had the best equipment and a veteran crew that was usually "high hook" (largest landings of fish) in a given season. Ted Lester, ten years younger than Bill, intensely curious and energetic, was the most innovative fisherman, and the most ambitious; he sold frozen bait (bunker chum and squid) to the charter boats and bait shops and shipped fish to New York from his Montauk Seafood, a fish-packing and storage house that was used by the Posey haul-seine crews in an effort to hold back shipments of fish until the Fulton Fish Market would offer a fair price. Whether they liked it or not—for even among his brothers, he was controversial—Ted Lester was the spokesman for the fishermen, not only in their running battles with the market but in their defense against sport-fishing groups, which had renewed a long war of attrition against the commercial men in an effort to prohibit the netting of striped bass.

A quick stocky man with a stiff brush of hair that stood straight up from his forehead, giving him an expression of surprise, Theodore Roosevelt Lester (born in a rock-ribbed Republican county in 1908) was always in a rush and often shouting, for want of a better way to let off steam. I met him first on a wet May morning in the 4 A.M. darkness of his yard as he hurried to start up his ancient silver truck, a former weapons carrier of World War II. The truck's hood had rusted out and fallen by the wayside, and because it had rained hard all night, the wiring was sodden. Ted Lester swore as he dumped gasoline on his engine and set it on fire.

The big silver truck, once the blaze was smothered, gave a shudder and exploded into life. Seeing my thunderstruck expression, Ted winked and said, "There's a lot of shit built into them things, bub, and the more you kick out of 'em, the less is left in there to kick you back." Ted's language—and Bill's and Frank's, too—was actually a lot less rough than that of the younger fishermen, and if one of his daughters, who listened to blue speech all day as the seine crews came and went to the freezer under the house, said so much as "damn," Ted would chase her right across the yard, yelling in the same strong language that the girls were forbidden to use, "By the Jesus, Vinnie [or Gloria or Ruth Ann], I hear any more of them damn words . . . !"

Years before, chased in this manner by his father, Ted's son Stewart had fallen in a woodpile, driving a hole through his cheek that survived as a permanent scar to the left of his mouth. The only son in a household of five daughters, nineteen-year-old Stewart was already contesting Ted's ideas on how things should be done. As strong, tough, and stubborn as four sons wrapped into one, he yelled back fiercely at his father until he went fishing on his own about five years later.

Jenny Bennett Lester, as lively and talkative as her husband, gave us peanut butter toast and coffee, as she would do each morning of good fishing weather for the next two months. It was still dark when we went down the back steps, hauled on stiff black bulky waders, squashed onto the hard front seat of the silver truck with its sweet smell of rotted fish scales, and rode down Indian Wells Highway to the ocean. Stewart followed in a Model A Ford with a winch mounted in front; this ancient and indestructible vehicle, replaced the following year by a Jeep pickup, was the last "A" that ever worked on the ocean beach. At the beach landing, Ted yanked his gears into four-wheel drive, stepped on the pedal that he called the "exhilarator," and headed east along the beach in the first light. Besides Stewart, John Cole, and me, Ted's steady crew that spring was brash young Richard, youngest son of his brother Frank;

Richard's brother Lewis, Milt Miller, and Pete Scott were among the men who filled in here and there on Ted's five-man crew.

On my first haul, at sunrise that May morning, we loaded up two truckloads of bass, and our shares on this haul came close to two hundred dollars—a very good week's pay in the early fifties. In our excitement, it was clear to John and me that commercial fishing was the path to fortune, but in the next two weeks, rising at 3 A.M. and fishing hard whenever the weather permitted, we scarcely made enough to pay for gas. Then the weather improved, we made money again, packing and icing fish until 10 at night, staggering out again five hours later, hands hot and swollen from fish spines and twine cuts and razor slashes from the sharp gill covers of big thrashing bass seized out of the bag by the eye sockets and tail and lugged up the beach to the trucks; sometimes I would be home after a half day's work by 8 in the morning. But on such days I would breakfast on butterfish, or shad roe fresh out of the ocean (Cap'n Ted declared that shad roe was disgusting, apart from being worth too much to be eaten by the likes of us). If the fish were in, and Ted wanted to rush back to the beach, Jenny Lester might send us off with a bellyful of her bluefish-and-pancakes.

On most days shortly after noon we would be back on the broad beach that stretched away westward for nearly one hundred miles, riding along on top of the nets in the dory's stern, washed by strong sea smells and new air of Atlantic springtime, on the winter-washed white quartz sand tinted red by feldspar and garnet. Here and there Ted would stop the truck, as if searching for fish sign, gazing out to sea under his long-billed Montauk swordfisherman's cap, the collar of his black-and-white wool shirt turned up in the cool wind, gnarled swollen-looking fisherman's hands clasped on his chest under his waders.

In early spring the presence of bass can rarely be determined from the beach; most often the set is made by old experience or instinct, some indefinable smell or feeling that the fish are there. (The long-nosed Posey Lesters are said to be strangely gifted with this instinct, known to other fishermen as "Posey smell.") As the water warms in early summer and schools of spearing and sand eels move inshore, gulls and terns attracted to the scraps of bait may indicate a feeding school; sometimes an oil slick from the carnage beneath gives its presence away. When there is fish smell on the wind, it may suffice to set around the dark shadow of a bait school driven into a compact mass by the slashing predators; sometimes the wet sand glistens with a sprinkle of sand eels, or spearing, chased into the translucent surf and cast ashore. Bait chased upward may be seen popping on the surface, and less frequently there are surface breaks—the hunters themselves swirl and are gone. Feeding bluefish—and bonita, too—erupt in sudden bursts of white, while the big bass roll their dorsals out, in heavy whirling.

In spring, such sign is very scarce, the cold ocean is closed and secretive, most sets are "blind." And Ted would say, "Better try 'em here, ain't that right, boys? See how we do." Or "Boys, ain't nothin doin here, don't look like; let's work back east'rd, hold that Eagle Boat set, try her again this evenin, before supper." But sooner or later Ted would "smell fish," sometimes where, for several hours, he had stared at the same faceless stretch of sea. "Let's try 'em, boys, let's go, let's go!" he would yell out, in a sudden hurry, backing the heavy boat trailer down to the water.

The handling of a loaded dory in the Atlantic surf is a stirring sight, and one not likely to be seen many years longer. "The ability to maneuver a rowboat through breaking waves will soon become a lost art among the Long Islanders," wrote Captain Josh Edwards's granddaughter in

1955. "A few men still draw seines for bass ... fewer still set trawls for cod from small dories in wintertime, but their ranks are thinning."[1]

In the fifties the boats were backed down to the water on a trailer, but once in the water they were still propelled by oars; the tactics of "going off" through the surf were much the same as those in the days of winter codfishing and shore whaling. Though heavier and a lot more leaky than most of its kind, Ted Lester's yellow dory was more or less typical, a sturdy high-sided double-ender of soft pine about sixteen-foot long (on the bottom) carrying three men and three hundred fathoms—about eighteen hundred feet—of netting, corks, and leads. The rest of his rig was also fairly standard, and the description of setting net that follows would apply to any of the seven or eight rigs that were active on the ocean beach until motors were put into the dories ten years later.

When the truck is backed down, the crew heaves up on the dory's bow to slide her off her trailer into the wash. Prior to launching, the dory is held steady by the crew while the two oarsmen, jumping in, row lightly to set up their timing and keep the bow headed up into the waves. To maintain that timing and be ready to go at a moment's notice, they must never glance back over their shoulders, nor do they need to, since everything can be read in the faces of the shore crew bracing the stern. One of these men holds the bitter end of a coil of line that will lead from this inshore end of the net up to the winch. As crew leader or captain— ordinarily the man who owns the rig—Ted is studying the seas, which usually arrive in a series of three; he looks for a likely interval, or slatch, between two series. As the third sea breaks, he hollers, "Go, boys!" and the men in the surf shove the dory out through the tumble of white water. In deteriorating weather and an onshore wind, the seas are choppy, with no slatch, and the oarsmen can count on a cold rinse down the neck to keep them lively.

Unless the sea is very calm, the beach crew shoves until the water is at their chests, at which point whoever will set the net hauls himself over the dory's stern; if necessary, he may grab up the spare oar to help propel the dory seaward. The oarsmen are rowing mightily, standing up at their seats to hurl their backs into the stroke, yet taking pains not to pop an oar—jerk it out of its oarlock—and spoil the timing; it is these next seconds, in rough weather, that will determine whether the dory will slide up and over the sea already capping or whether the sea will break over the bow into the boat. Filling up—an inevitable experience—means wallowing or worse until the dory can be beached, bailed, and refloated, and is especially disagreeable in the dark of a cold spring or autumn morning. Sometimes the dory will broach to—swing parallel to the wave and capsize, dumping the net—or, worse still, climb the wave too late and pitchpole in a backward somersault, with a great risk of serious injury to the crewmen. In either case, men in heavy waders are floundering in the icy surf, struggling to escape the swirling net.

Usually the dory goes off in good style, and one of the shore crew drives the truck and trailer to the point on the beach where the boat may be expected to come ashore. (Beach trucks, which range from converted war vehicles to old pickups, are all equipped with four-wheel drive, large semideflated sand tires, and a winch operated by a power take-off gear from the truck's transmission or by a separate donkey motor with reduction gear that is bolted to the truck bed.) The second vehicle remains at the launching place, hitched to a line that trails out to the moving dory. At its seaward end, the line is bridled to the jack, a stout pole that serves as a hauling purchase and also to spread the cork and lead lines of the net to keep them from fouling, or rolling, in the seas. Once clear of the surf, the man setting net heaves the jack overboard; it is then hauled back into the surf by those on shore to close the net to any fish that might try to slip past, inshore.

The dory has headed out to sea as the man in the stern pays out the net, heaving out coils of lead line with loud slaps that, in fog, carry back to shore. The cork line follows of its own accord, corks bouncing lightly over the gunwales, as he checks to make sure that the mesh is hanging straight, without a snarl. Still inside the bar, the dory turns parallel to the beach, bearing west in the springtime, east in the fall, in order to draw the net across the path of the migrating fish. Not long thereafter, the bag is set, together with a red or orange buoy to indicate its location to the trucks during the hauling. The bag, or cod end, is a large tubular pocket in the reinforced center section of the net, known as the bunt. As the net is hauled, the trapped fish collect in the bunt and bag, where the twine is necessarily much heavier than it is in the quarters of the net, which adjoin the bunt, and in the wings or outer sections, which are usually tapered toward the jacks so that they will "wade" in shallow water. The net is three-inch "mash"—each diamond-shaped mesh, pulled straight, is three inches long—and the leads are spaced about eighteen inches apart on the wings and about twelve along the quarters.

Once the bag is set, the net is paid all the way out parallel to the beach, although a slight hook toward shore is often made before the second jack is thrown. This offshore wing is rarely returned close to the surf, not only because heavy net would be dangerous in case of a mishap in landing, but also because the net can be left open a little longer in case fish are still moving down the beach. The offshore jack is secured to a long line coiled in the bilges, which is used for hauling the net and as a safeguard: if the timing is bad on the run for shore, this line can snub off the dory's headway and haul her back to safety outside the breakers, and it can also serve to keep her stern into the seas so that she will not yaw dangerously, broach to, and capsize.

"Although the dory is capable of riding wild seas, it is

not tolerant of handling error. When nearly empty, it is a skittish platform for experts only. . ."[2]

Timing is critical as the dory nears the breakers. She must ride to shore on the back of one sea without losing headway and wallowing helpless in the trough; but if she rides too far forward on this wave, picking up speed, and plunging down its face as the wave is breaking, she may jam her bow into the sand and pitchpole in a very fast violent forward somersault as the wave carries the stern up and over, bringing the dory down on the three men.

On shore, the winch is already started, and a crewman is ready with a haul line to secure to the dory when she comes ashore. Once the dory is committed to the surf, the oars are boated, and the net man does his best to hold the line burning out over the stern. When her bottom strands, the man on the beach seizes the bow and the crew jump out and fight to hold her perpendicular as they rush the empty boat as far as possible up the beach on the next wave, then run a line from a ring bolt in her bow stem up to the winch. Once safely ashore, the boat is spun and hauled stern foremost onto her trailer. Ordinarily the man who sets the net also loads the net into the dory, to make certain it will pay out cleanly and hang properly on the next haul.

Sometimes at midday in fair weather, the net is left offshore to fish a while, but usually the jack on this open wing is drawn ashore as soon as the boat is beached. With both jacks in the surf and the cork line lying in a half-circle, the winch at the inshore end is started up, and the net is hauled from both ends simultaneously; as the half-circle diminishes, the trucks are moved closer together. Care must be taken that the large red or orange buoy marking the location of the bag stays at dead center, for otherwise the net will lie askew, and the lead lines may be pulled up off the bottom, permitting the quick, nervous fish to slip beneath.

The net, in hanks, is winched onto the beach by means

of a long "whipping line" secured by a nonbinding hitch to cork and lead lines where they come together at the water's edge; when it nears the winch, this hitch can be cast off quickly and the free end run back down to the waterline and resecured to another length of net. This process, known as tying-on, is repeated until the bunt and bag are just behind the surf. From this point on, unless it is too heavy for five men using the lift of the waves to ease it ashore, the net is "bunted up"—worked in carefully by hand, slacking the strain as each wave rises so that the lead line won't be lifted off the bottom. The men on each side shout across the surf as they struggle to control the bag, holding the cork lines up and the lead lines down, for whatever fish the net contains are now packed into a small area and would quickly shoot away through any opening.

Although a few fish may be gilled in the wings and quarters, it is rarely clear until late in the haul whether the crew is "around a charge of fish" in commercial quantity. The men peer into the sea for the first signs of a good haul—fish shadows in the rising wave, a surface whirl, a silver skittering in the wash. "There he is!" somebody yells, and the cry releases meaningless orders, oaths, and imprecations that accomplish little besides easing the suspense. Then the bunt is washed into the shallows. The men seize the heavy mesh and, heaving upward, pour the skittering fish into the bag; soon a hitch is taken, and the bag is winched onto the sand, where the "puckerin string" that ties the bag is loosened, and the bag unloaded. This string is retied as the net is loaded back into the dory, and when fishing is good, the same man always ties, to ensure good luck.

In early spring there is sometimes a limited market for the blueback (or round or English herring) much valued in Europe, which is the first "money fish" to arrive; black-back flounder, mackerel, and squid also come early. The most valuable spring species are the American shad, the weakfish, bluefish, and the small striped bass.

Traditionally, the arrival of the shad coincides with the spring blooming of a wild member of the rose family, which is called shad, or shadblow, for that reason, and the adult females ordinarily contain two kidney-shaped sacs of firm, pink-brown roe—the only roe besides that of sturgeon and salmon (and a mushy facsimile produced by the ocean lumpfish) that has any significant commercial value. Sturgeon showed up occasionally in the spring nets—with or without roe for caviar, they have a certain value as smoked fish—and sometimes there were hauls of butterfish and the northern puffer (or bottlefish or blowfish).

The small striped bass appears on the ocean shore in the last days of April. Not until the time of lilacs in late May or early June, say the old people, will the bluefish arrive, in company with large striped bass, and "the height of the bass" comes later in the month, with the white flowers of the new potato plants. Rounding Montauk Point, the migrant species scatter through the bays and islands. Though some will remain along the ocean shore; many more continue north and east along the New England coast.

In spring as many as forty species may appear at one time or another in the nets—the thirty-three that I recorded in 1953–1956 did not include the many creatures such as spearing, eels, sand eels, and others that slip easily through the three-inch mesh. The shining heap on the ocean beach, catching the first red of a cold sun that rises in roaring silence out of the ocean, may include small dogfish sharks, big stingrays, skates, assorted members of the herring and flounder families, two species of sea robins, and the angler fish, or monkfish, known to the commercial men as mollykites; the extraordinary angler lies on the bottom like a large cow patty, waving a yellow flap of skin on its first dorsal spine to attract prey to its huge mouth. Ordinarily large sharks and porpoises rush straight through the net, leaving big holes, but I recall a day when a large thresher shark became entangled. Now and again there is an exotic species such as the spiny boxfish, or porcupine fish. (In the fifties, Suffolk County was still a Republican stronghold— the only county outside Vermont and New Hampshire, it is said, that voted for Alf Landon against Franklin Roosevelt—and these rare, prickly, and inconvenient creatures, together with the horned sculpin, were known to the staunchly Republican fishermen as Democrats.)

Throughout the spring, the unmarketable herrings— skipjacks, alewives, and menhaden (the menhaden and the closely related skipjack are valuable only in huge quantity)— the delectable sand dab, or daylight flounder (so-called because light can actually be seen through its thin green-spotted disk), the anglers, sea robins, dogfish sharks, the rays and skates, are dumped out of the bag into the shallows. Many strand on the beach or wash ashore again, killed by the nets, and although the gulls, crabs, snails, and sand fleas will put them to good use, the fishermen are blamed for this sad waste that is caused by a fussy American market.

Captain Ted Lester, when time permitted, would scuttle around the beach, quick as a sandpiper, gathering herring to slip down the throats of our big bass to increase their weight; sometimes he used a water hose for the same purpose, back at the freezer. All the fishermen resorted to such tricks to combat the crooked dealers at the Fulton Market, who not only paid the bare minimum for fish, but sometimes reduced by 10 per cent the weight indicated on the shipped boxes, yelling over the telephone each morning that the fishermen's scales must all be wrong. "Market don't give us nothin for thim herrin, boys, but it don't seem right to let 'em go to waste," said Ted, whose obsessive energy needed an outlet when there were no "money fish" to lay his hands on. However, not all of the fishermen, even in hard times, would pick up herring left behind by other crews.

Ted was both thrifty and hard on his gear, which he would patch relentlessly but not replace; his reputation as a scavenger of discarded odds and ends, including trash fish, had won him the nickname Cap'n Seagull. "Out of the fog come Cap'n Seagull and all thim Poseys," as a Bonac bayman said, in one of the many stories that expressed a kind of carping respect for this driven man. Yet without Ted Lester's scavenging habit, outsiders such as Scott, Cole, and myself might never have found work on a Lester crew. Until recent years, Ted was the only Posey who would take on "people from away," mostly because—so his detractors said—outsiders were less likely to resent the makeshift gear that kept his rig in near-constant emergency.

On June 9, 1954, we made a set just before light east of the boarded-up Coast Guard station at Amagansett, which is the set closest to Poseyville.[3] This home set was chosen because the silver truck had broken down, and we had only the Model A to work with. In addition, we had torn up our new nylon bunt on the Erdmann's set the day before—the captain was furious because Richard and Stewart had put too much strain on the net when it got mudded—and Ted had replaced it with a bunt of tattered cotton.

That morning the water's edge was sprinkled with driven bait, and the light fog was heavy with the sweet oily smell of fish, and we had scarcely begun to haul when the water just inside the corks farthest offshore began to shiver. In the dim light, still uncertain of what we were seeing, unable to believe that the whole crescent of smooth gray sea inside the corks was somehow stirring with uneasy life, we kept on hauling in dead silence, tying on sections of incoming net, trudging up the soft sand hill to the winch to untie the line from the last hank, hurrying back down to the water to tie on again. The fish were showing up too soon, gilled far out on the net's wings, and very early a fish swirled on the oily surface of the long slow swells. A minute later, when a fair-sized bass actually flipped over the corks, everyone yelled out all at once. The net was scarcely halfway in, and it was already so packed that the roiling bass, seeking escape, could be felt thumping up and down the length of it.

In the new light, we could see that the water was browning with churned sand, what the fishermen call sand rile. Then somebody yelled out, "They're going through!"

We plunged into the surf over the bibs of our heavy waders, struggling to hoist the old bunt out of the water and horse the net ashore at the same time. By now, the whole surface was broken by swirls and slapping tails, and Bill Lester's crew, sighting the tumult from a mile away at Two Mile Hollow, came burning down the beach from the westward. Seeing the fish going through, they set around us, but even as they backed their dory down into the water, one of Bill's crewmen, Lindy Havens, was cursing Ted at the top of his lungs: "Goddamn you, Ted! Maybe *now* you'll get rid of that old cotton shit, goddamn you!"

Big Lindy, a tall man with big ears, black-haired country good looks, and a hot temper, had tears of exasperation in his eyes; he felt things strongly. One morning on the beach at Wainscott he offered to throw into the surf our local congressman, who had never helped the fishermen in their struggle to survive in a resort economy, yet had dared to chastise Bill Lester's crew for setting a net around such an important surfcaster while he was relaxing in the out of doors in his lightweight trout waders. When we came along, Lindy was still hurling obscenities at the empty dunes into which the alarmed legislator had fled.

On this June morning, Lindy's howl of pain was mixed with Ted's own anguished screeching and the grinding of truck gears and the thump of soft breaking seas in the morning mist. But it was too late; the old net tore in our hands, and Bill salvaged little from the slapping tumult

pouring through Ted's bunt as most of what Lindy called
"the biggest charge of bass I ever seen on this goddamn
beach" moved back offshore. All we saved were those fish
driven by the others into the heavy mesh of the nylon bag,
two tons of cow bass, thirty-three boxes, scarcely a fish less
than forty pounds and a good many over sixty.

The old cotton in the net was shot; the tattered mess
was nothing that could be mended, since the twine was rotten ("Twoine's some tender, ain't it, Cap?" as the Poseys say,
snapping a bar of mash between gnarled fingers). We were
out of business for two days while Ted went to Greenport
after netting, hung new quarters, and sewed his old bunt
into the center, rerigging the cork line and the leads.

# 7.

# A Delicate, Fine,
# Fat, Faste Fish

O n Thanksgiving Day, 1923, the keeper of the Montauk Light noticed a big school of striped bass off the rocks; in just over an hour, with fifty-seven casts, he horsed in fifty-six bass up to twelve pounds each. "Striped bass fishing is nowhere better," the East Hampton *Star* reported at the end of that season. Yet the bass had been very scarce since the 1880s, and a few years later the species was so rare that its probable extinction was predicted, lending support to a growing movement among sportsmen to eliminate commercial fishing from Long Island.

As early as 1924, in an amendment to the state marine fisheries conservation law, it was proposed that all dragging or trawling of any kind be prohibited in state waters, and that all other netting be so severely curtailed that, in effect, all fishing except angling would come to an end. Among those who denounced this drastic measure was Captain William Tuthill of Montauk, an old-timer who was able to point to extreme cycles of scarcity in numerous migratory fish species:

In the year 1870 there was a large run of weakfish at Montauk, but for some unknown reason they never came up bay. In 1906 and 1907 there was another large run of weakfish. But where have the bonitas gone? No one can tell. They may be and probably will be back, because other fish have gone and come the same way. I remember one day off Montauk Point as far as the eye could see in every direction bonitas were jumping out of the water. This was in 1914. . . . I remember in 1865 there were very few sea bass caught. In 1870 they came on again in large numbers, and in 1890 there seemed to be no end to them. . . . They were caught off Gardiners Island on October 15. A few days later, we didn't get a fish. It is just the same with other fish—they come and go, and no man or set of men can control the movements of salt water fish. . . . Where would the public be but for the net fishermen? They never could have a fish to eat. And yet we have to go to Albany to fight for our rights.

Eventually the bill was defeated in the legislature by a vote of 45 to 3. The sportsmen's mutterings continued, however, and a decade later their delegates in Albany were back again with a similar bill: "It shall be unlawful for any person or persons to take fish in any of the tidal waters of Long Island by means of nets, fish pounds [traps], set lines [trawl lines], or beam trawls [dragging], except that minnows or shrimp may be taken for bait. . . . This act shall take effect immediately." Other proposed measures that year forbade the sale of striped bass and bluefish under a certain size, and all commercial hand-lining for weakfish in Peconic Bay, where in the years of striped bass scarcity, weakfish sustained a profitable catch in April, May, and June. Eventually this legislation was defeated too, not only because weakfish were plentiful, but because it was clear that recreational fishermen were taking many more than the commercial men. However, very similar attempts to limit the commercial catch were to be repeated with striped bass in the decades to come. As Captain Charles L. Tuthill wrote in the East Hampton *Star*, Feb. 2, 1934:

> The sports fishing organizations are seeking such legislation here on the east end of Long Island as our people do not want. It affects the freedom of our bays to everybody and permits only such fishing methods as their bill might approve.
>
> Is it not a fact that those who have been using our bays for generations are better qualified to judge if protective measures are necessary? This sudden fear of our marine resources being abused and exploited by the commercial fishermen is nothing but a state of mind without any foundation in fact, and brought about by propaganda and misguided ideas as to conservation needs. There have been years of plenty and years of scarcity of practically all kinds of migratory fish, which the oldest fishermen can testify to, and why, no man with certainty can tell. We are going to make the prediction that this fine run of weakfish which have been coming for the past few years will turn in some other direction in the not far distant future only to come back again when natural conditions are favorable, and this without any futile attempt at regulation by man. . . .
>
> We would like to believe that the anglers' grievances concerning commercial fishing methods, the supposed need of conservation measures, are due to a lack of painstaking efforts to get at the true facts. But if this is not the case, the only sane conclusion to which we can arrive is that this whole conservation propaganda is nothing more or less than a mask behind which is a desire to monopolize Peconic Bay for sports activities alone.

In 1934 an anti-netting measure was "narrowly forestalled" in the legislature, according to the East Hampton *Star*, which made this comment on December 20 of that year: "Last year when there was agitation in the state assembly for various regulatory laws for commercial fishing for the benefit of sport fishing, the assertion was made that all trap fishing should be stopped on the south shore of Long Island, as they were catching such huge quantities of fish that they could not survive. Investigation of the true condition disclosed that there were only a few traps and that they did not take in a week the quantity taken by the sports in a day. A suggestion to stop hand-lining up-bay during spawning season of the weakfish, on the other hand, met with loud opposition from the sport boat captains. It all depends on whose bull is being gored."[1]

Nevertheless, large commercial hauls continued to outrage the recreational angler, and particularly that species called the surfcaster, whose primary habitat in New York State is the coastal stretch of rock and beach on both sides of Montauk Point. Except for the experts, surfcasting for stripers is one of the least efficient methods of angling ever devised, due to the self-imposed limitations of the caster. He cannot, first of all, reach the more productive depths available to a man trolling from a boat. Also, his range is much more limited, and his lure spends less time actually at work. Even when a fish is hooked, it must be landed through the rocks or surf and is therefore lost at least as often as it is brought slapping from the water. The expert, of course, can reach out farther and place his lure just where he wants it, at a known rock or hole or eddy, and he does not waste time casting blindly but moves from one known spot to another. It is said, with some justice, that 5 percent of the surfcasters catch 95 percent of all fish taken from the shore.

Even for he who spends months or years, often at night or in foul weather, lashing the water white in quest of a large fish tasting of iodine that has already cost him a great amount of time and money, this sport has an uncanny attraction. The unseen quarry and mysterious dark water, the pleasure taken in the strong and skillful cast, the sound and smell of sea and weather, the healing solitude, and the suspense, are reward enough to the true sportsman who seeks no profit from his hobby, and surfcasting for striped bass probably claims more fanatics than any other form of saltwater fishing.

Whether novice or expert, surfcaster or boatman, the angler reacts to a truckload of big "trophy fish" as a gourmet might to a trashcan full of caviar, and his distress is understandable, though not well-founded. His wily foe loses dignity in the mass, especially if the angler has passed the whole of a rainy night without a strike only to be confronted at daybreak with a bag of stripers as large, or larger than his car. In that bag, it seems to him, gasps "the fish that had my name on it," and even in years when bass are plentiful, he interprets the large haul, not as good news of bass prosperity, but as evidence of exploitation and overfishing.

In fact, however, there have rarely been more than eight or ten haul-seine crews at work in one season on all of the South Fork, and few if any farther to the west. This is mostly because—on this hundred-mile beach—there are so few places that it pays to fish. To the west, the fish migration along shore is too sparse to justify the effort; to the east, near Montauk Point, rocks and sunken ships, struck on the bar and emerging intermittently in the wake of storms, have become obstructions, known as hang-ups or fasts. There are also stretches where storm has carved away the sloping sand, leaving a beach too steep to work from, and mudholes, where the seine is fouled by storm-exposed peat from an older shoreline farther out to sea.

Therefore the seiners are confined to specific locations, or sets—the Georgica set or the Ditch Plains set or the Eagle Boat set[2] or the Towers set off the ITT radio towers on the Napeague stretch, still known from the days of the old fish depot platform as Napig Station. (One set in this stretch was spoiled by the crash of a 707 in the sixties, the motors of which emerge as hang-ups to this day. Bill Lester agreed to haul seine for the bodies, and landed parts of more than one: "Supposed to get paid for 'em, too," he says today. "Ain't paid me yet!")

Excepting a clear mile of Napeague Beach, east to Hither Plains, there are only a half dozen places between Amagansett and the Point where a net can be put with confidence into the water. There are three sets in Amagansett, then another clear stretch of East Hampton beach from the Eagle Boat set west of Two Mile Hollow Road to the old "Pots 'n Kittles" whale works location off the middle of Hook Pond. There is also a clear stretch at Wainscott, and a few good sets at Sagaponack, Mecox, and Flying Point, in Southampton Town. But many of these locations are considered dead spots, while other spots "where the bait seems to lay or somethin" produce fish year after year. Probably there are no more than eighteen good sets in all of the thirty-one miles of beach between Shinnecock Inlet and Montauk Point.

(The term "set" also refers to the direction of the long-shore current, which is much increased by wind. Unless wind from another quarter rises to check it, an easterly or westerly set can run for days at a time, roiling the channel between the beach and the outer bar. Even in otherwise fair weather, when a dory can go off safely, a strong set eliminates beach hauling, since it pulls the net sideways down the beach and washes it ashore.)

In September the striped bass regather, on their way to winter grounds. Once in the ocean, the bass move gradually southwestward; the great body of fish passes mostly outside the bar, moving inshore only irregularly. In a long warm fall of steady weather, haul-seining may be very good (although a dry haul, with scarcely a fish of any kind, is not uncommon). But autumn storms limit the fishing, and an average of four work days a week is probably high. Since the number of sets is very limited, since the seine works only during the time it takes to haul, and since there may be no weather for hauling for days at a time, one can understand the haul-seiners' conviction that these few hours out of every week scarcely diminish the migrating schools. On the other hand, after World War II, numerous anglers became adept at hooking bass with baits, jigs, plugs, lures, and live eels, and both boatmen and surfcasters began selling their fish, until many more bass in the commercial markets were being caught by hook and line than were caught in nets. Under the circumstances, the commercial men found it difficult to understand the unrelenting attitude of certain sportsmen, whose hostility seemed to grow as the bass increased.

Entirely oblivious to the controversy is the placid and handsome marine vertebrate known in the South Atlantic states as the rockfish, or rock, and in the Northern states as the striped bass. The biologist classifies *Morone saxatilis* as an anadromous and tolerant member of the family *Serranidae*, or sea bass, a group that includes the anadromous white perch of the coastal ponds and is closely related to freshwater perches. By anadromous is meant the characteristic of ascending from salt into fresh water to spawn. By tolerant is meant a considerable adaptability to a wide variety of conditions, including changes in salinity and temperature, turbulence, man-made pollution, and food. (Though they favor small fishes, striped bass also eat lobsters and crabs, soft clams and mussels; while in the estuaries, they are partial to *Nereis* worms.) An early—and striking—example of striped bass tolerance was the shipment by rail in 1879 and 1881 of a total of 435 small fish from New Jersey to California for transplanting in San Francisco Bay. Within two decades, the commercial landings of a species heretofore unknown in the Pacific totaled 1,234,000 pounds, and the bass has since spread to southern California and to British Columbia.

Left to itself, this strong silver-white fish with black lateral stripes from gills to tail (the dorsal area is often greenish, and the silver scales glint with tints of brass) aspires to an age of thirty and a weight of 125 pounds. Its broken stripes tend to blur and fade with age, and a larger fish often acquires a pot belly. Widely celebrated as splendid game and table fish, these mighty bass are known to awestruck anglers as stripers, greenheads, lunkers, line-siders, soakers, tackle-busters, and the like. Since almost all of the big fish are aging females, they are known to the commercial men as cows.

More than a few of the larger specimens have little more fight than a foul-hooked copy of the Sunday *New York Times*, with taste to match. Nevertheless, their great weight and thrash, in conditions of surf and boiling rocks, make them a redoubtable foe when hooked from shore. Armored by thick scales and gill plates and propelled by a strong heavy tail, the bass is beautifully designed for rough white water, and seeing one whirl out to strike a lure will make a man a surfcaster for life. The small bass (five pounds and under in market terms; the medium bass is five to fifteen pounds, and the large bass is any fish above that size) is vigorous and very tasty; it has been called the most desired food and game fish on the Atlantic coast.

Sport-fishing writers habitually refer to stripers as wily, crafty, even wise, and although this wisdom might also be perceived as lethargic indifference to lures, live baits, or other enticements designed to remove them from their natural environment in river estuaries and along the coast, the commercial men also will testify to their sagacity; the bass, they say, is the first species to find its way out of a fish trap, and the first to escape through any opening when a net is hauled.

On the Atlantic coast, the hardy bass is found not only in estuaries, bays, and along the ocean shore, but as far inland as it can swim up any stream that empties into the sea. It ascends the Hudson 160 miles to Albany, and it is also found three hundred miles inland at Rhodes Landing, Georgia, as well as in the Santee-Cooper Reservoir, in South Carolina. There Lakes Marion and Moultrie, created in 1941 by a federal power project and invaded by the ubiquitous bass by way of the Pinopolis locks on the Cooper River, yielded a conservative estimate of 100,000 pounds to astonished anglers in the three months preceding Christmas 1954. Since they now spawn there, it can be assumed that the bass readily become landlocked fish, with no biological dependence on salt water. By comparison, the anadromous Atlantic salmon is so intolerant of dams and pollution that it has vanished from almost all of its ancestral streams.

Striped bass spawn in a shifting and variable environment where the salt tides meet the freshwater spring rains in the large estuaries. A successful spawning, producing what biologists call a dominant year-class, depends upon a complex balance of conditions, including rainfall, salinity, water temperature and cleanliness, available nutrients, wind, currents, and weather, and the fact that one female may lay several million eggs is less significant in the survival of the species than the aquatic conditions that surround the hatch and determine the ratio of survival. But the long-lived bass is well adapted to patterns of drastic population fluctuation. For a decade or more it may all but disappear; then, in a single spawning season when conditions are harmonious, a relatively small number of adult females may produce an immense stock of new fish.

Striped bass spawn in the spring at the freshwater-saltwater interface of major estuarine systems. Probably no aquatic environment is as variable from one year to

the next . . . in response to spring freshwater flow. . . .
The chances for annual spawning success in such an
unpredictable environment are relatively poor, with the
high probability that there will be far more poor years
than good ones. Therefore, in order to survive as a species, it had to become long-lived and very fecund, so that
it could sustain itself for ten to fifteen years at a time—
if need be—between successful spawning years. Historical records seem to bear this out. Prior to 1900, there
are reports of both scarcity and abundance. In fact, the
N.Y. State Fish Commission, about 1895, noted that because bass were so scarce at the time, a hatchery at Cold
Spring Harbor was recommended. We know from personal knowledge and commercial fishing statistics that
there have been extreme population cycles throughout
this century.[3]

Populations of bass at the north and south ends of its
long range—the Canadian populations from Quebec southward, and also those from southern North Carolina to north
Florida and in the Gulf of Mexico west to the Mississippi—
are mostly estuarine and riverine in habit and do not appear
to migrate, although some will ascend hundreds of miles
upriver in the spawning season. There are also nonmigratory populations in the Chesapeake and other areas in the
center of the range. But for reasons not well understood,
large numbers of Mid-Atlantic bass from Cape Hatteras to
the Hudson, and particularly from Chesapeake Bay, move
out of the estuaries to travel north and south along the
coast. The great majority of these migratory fish are females
between two and four years old. Small school bass, appearing on the east end of Long Island in late April, are followed
in May by the medium fish; the large bass, most of them
spent spawners, do not ordinarily appear until early June.
By early July, the migration has passed to Massachusetts

and the Gulf of Maine, leaving small concentrations in such sportsmen's haunts as Montauk Point, Block Island, Watch Hill, Point Judith, Cuttyhunk, Nantucket, and Cape Cod.

In late summer the bass start to move south again, while those in Long Island Sound move east, heading seaward through the passages at Plum Gut and the Race. Throughout the autumn, striped bass congregate around Montauk Point, where they fatten for the winter on the shoals of bait fish. By Thanksgiving most of them are gone, though a few small bass may persist along the beach until the first snow in early December. Once they leave Montauk, their distribution is incompletely known. In 1953 one authority speculated that "a good proportion of these bass that come from the south when they are three or four years old may remain in the north for the rest of their lives."[4] Some fish overwinter in deep tidal channels of the coastal rivers, and some, it appears, move offshore to deep water of the continental shelf (in February 1949, a small bass was picked up by a trawler in the open ocean about sixty miles south of Martha's Vineyard). But bass schools are never seen on the surface more than a few miles offshore, and most fish, it was thought, seemed to return south to the Chesapeake, with a good number moving farther still, to inshore waters between Cape Henry and Cape Lookout.

The Chesapeake and Hudson appear to supply almost all the migratory bass in the Northeast,[5] but in other days large populations in such places as the Roanoke River of North Carolina, the York River of Virginia, and the Delaware Bay doubtless contributed to the migrations. Before the nineteenth century, when many rivers were despoiled by dams, industry, and untreated sewage, this prosperous species must have spawned in almost every estuary on the Atlantic coast, and small endemic races still persist all the way north to the St. Lawrence River and all the way south to the St. Johns River in Florida, in addition to the northeast Gulf Coast populations (entirely isolated from the fish of the Atlantic coast by the emergence of the Florida peninsula after the Ice Age), which occur as far west as Lake Pontchartrain, Louisiana. While these races may vary in such minor morphological traits as the number of soft rays, or spines, in the dorsal, pectoral, and anal fins, and the number of scales along the lateral line, all are local populations of the hardiest and most widespread food fish species in the coastal waters of North America.

Before the ruin of the rivers, striped bass numbers must have been more consistent than they are today. The bass helped to sustain the Pilgrims in the Massachusetts Bay Colony and astounded Captain John Smith, who wrote in his journal of that coast (1614), "I myself at the turning of the tyde have seen such multitudes pass out of a pounde that it seemed to me that one might go over their backs drishod."[6] One of Smith's contemporaries called the bass "a most sweet and wholesome fish as ever I did eat . . . altogether as good as our fresh Sammon. . . . Our Fishers take many hundreds together . . . yea, their Netts ordinarily take more than they are able to hall to Land."[7] Twenty years later, William Wood, in his *New England's Prospect,* called the bass "one of the best fishes in the Country . . . a delicate, fine, fat, faste fish. . . . The English at the top of an high water do crosse the creek with long seanes or bass nets which stop the fish; and the water ebbing from them, they are left on the dry grounds, sometimes two or three thousand at a set, which are salted up against winter, or distributed to such as have present occasion either to spend them in their homes or use them for their grounds." The Pilgrims also caught them "with hook and line, the fisherman taking a great cod line to which he fasteneth a peece of lobster and threwes it into the sea. The fish biting at it, he pulls her to him and knockes her on the head with a sticke."[8] (The passage also testifies to the abundance of lobster, which nobody would use today for fish bait.) But as early as 1639, in the first conservation law passed in the New World, Massachusetts forbade the use of this delicate, fine, fat, fast fish for fertilizer, which suggests that its multitudes had limits, even then.

Colonists from Massachusetts who settled the east end of Long Island in this period apparently found bass common on the Long Island coasts, but in the last half of the eighteenth century a decline was already noted in the Gulf of Maine. The fish recovered somewhat in the first part of the nineteenth century, but a history of Cape Cod published in 1862 described the species as much less plentiful than formerly. Though still abundant in the Mid-Atlantic states in the 1870s, bass became so scarce north of Boston that in certain years there was no commercial catch at all (the non-migratory populations farther northward were more stable), and a decline was soon apparent to the southward. In the half century and more of increasing striped bass scarcity after 1880, dams, dredging, and pollution ruined the spawning grounds, as more and more estuaries, rivers, and creeks were removed from the species' range.

Amagansett men "occasionally fish with seines for striped bass and other species on the Atlantic side. The bass have been scarce this year," says an observer of a century ago, in 1880;[9] he cites a Talmage of Sag Harbor, a Ludlow of Bridgehampton, and a Burnett of Southampton, all of whom agree that the striped bass was scarce and growing scarcer. Between 1880 and 1897, the highest yield of bass in a single year was 200,000 pounds as compared to a high of 2,500,000 pounds for weakfish. There seemed no cause for alarm, however. "Though the striped bass has undoubtedly decreased greatly in abundance during the century, it is still an abundant fish," according to turn-of-the-century authorities.[10]

To judge from the recollections of the Lesters, the first decades of the present century were progressively poorer. Between 1921 and 1938, the highest annual bass catch for all Long Island was 120,000 pounds,[11] a tiny fraction of the annual Long Island landings of all finned fish species, which in 1938 came to fifty million pounds. In 1928, when a fifth dam was built on the Chesapeake's main tributary, the Susquehanna, the bass stocks in the bay quickly diminished, and by the early 1930s it was actually said that the species was becoming extinct. But the enlargement of the Chesapeake-Delaware Canal a few years earlier had flushed out much of the stagnation in the upper bay, preparing the way for successful spawnings in 1933 and 1934; the great year-class of 1934, in fact, was the largest in the memory of man.

With the reappearance of small bass a few years later, measures were taken to avoid another precipitous decline. In 1939, following the recommendations of Dr. Daniel Merriman, director of the Bingham Oceanographic Laboratories at Yale University, the size limit on coastal bass taken in New York (and most other North Atlantic states as well) was raised from fourteen to sixteen inches, or about two pounds, at which size the young female fish first spawns. But on the Chesapeake fishing grounds of Maryland and Virginia, where over half of the Atlantic coast striped bass were harvested, the size limit remained at fourteen inches, and in Delaware and North Carolina, it was twelve.

Throughout the forties the striped bass grew more abundant, but rod-and-reel fishermen were now abundant, too. Schooling up in large lobbying aggregations, they began to put pressure on the politicians for legislation to reserve the bass for recreational anglers, who could round up far more votes than the commercial men. This campaign, led by the rugged fraternity of surfcasters (which produced its own dominant year-class with the advent of beach buggies and sophisticated spinning tackle after World War II), was generally endorsed by small boat fishermen. Similarly, the charter boatmen felt obliged to support their excited customers, though most of them knew there were plenty of bass and that restrictions on small local net fisheries that were harvesting migrating fish would not significantly affect the far greater numbers taken on rod and reel.

In 1945 the sportsmen triumphed in Massachusetts, where all netting of striped bass was now prohibited; the sportsmen could and did point out that good surfcasting and bass boat fishing at Cuttyhunk, Cape Cod, Nantucket, and many other excellent locations produced far more income for local communities than the marginal net fisheries, and far more votes for politicians, as well. The commercial netters, in effect, had been put out of business by commercial rod-and-reelers, who now had a monopoly on peddling bass, and this new breed of money-minded sportsmen organized effective lobbies that put strong pressure on sportsmen in other states to fight for complementary legislation. Maine, New Hampshire, and Connecticut, where netting was insignificant, fell into line (though bass laws vary in each state), but New York and Rhode Island, with important local fisheries, refused. No reputable biologist seemed to feel that such discriminatory legislation was desirable, and even the anglers' magazine, *Salt Water Sportsman*, had certain doubts about the proposed restrictions. In 1948 it offered the views of the leading striped bass expert, Dr. Merriman, who wrote in part: "The fluctuations in abundance are due more to the environment than to the size of the adult stock. . . . Indeed, an awkward problem is posed by the fact that the dominant year-classes [such as the one in 1933] have a nasty habit of turning up when the adult stock is at the lowest level. In the case of the striped bass, there is no evidence that an increase in stock will produce more young. Since all evidence indicates that the stock of striped bass is adequate for both commercial and sporting interests, the efforts of the sportsmen to eliminate commercial fishing is in no way justified from a conservation point of view."

"In the case of the striped bass," declared another bass

biologist, Dr. James R. Westman, chairman of the Department of Wildlife Conservation at Rutgers, "hook-and-line fishing is inadequate for harvesting anything like the quantity of stripers that can be quite safely taken each year. The present net harvesting of striped bass, for example, is some eight million pounds per year throughout its Middle-Atlantic range from Virginia to Massachusetts, and yet the supply of striped bass has been increasing, irregularly, since 1933. . . . At present, the elimination of commercial netting for striped bass would not only be unjustified from a conservation point of view but would actually be wasteful."

In June of 1952, alarmed by the sharp dispute that year in the state assembly, the magazine of the New York Conservation Department (now the Department of Environmental Conservation, or D.E.C.) published the opinions of Drs. Merriman and Westman, who were growing weary of having their findings ignored. "It is a curious anachronism," Dr. Merriman observed, "that the unusual abundance with which we have been blessed has, in a round-about way, resulted in frequent acrimonious disputes between commercial and sporting interests." And the *Conservationist* commented, "In this controversy the department found itself, as it often does, being pressed to throw overboard the findings of the country's best biologists, who in this case do not recommend reserving the striper solely for the angler." As will be seen, the pressure had scarcely begun.

Already a great amount of research on the striper was being implemented, organized, and published by the Atlantic States Marine Fisheries Commission, which was subsidized, in part, by an excise tax on fishing tackle. The commission, which concerns itself with all fish and shellfish problems on the Atlantic coast, coordinates the findings of the marine biological laboratories, the state research programs, the university departments of conservation and biology, the Fish and Wildlife Service, and interested anglers and commercial men whose aid is conscripted in fish-tagging surveys and other studies contributory to the understanding and management of this resource. The chief function of its striped bass committee is to discover and promote conservation practice and state legislation beneficial to both bass and man.

In 1953 the commission made this statement on the general subject of legislation in the fisheries: "During the past thirty years there has been a growing trend toward social legislation in the marine fisheries of the several Atlantic states. Except in rare instances, such social legislation seeks to protect one particular fishery interest at the expense of another. . . . Such acquisitive attempts often claim conservation and sound management as their objectives. Rarely, however, is there sound scientific evidence to back these claims. Accordingly, this commission now feels called upon to indicate the possible results and danger that such legislation may hold and to point out that unless this trend is checked and far greater consideration given to scientific data and warranted conclusions, the longtime result may well be a gross mismanagement of our marine fishery resources. . . ."

But none of these sensible observations eased the dispute, which was to fester for the next thirty years. Old-fashioned sportsmen had largely been replaced by the "meat fishermen," who accused the commercial men of ravaging natural resources, a cry taken up by fishing columnists and sportsmen's magazines. Wrongly encouraged in such prejudices, as one observer commented, "the angler, in company with his friends, will start a crusade against some innocent group of people who make their living from the sea." It was not an apologist for the commercial men who made this comment but Dr. Edward C. Raney of Cornell, who would inherit Dr. Merriman's position as the foremost authority on the striped bass. I happened to know Dr. Merriman quite well and had spoken and corresponded with Dr. Raney, who came to Long Island several times to observe the haul-seining operation; both biologists deplored the unsporting crusade against the commercial men that was already well under way in the early fifties.

# 8.

# Under Montauk Light

I n the early summer of 1954, a power boat with the most beautiful lines I had ever seen was riding at anchor in the harbor of Rockport, Massachusetts. Her designer turned out to be a local sailmaker who had built her as a tuna harpoon boat; she was the only one of her kind, and she was for sale. The following day I took the helm on a run around Cape Ann, as the owner ran forward to the pulpit and harpooned a small harbor seal (bountied in Massachusetts) with an astonishing throw of the clumsy pole. In Ipswich Bay, giant bluefin tuna were carving circles on the surface, and the sailmaker showed me how to approach them, how much to lead the swift fish on the throw, how important it was that everyone aboard stay well clear of the line tub when the fish was struck, but because he was selling his beautiful boat, he seemed too disheartened to pursue them.

With her high bow and deep hull forward, her long low cockpit and flat stern, the thirty-two foot boat looked like a trim and elegant Maine lobsterman, and she handled well in any kind of sea. Powered by a 120-horsepower Buick engine adapted to marine use (automobile engines, readily and cheaply acquired at wrecked-car yards, are often adapted by commercial fishermen), she came equipped with spotting tower, outriggers, harpoon stand, harpoons and line, a heavy tuna rod and reel and fighting chair, boat rods, shark hooks, and miscellaneous gear of all descriptions. At five thousand dollars, she was a bargain even in those days, and I knew from the first that she was my boat, though I had to borrow to obtain her; she was the most compulsive purchase of my life.

Signing the papers, the sailmaker was close to tears. He had designed and built this lovely craft with his own hands, he was losing her for an unworthy purpose (his wife desired a breezeway for their house), and throwing in all the fishing gear was an acknowledgment that a vital aspect of his life was at an end.

A few days later I ran the boat southward down the coast off Salem and Boston and on through the Cape Cod Canal and Buzzards Bay, putting in at Block Island late that evening, and continuing on to Three Mile Harbor the next day. By that time it had come to me, a little late, that writing and commercial fishing were barely paying my household expenses, that there was nothing left over for boat insurance, berth fees, maintenance, or even gas for a boat this size (the one-cylinder engine on my scallop boat ran mostly on air, and the rude hull could be berthed on a mud bank, invulnerable to theft or serious damage). And so, within a few days of her arrival, the beautiful boat I had rechristened *Merlin*—after the small swift falcon of that name as well as the celebrated magician—was sailing out of Montauk as a charter boat, with John Cole as mate. For the next two summers, often twice a day, we headed east along Gin Beach, rounding Shagwong Point and running south to join the fishing fleet off Montauk Point, or continuing offshore to the tuna grounds at the eighty-fathom line, where one misty morning of long and oily swells, many years before, I had seen the first whales of my life, the silver steam rising from the silver surface, the great dark shapes breaking the emptiness of ocean sky.

For many years as a boy in the late thirties, I had gone deep-sea fishing off Montauk with my father, and to this day I cannot see that high promontory of land with its historic lighthouse without a stirring of excitement and affection. Montauk is essentially a high rock island, cut off from the glacial moraines of the South Fork by a strait four miles wide. This strait, now filled with ocean sand, was known to the Indians as Napeague, or "water land"—old-timers speak of going "on" and "off" Montauk[1] as if it were still an island—and the headland at Montauk's eastern end was known to the Indians as Wompanon.[2] A lighthouse fired by sperm whale oil was constructed at Wompanon in 1795 by order of President George Washington, who proposed that it should stand for two hundred years.

Montauk's access to swift rips and deep ledges, to the wandering Gulf Stream, forty to seventy miles off to the south, has made it a legendary fishing place since Indian times. It was the fishing that attracted the developer Arthur Benson in 1879, when New York sportsmen were establishing striped bass fishing clubs in New York and Rhode Island. In 1880 some visionary anglers caused the construction of an iron fishing pier[3] over seven hundred feet long on the ocean beach at Napeague, only to see it torn away in its first winter.

Meanwhile, a small camp had been established at Fort Pond Bay by commercial fishermen from the North Fork. In the early 1880s, fishing was poor, and most of them transferred their operations to Rhode Island. Three years later, when the Rhode Island fishery declined, they returned to Montauk, finding the fish "more plentiful than was ever known before."

Then, at the turn of the century, a William J. Morgan, surfcasting under the Light, landed a seventy-six-pound striped bass that made Montauk famous. Wherever this hero went thereafter, it was said, people would point and say, "That's Morgan!" But Morgan was no doubt well aware of the 101-pound specimen taken off East Hampton in this period by Nathaniel Dominy's haul-seine crew. Cap'n Dominy laid the monster out in style in a farm wagon and trundled it around East Hampton and Sag Harbor, charging the villagers ten cents each for a good look before selling it for five dollars to a Sag Harbor hotel; no doubt people draw breath today whose forebears dined on that historic fish. The obsessed Morgan, who tried for the rest of his life to catch one larger, built a house on Montauk overlooking a surfcasting site that was known as "Morgan's" for decades thereafter.

Within a few years of the arrival of the railroad in 1895—and despite Montauk's meager population and facilities—the fishing community at Fort Pond Bay became the principal fish shipping port on the East End, with hundreds of tons of black sea bass and other species shipped every day. Tracks were built onto the dock for a special fish train that was loaded directly from the boats. It left Montauk at 4:30 P.M., picked up boxes of fish at the depot platform known as Fanny Bartlett's, or Napeague Station, as well as at Amagansett and East Hampton, and arrived in the New York markets before daylight.

For years to come there was no paved road across the sands of Napeague,[4] and Montauk's shantytown of fishermen and fish packers remained clustered on the eastern shore of Fort Pond Bay, with four or five pioneer summer cottages on the dunes opposite. Mrs. Agnew's Tea Room was the only building on the wagon road between the settlement and Montauk Light. The fishing community, notably the Parsons, Edwards, and Hulse families from Amagansett and the large Tuthill clan from Orient and East Marion on the North Fork, in addition to some people from Connecticut, would usually arrive in early May and go home

in fall; most of them lived in simple shacks constructed from
"fish box boards"—the big sugar boxes, made from sugar
pine, that would carry ten bushels of skimmers or six
hundred pounds of fish. Since Fort Pond Bay was relatively
unprotected, the fishing boats were moored to spiles, or
stakes, offshore that were limber enough to bend with the
strong winds. The Parsonses and Tuthills ran their own
boats and kept their own fish houses on the east shore of
the bay; the fishing company on the south shore belonged
to J. C. Wells.

The Edwards Brothers, running ocean traps off Amagansett, unloaded their catch at the Tuthill dock. In early
April, four to ten ocean traps, or barrel traps—a leader or
wing turned fish offshore into a series of funnels and pens—
were set up to a mile offshore in about seven fathoms of
water, to catch whatever came along in the strong spring
run. The ocean trap was similar in design to a large pound
trap but used anchors instead of stakes. A crew of forty, in
four seine boats, was required to lift these traps, from which
twelve tons or more of edible fish might be harvested each
day. When the ocean traps were taken up, about June 1,
the crews were switched to the big bunker steamers, which
sailed from the Edwards Brothers docks near the menhaden factories (called Bunker City) now concentrated in
the vicinity of Promised Land, west of Napeague Harbor.
In the twenties, the Tuthills and Jake Wells hired summer
help from Nova Scotia to work in the packing houses and
on the docks, and some of these men moved down to Promised Land to crew on the Edwards Brothers boats. A Montauk colony of Nova Scotia families—including such fishing
clans as the Pittses and Beckwiths—are part of the Montauk
community to this day.

Most of the early Montauk fishermen were trappers, and
the Tuthills lifted their fish pounds, or traps, on Gardiners
Island as well as in the environs of Fort Pond Bay. On a
map made early in the century, nearly three hundred traps

are shown between North Bar at Montauk Point and Eastern Plains Point on Gardiners Island, a far denser concentration than exists today.[5] Captain Nat Edwards, son of Cap'n Gabe, ran a dozen pound traps between Shagwong Point and Water Fence; Captain Sam Edwards and other fishermen ran small low-powered draggers, thirty to thirty-five feet long, or set lobster pots, or hand-lined for pollock, sea bass, and bluefish.

Throughout the Hamptons, small scallop boats and other craft had been catering to summer fishing parties since the turn of the century. Montauk draggermen did well with swordfish (by August 7 in the summer of 1925, Captain George Beckwith had harpooned thirty-seven) and in the late twenties and early thirties, when Montauk was developed as a resort, many draggers joined the early charter fleet. In 1927 the first swordfish ever taken on rod and reel was brought into Fort Pond Bay by one of the Florida fishing guides drawn to the area. The following year the former Great Pond, rechristened Lake Montauk, was permanently opened to the bay, creating an all-weather harbor.

In the mid-twenties, when agitation to restrict the activities of commercial men had already started, a federal hatchery for production of lobster, codfish, flounder, and pollock was proposed for Fort Pond Bay, and a freezing plant designed to market prepacked fish was already under construction. But these enterprises were abandoned with the opening and development of Great Pond. Although certain old-timers stuck to Fort Pond Bay for another twenty years, the construction of additional docks, and the protected anchorage, had drawn most of the fleet to the new harbor. The Napeague road was long since paved, and the fish train was now replaced by truckers. Commercial men such as Gus and Fred Pitts (of the Nova Scotia colony), draggermen Dan Grimshaw and Harry Conklin (who took out President Herbert Hoover), and the Beckwith, Erickson, and Tuma brothers soon adapted their work boats for chartering; even Captains Sam and Bert Edwards, and later Sam's sons Kenneth and Dick, took time off from bunkering to join the fleet. Before long, big bottom-fishing boats were developed that would attract thousands of people to Montauk every year. More than five thousand customers were recorded in 1932, and this number tripled the following year and doubled again in 1934, when the Long Island Rail Road established daily excursion trains from New York and Brooklyn. S. Kip Farrington of East Hampton (ignoring the surfmen) described the pioneer fish guides of the thirties as the rightful heirs of Captain Josh Edwards and the shore whalers; as a big game fisherman and sport-fishing writer, he did more to advertise the new craze for deep-sea fishing than anyone else before or since. By the mid-thirties, special deep-sea fishing boats with twin screw engines and flying bridges had been designed for working the Gulf Stream, sometimes as far as seventy miles offshore; the fish prized most were swordfish, marlin, and the giant bluefin tuna, moving north and south from its summer grounds off Wedgeport, Nova Scotia.

The 1938 hurricane created the Shinnecock Inlet, now a fishing station, but it mostly destroyed the Montauk fishing village at Fort Pond Bay. The railroad depot is still there, however, and so is the fish company founded by E. D. Tuthill and owned today by Perry Duryea, Jr., whose father married Captain Ed Tuthill's daughter. The hundreds of boats that once littered the bay are now in Montauk Harbor, which by the time of my arrival in the early fifties was already home port for one of the largest sport-fishing fleets on the East Coast.

That summer of 1954, the charter season was well under way when the *Merlin* arrived. There was one slip left at the town dock, right across from one of the pioneer charter men, John Messbauer, and we soon found out why nobody had wanted it; the current was strong and the approach narrow, and the one way to back a single-engine boat into this berth was a sequence of swirling maneuvers at full throttle. Unless executed with precision, these maneuvers would strand the boat across the bows of neighboring boats, held fast by the current, while the customers wondered how their lives had been consigned to such lubberly hands. Before I got the hang of it, there was more than one humiliating episode, not helped by the embarrassment of my trusty mate, who would shrug, wince, and roll his eyes, pretending to the old salts along the dock that if only this greenhorn would let him take the helm, he could do much better.

At thirty-two feet, the *Merlin* was small by Montauk standards, and she lacked the customary flying bridge, not to mention upholstered fighting chairs, teak decks, and chrome. We had no old customers to depend on, and no big shiny cockpit to attract new ones, and Captain Al Ceslow on the *Skip II*, for whom John had worked as mate the previous summer, was the only man in the whole fleet of forty-five-odd boats who would offer advice or help of any kind. However, it was soon July, and fish and fishing parties both abounded (and were biting hard, said cynical Jimmy Reutershan, who was bluefishing out of Montauk in his Jersey skiff, and who believed strongly in lunar tide tables as a guide to the feeding habits of fish and man; he had noticed, he said, that *Homo sapiens*, wandering the docks with a glazed countenance, would suddenly stir into feeding frenzy, signing up boats with the same ferocity—and at the same stage of the tide—that *Pomatomus saltatrix* would strike into the lures around the Point).

And so, from the first, the *Merlin* did pretty well. We made up in eagerness and love of fishing what we lacked in experience of our new trade, we worked hard to find fish for our clients, and except on weekends, when we ran two six-hour trips each day, we sailed overtime without extra charge whenever the morning had been unproductive. Also, unlike many of the charter men, who seemed to feel that anglers of other races belonged on "barf barges"—the party or bottom-fishing boats—we welcomed anyone who came along. One day we sailed a party of Chinese laundrymen from up-Island, each one equipped with a full-sized galvanized garbage can. Their one recognizable utterance was "Babylon." Conveying to us through their Irish-American interpreter that trolling for hard-fighting and abundant bluefish did not interest them, they said that they wished to be taken to the three coal barges sunk southwest of the Point in a nor'easter, a well-known haunt of the black sea bass so highly esteemed in Chinese cookery. Once the hulks were located, they set out garbage cans along the cockpit and pin-hooked sea bass with such skill (to cries of "Bobby-lon!") that every man topped off his garbage can. The half ton of sea bass that they took home more than paid the cost of the whole charter, while gladdening every Oriental heart in western Suffolk.

Another day, three Shinnecock Indian chiefs in quest of "giants" (they were soon off to Alaska, they declared, to shoot giant brown bear) took us all the way to Rosie's Hole off the coast of Rhode Island in vain pursuit of giant bluefin. Because of the fuel, the barrel of bunker chum bought at Ted's freezer, and the installation of the *Merlin's* heavy tuna chair, the trip was expensive even for car dealers from Washington, D.C., where the three chiefs spent most of the year, passing themselves off as black men. The chiefs liked us because the other boats had refused their trade, and we liked them because they spent their money cheerfully, though they saw neither hide nor hair of giants.

No other boat got a bluefin that day either, and John and I were relieved as well as disappointed; in theory, we knew what to do once the huge fish took the mackerel bait that we drifted down the current (crank up the engine, cast off the buoy on the anchor, and chase after the exhilarated fish before it stripped the last line off the reel), but being inexperienced with giant tuna, we foresaw all sorts of possibilities for dangerous error. Big bluefin may be ten feet long, and nearly a half ton in weight, and the speed and power of these fish are awesome. (In the *Merlin's* former life in Ipswich Bay, a passenger had come too close to the blur of green line leaving the tub after a horse mackerel had been harpooned. The line whipped around his leg and snapped him overboard and down thirty feet under the sea before someone grabbed a hatchet and whacked the line where it sizzled across the brass strip on the combing. Had that hatchet not been handy, and wits quick, the nosy passenger would have lost his life.)

Toward the end of the homeward journey across Block Island Sound, I encouraged the chiefs to stop on Shagwong Reef and pick up a few bluefish to take home for supper. The thwarted giant-killers had consoled themselves with gin on the long voyage, and one man agreed to fish for blues if we would strap him into the big fighting chair and give him that thick tuna rod to work with, so that he could imagine what it must be like to deal masterfully with one of those monsters back at Rosie's Hole. When the strike came, it failed to bend even the rod tip, but the angler, cheered on by his friends, set the hook with a mighty backward heave into the fighting chair. "It's charging the boat!" his assistants yelled as something broke the surface; the only porgy in the *Merlin's* history that ever went for a trolled bluefish lure had been snapped clear out of the water by that heave and skimmed through the air over the wake in a graceful flight that a flying fish might well have envied.

So much did all three chiefs enjoy this exciting fishing experience that they felt obliged to lie down in the cockpit, collapsed with laughter. "No mo' bluefishin," they cried helplessly, waving us on. "Giant pogie's good enough!" Once ashore, they gave both of us giant tips, thanked us as "scholars and gentlemen" for a splendid outing, and went off merrily down the dock with their souvenir porgy. Next time they visited these parts, they said, they would bring their girlfriends down to meet us (which they did).

Not all our clients were such good sports as the three chiefs. A charter demands six hours at close quarters with company that is rarely of one's choice, and often there are two charters each day. While most of our people were co-operative and pleasant, others felt that their money entitled them to treat captain and mate as servants, and one ugly customer advised me even before the *Merlin* cleared the breakwater that he knew all about the charter men's tricks and cheating ways. I turned the boat around, intending to put him on the dock, but his upset friends made him apologize.

Another day the motor broke down on Shagwong Reef in clear, rough weather of a northwest wind. A cockpit full of queasy passengers wanted to know why I did not call the Coast Guard. The truth was that their captain, having had no time to go to New York and apply to the Coast Guard for a captain's license, was running a renegade boat, and was stalling for time until Al Ceslow on the *Skip II* could finish his morning charter and tow us in. One of the men, under the horrified gaze of his newlywed wife, actually panicked, shrieking at the other passengers that the captain's plan was to put this death craft on the rocks; I had to grab him by the shirtfront and bang him up against the cabinside to calm him down. (On another charter boat one morning— we could hear the shouts and crashing right over the radio-telephone—a disgruntled client had to be slugged into sub-mission, with the skipper bellowing for police assistance at the dock.)

The *Merlin* was plagued by persistent hazing from two charter boats that now and then would turn across our wake, out on the Elbow, and cut off all four of our wire lines; no doubt other new boats were welcomed in this way as well. Wire line, lures, and leaders are expensive, and because wire line is balky stuff, it often took most of an hour of good fishing tide to re-rig the lines for the unhappy customers. The two big captains of these big boats (both of them sons of earlier big captains who now ran big enterprises on the docks) were successful charter men who had nothing to fear from the small *Merlin;* often this pair trolled side by side, chatting on radio-telephones from their flying bridges. One day off Great Eastern Rock,[6] heart pounding with mixed fear and glee, and deaf to all oaths and shouts of warning, I spun my wheel and cut across both of their fat sterns, taking all eight of their wire lines at a single blow.

In the long stunned silence on all three boats, John Cole said quietly, "Oh boy," and suggested a long detour to Connecticut. "Those guys are going to be waiting for us on the dock," he said, "and they are BIG." But there was no reception party, and our lines were never cut again. Not long thereafter one of these skippers called the *Merlin* on "the blower," passing terse word in the charter man's way that he was into fish: "See where we are, Cap, down to the east'rd? Better come this way."

One day on the ocean side, working in close to the rocks west of the Light, we picked up a striped bass on the inshore line and a bluefish on the outside; we did this on three straight passes, and probably could have done it again if we had not been late for our afternoon charter and had to head in. So far as we knew, those three bass, and three more the next day from the same place, were the only stripers taken out of Montauk for nearly a fortnight in the bass dog days of late July. From that day on, we had to wait to fish this spot until the fleet went in at noon, because other boats began to tail us with binoculars, in the same way that the *Merlin* sometimes tailed Gus Pitts when the *Marie II* worked the striper holes along the beach, watching his mate strip out the wire to guess the depth at which Cap'n Gus was trolling, or glimpse what lure he was rigging to his rods.

On days when we had no charter, we went out handlining for blues, heading west past Culloden Point[7] and Fort

Pond Bay to Water Fence, at the western boundary of the land acquired by the Proprietors of Montauk, where the cattle fence that once kept East Hampton's livestock on the Montauk pastures during the summer had extended out into the water; past the walking dunes, a sand flow at the old forest edge on the north side of Hither Hills; past Goff Point and the fallen chimney of the abandoned bunker factory at Hicks Island.[8] East of Cartwright Shoal, the shallow waters teemed with small three-pound "tailor" bluefish that bit as fast as the hand lines were tossed overboard, and brought a good price on the market.[9]

The *Merlin* was no longer a renegade boat (I got my license in late summer), and no one ignored her radio queries or disdained to call her; she had already built up a list of clients who wished to charter her again the following year. The bluefishing was strong and steady, and offshore the school tuna were so thick that by leaving one fish on the line while boating the other three, we could keep all four lines loaded almost continually until the box had overflowed. On some days, poor John, skidding around on the bloody deck, exhausted from pumping the strong tuna off the bottom for the weary customers, would send me wild-eyed signals to get the boat away from the goddamn fish, maybe show the clients a nice shark or ocean sunfish.

But there were days in that first summer when the *Merlin* sat idle at the dock, and in August the price of bluefish was so low that hand-lining would not make us a day's pay. Bass remained scarce in the dead of summer, and one morning when his boat was hauled out for repairs, we decided to show our friend Al Ceslow our secret striper spot on the ocean shore west of the Light.

In the days before, there had been offshore storms, and the big smooth swells collapsing on the coast would make it difficult to work close to the rocks. We also knew that Cap'n Gus, widely regarded as the best striped bass fisherman ever to sail under the Light, had put three boats on those rocks in his twenty years of hard experience. And so we rode in as close as we dared on the backs of the broad waves, letting the lures coast in on the white wash. We were not close enough, and tried to edge in closer, keeping an eye out for the big freak sea that would break offshore and wash us onto the rock shore under the cliffs. Unlike the established boats, we were not booked solid a full year in advance, and the loss of the *Merlin*—we could not yet afford insurance— would mean the end of our careers as charter boatmen, apart from endangering our lives.

The wave we feared rose up behind us, sucking the water off the inshore rocks, and as Al or John shouted, I spun the wheel and gave the *Merlin* her full throttle. With a heavy thud, our trusty boat struck into the midsection of a high, clear, cresting wave, and for one sickening moment, seemed to lose headway. Then the wave parted, two walls of green water rushed past the cockpit, over our heads, and the boat sprang up and outward, popping free. If we ever fished that spot again, I do not recall it.

Hurricane Carol, on the last day of August 1954, blew so hard at Montauk that I ran the *Merlin* at eight knots in her slip in order to ease the pressure on her lines. At high water, only the spile tops on the town dock were visible above the flood, which carried loose boats and capsized hulks down toward the breakwater. In leaping from the stern to fetch more lines or lend a hand with another boat, one could only pray that the town dock was still there.

The hurricane's eye passed over about noon, in an eerie silver light and sulfurous pall. Then the winds struck in again, subsiding only as our fuel ran low in midafternoon. By evening we felt free to leave for home, but could not get there; the storm seas, surging through the dunes, had reopened the old strait in a new channel into Napeague Harbor, knocking down one of the radio towers that transmitted to the ships at sea. Until late that night, when the tide turned and the sea subsided, we were stranded on Montauk, which was once again an island.

I was not sorry when the season was over and I ran my boat back west to Three Mile Harbor. To judge from the sour, contemptuous remarks that were traded back and forth on the radio-telephones, a lot of charter men were opportunists, out for an easy dollar that was not forthcoming. Almost all of us made good money between July 4 and Labor Day, but only the best boats in the fleet, with the longest lists of faithful customers (these were the charter captains we admired, the skilled and happy ones who loved to fish) could make it in the colder days of spring and autumn. The *Merlin* was not yet one of those boats, and we quit right after Labor Day, to make the most of the first weeks of the scallop season. It was a poor season that year, with so many scallops destroyed by Hurricane Carol.

The *Merlin*'s summer in 1955 was busy and successful, but I ended my second year of chartering with the same feeling. I chartered because it paid for my boat and I made a living out of doors in the season between haul-seining and scalloping; I scalloped and hauled seine because I liked the work, and liked the company of the commercial fishermen, the baymen.

# 9.

# Amagansett Winter

T he South Fork of Long Island is the windiest reach on the Atlantic coast, not excluding Hatteras, and 1954 must have been one of the windiest on record. Eleven days after Hurricane Carol came Hurricane Edna, but this time there was advance warning, and I ran the *Merlin* to the sheltered cove at the head of Three Mile Harbor. Here the main threat came from a large dilapidated craft hitched casually with old clothesline to the town bulkhead; but for the emergency lines set by other boatmen, she might have broken loose and done great damage. Perhaps she was meant to sink, since her hull was flooded—I assumed the petcocks had been opened. Held fast (and afloat) by a cobweb of spare lines, she wallowed lopsided on the surface, to the great consternation of her owner, whose pale face was seen several times during the storm, peering out from behind his windshield wipers, at a loss to understand why his plan to cash in on his insurance was a failure.

During this storm, the tough old *Vop-Vop* was tied up across the cove, opposite the boatyard, where the heavy gales banged her remorselessly against the bulkhead. Because there was no way to protect her, Pete Scott suggested that I sink her, which I did. Two days later, we floated her

again, she was undamaged, and my coot-shooting cronies
George Rosen and Eddie George, who did boat engine work
out of their garage at Olympic Heights, yanked her simple
engine. Washed with fresh water and sprayed with oil, it
was installed again, as good as new.

We used the *Vop* for scalloping that autumn, and Pete
used her at Montauk all that winter. On days of wind, she
pulled the dredges well with her gaff-rigged sail; on other
days, on the silver stillness of Lake Montauk, she seemed to
be moved mysteriously by unseen powers. As on most auxiliary boats in the scallop fleet before "powerin" became per-
missible by law, her motor was just "tricklin over," with an
inner tube rigged over the exhaust pipe to carry sound away
under the water. Knowing that these were hard months for
the fishermen, the bay constable, Jack Conklin, rarely paid
these boats' peculiar progress much attention.

When the scallop crop diminished in the local harbors,
the haul-seine crews returned to the ocean beach. I was
trying to get some writing done, and except to fill in here
and there, I rarely went seining in the autumn, though I
went gunning at every opportunity. On those golden-and-
blue days, using canoes, we jumped teal and black duck
from the coves of Georgica. We walked the glacial kettle
holes in the warm October woods west of the old road between Sagaponack and Sag Harbor; when the weather
turned to rain and wind, we set out decoys in Hog Creek
and Accabonac. In colder weather we dug pits on Sammis
Beach and on the sand spit leading out to Cedar Point, pass-
shooting for golden-eye and the scoters, or coot, that
crossed over from the harbors to Gardiners Bay. The best
spots were claimed by hard-bitten old "swampers" down out
of the woods with antique ten-gauge fowling pieces that shot
nuts and bolts and belched out yellow smoke, George Rosen
swore, and were capable of wild towering shots that brought
the swift sea ducks down out of the clouds like missiles. As
the season progressed and the birds flew higher, or veered

away to fly over the channel between Cedar Point and Shelter Island, we trailered sharpies across the Northwest Woods to the landing at Alewive (pronounced "Elly") Brook, where the first settlers at Northwest had their anchorage. George and Eddie and our friend Herb Latshaw from the Three Mile Harbor Boatyard and old Joe Ambrose from Soak Hide Road and other regulars would gather before light at the Elly Brook landing, and the flat-bottomed sharpie fleet would bang out across the chop to string the Cedar Point channel for coot and old squaw.

One December day, when the black duck had grown scarce and wary, Pete Scott and I lugged waders and guns and shells and decoys in burlap bags from Skunks Hole on the east side of Napeague, where the road ended, to the ponds beyond the walking dunes, just west of Water Fence; it must have been an hour's walk in hard wind and cold. At dusk, with red, stiff, frozen hands, we picked up the ice-glazed decoys from the ice-skimmed water and trudged back to Skunks Hole without having fired a shot at a single bird.

Then the gunning season was over, and the long quiet winter set in. Even those city people who came out from New York for Thanksgiving or Christmas were gone until late spring; Main Street was empty. Lacking the stone hands of a fisherman, I was content once more to be a writer.

One early winter day, in a cold twilight, John Cole and I stopped in Francis Lester's yard, where Francis was emptying fish from his ancient truck. In the old days, cod had been plentiful by November, coming in so close to the beach that at the end of the haul-seining season a few would appear among the bass, but now they were fewer and farther off the shore. That afternoon Francis had lifted his cod trawl in the ocean, and this cold, arduous, and dangerous work had rewarded him with just three cod, which he tossed in disgust across the yard; he was wet and cold, and maybe he'd box and ship them in the morning. But that night there was heavy snow, and in the morning he could not find the codfish. He forgot about them until late February or March, when their woebegone eyes and broken tails emerged after a thaw. In a forlorn gesture of protest and futility—though he could ill afford the waste of money—Francis boxed and shipped the half-rotted cod to the Fulton Fish Market. "B'god, boy," he told John later, "got full price for 'em, too! Them people don't give us nothin until fish is scarce, and then they'll buy goddamn near *anything!*"

In a good bass year, most of the fishermen take most of December to go gunning, pay attention to their families ("Your family comes before everything else," Milt Miller says), and enjoy the holidays. Otherwise, until mid-March, the fisherman's life is a hard, marginal existence, scouring the cold bays for scattered scallops, tonging clams from the stiff bottoms, seining whitebait in Georgica and Sagaponack Ponds, and in dead of winter probing for mudded eels with spears through the ice of the frozen harbors. The men are usually obliged to invest up to one third of their year's income in equipment, and they work unpaid for weeks on end to prepare their battered gear. New nets are hung and old ones mended, boats caulked, beach trucks overhauled. Not until the February thaw, when the harbor seals vanished, would a few men set flounder fykes in sheltered waters; eelpots were scattered in the salt ponds in the month of March. Now boats were painted and trap stakes cut from tall white oak and hickory saplings, in wood lots that were harder to find each year. Until late April, when the traps were fishing, and the spring run appeared along the beach, the men had to "grind it" to scrape up a day's pay, and only the most dedicated fishermen, supported by strong dedicated wives, were able to endure year after year.

The winter stretched away without an end, and at the heart of it, even in storm, was this dead quiet, all the more so on white days of heavy snow. One Saturday night, escaping the pressure of a second novel, I got mixed up in a free-for-all in what was then the Elm Tree Tavern in Amagansett. In the tumult I went down, and an excited stranger I could not recall having offended, or met previously, was astride on my chest, getting in some licks, when he was picked up and thrown aside by a tall, rangy rescue party whom I recognized with gratitude as Lindy Havens. A man who had always enjoyed hard drink, Lindy resided in a room over the bar, and no doubt he had been attracted down by the sound of brawling. Perhaps he acted on a simple-hearted wish to join the action, but I like to think he helped me out because I was a member of Ted Lester's crew, and therefore an honorary fisherman; and the fiercely independent fishermen, with their old trucks and autos and disreputable front yards, their hell-raising and their aversion to orderly hours, had to stick together.

To the up-street solid citizenry of East Hampton, independence was no excuse for poverty. A black lady who cleaned our house informed my wife that my profession and the company I kept was a threat to her own standing in her community, which was based on a long ancestry in East Hampton; her middle-class clan had come long ago as slaves of the "first families." The fishermen, also of first families, were quite aware that these established black people were often more prosperous than themselves, and the use of such terms as "nigger rich," "nigger geese" (for cormorants), "niggerhead" (a winch), "nigger work," or "good enough for niggers and Bonackers," reflects their wry, laconic bitterness about their diminished standing in town.

Ralph Carpentier, now the director of the excellent Marine Museum in Amagansett, is an "outsider" who fished with Ted Lester in the early sixties. One summer day Ted informed the crew that they were going to make the Napeague Station set, although they had been doing well farther east. His son Stewart was with the crew that day, and as they were hauling, Stewart suddenly stopped winching on his end, where he was working with Jimmy Reutershan. "Ted started hollering," Ralph says, "and Stewart hollered back: a human body had turned up in the net! 'Well, take him out,' Ted yells, 'and keep that net coming.' But Stewart was really spooked and he yells at his father, '*You* take it out!' So Ted says, 'Come on, Ralph,' and goes running down there, and sure enough, there's this young guy in bathing trunks, covered with little black snails. He was all stiff with rigor mortis, hands pointing kind of funny at the wrists. Jimmy didn't mind him much, but Stewart was green, he just wouldn't go near him. I don't blame Stewart for being spooked, I was spooked myself. So Ted grabs one end and I take the other and we set him aside, and Stewart is yelling at his father, 'You made this set on purpose, you *knew* he was going to be here!' Because this guy had drowned two days before at the State Park, and Ted had known about it. So we go back down to our end to finish the haul, and I asked Ted if what Stewart said was true, and he admitted it. 'I knew he had to be along in this stretch somewhere. There was no other way them people were ever goin to get their son back. Why, hell, I'd do the same thing for a nigger.' "

Though Ted notified the police after the haul, he advised Ralph to keep quiet about it; it wouldn't be so good for business, having dead bodies in the nets. But a few days later, an interview with Captain Ted Lester appeared in the paper, telling all about it. "That's the way Ted was," Ralph remembers, laughing. "He was great and terrible at the same time; you loved him and hated him. I used to protest when he used that word 'nigger' but he'd just wave me off, like it wasn't serious. Not that he was any worse than the other guys, they all have the same blind spot on the subject."

The truth is, Stewart Lester says, his father was less prejudiced than other Poseys. According to Stewart, the resentment of blacks occurred in the Depression, when many women in the fishing families, his grandmother included, "had to work for rich people—that's all there was." Mary

Lavinia Lester was convinced that blacks were taking all these jobs, and proving their inferiority by working for less than a fair wage. Although race prejudice in the local community—by no means confined to fishermen—has much diminished, these views still prevail among certain members of the present generations. As usual, one group of poor was being set against another. As Stewart points out, there was also strong prejudice against Irish house servants, or "pot-rasslers," and Milt Miller says that the first Italian families who settled the east end of Amagansett didn't fare much better.[1]

When pale spring came and the ospreys reappeared, and black-backed flounders nosed along the harbor bottoms, tracing the bloodworms and orange mussel baits on the rusty hooks of old chafed men in rowboats, I slapped copper paint on the *Merlin's* hull at the Three Mile Harbor Boatyard. When the shadblow bloomed and the spring life in the sea brought strong fertile odors to the ocean wind, I got out my black waders once again, my long-billed swordfish cap and dark blue parka with its sweet smell of ancient fish gurry, and went on south across Abraham's Path to Poseyville. "Better try 'em, ain't we, boys?" Cap'n Ted would say, looking up briefly from mending net to squint at us. And I realized that watching those blunt weather-glazed hands slipping that net needle through the twine with such speed and deftness was one of the great many small pleasures of life on the beach that I took for granted. (Ted taught us some basic cutting and mending for emergency repair—three-leggers, laggers, zagging and the like—though not the goring and other skills required for big tears caused by hang-ups and sharks.) Across the broad littered yard toward Francis's house, the big silver beach truck was waiting. We turned the dory right side up and slid her up onto her trailer, then loaded the net that Ted had spread to dry on the new grass. "Get started early in the mornin, now, you fellers can tell them pretty wives of yours"—Ted's nudge and wink were boyish and naive—"you'll be back home time for a matinée, ain't that right, Johnnie?"

Ted was innocent and generous-spirited, and also sly and sharp-eyed as a gull; he had worked hard to make Montauk Seafood a good business and had not stopped there. On the floor above the freezer, he opened a retail seafood shop, run by Jenny Lester and her daughters, and in the sixties he would use the proceeds from these enterprises to open Lester's Liquors out on the highway. Among all the baymen I knew personally, this man alone had accumulated money. Baymen are exceptionally conservative, wary of change, and perhaps it was Ted's transgression of a favorite saying that "No one has ever come across a rich fisherman" that was not forgiven.

It was often suggested, for example, that Ted Lester cut corners in sharing receipts from the Fulton Market. (No fisherman ever works on salary, which is one reason why these doggedly independent men do not speak of themselves as "working," far less "taking a job." Income from the catch is divided into shares, one for the rig and one for each man on the crew.) "I quit Ted because he never whacked up fair with his crew," one man told me. "That's how come he took on people from away. Don't know if you knew it or not, but you fellas was gettin a half share all them years you fished with Ted, and he done the same thing to the rest of us, so after a while he couldn't get no Poseys to go with him. Old Ted! But we had some fun in them days, ain't that right?" Yet we knew just how many boxes we had packed, and Ted always showed us the receipts that came back with the checks a few days later. Almost all the best fishermen now on the beach had worked with Ted at one time or another, which they would not have done if he had cheated them; and fairly or not, the man quoted above had the same reputation he ascribed to Ted, and sometimes had trouble finding men to fish with him.

Most men quit Ted because he was such a relentless driver, not because he was dishonest; as his son says with mixed pride and exasperation, "He went through 'em all." When there was fit weather to go off, we made two early morning sets and at least two more in the afternoon; a lone fish in the net would inspire Ted to go out after its brothers, whereas most crews would give up and go home. Only the hard-core fishermen and inspired amateurs were willing to work this way on bad days as well as good, especially in the fifties, when most days were bad.

In the spring of 1955, at dawn on a rough April day, we were heading east from Napeague Lane in search of a set. "No weather today, boys," Ted kept saying. "Wind's pickin up out of the east'rd." But the whole crew had bills to pay, and so we went looking for a stretch of surf where we could launch the yellow dory. Cap'n Frank's crew was even hungrier; we saw the black lumps of four trucks in silhouette on the beach at Hither Plains, where another crew was helping Frank go off. In the ocean distance, the black figures were up to their chests in the white surf, which twisted the dory as the wash rushed high onto the beach. Then, too slowly, the boat drew away. She took a buffet— the white spray shot up, and she staggered. It seemed certain that the next wave would break right into her. She kept moving, and rose slowly on the wave face. But she had lost too much momentum, and the wave was too big, and the bow kept rising on the gray daybreak sky, the dory poised for a long awful moment, cocked on end. Then the wave, breaking, hurled her over backward.

Ted had already smelled disaster; the silver truck was howling down the beach, burning its gears. A minute later, we were out on the dead run into the sea, hauling at the net. Ding-Ding (Frank's son Harry) had been thrown clear, but the two other men were missing. They might have been struck by the crashing dory or caught under the net, which was unwinding in long tentacles along the beach with the set to westward, perhaps dragging stunned men in waders beneath the surface.

Then a dark shape rolled out from beneath the dory, disappeared, popped up again; he was seized and dragged ashore. It was Richard, who had left Ted's crew to go back fishing with his father. In the tumult, trying to keep our footing, trying not to get entangled or go under, we might easily have failed to notice him.

Fear for the third man was rising like panic when someone thought to look beneath the dory. The man who turned up, scared but unhurt, was Cap'n Frank's grandson, Walter Bennett, who swore that day that never again would he go off in a dory.

On most fair weather days just after noon, the warm air rising from the fields is replaced by cold air off the ocean. The wind backs around and comes onshore behind short choppy seas out of the southwest. The cold surface water retards spring growth (which is two weeks behind the foliage on the bay side) and causes the dense fogs of June as the air warms. In fall, the process is reversed, as the ocean's gathered heat extends the blue and golden warmth of Indian summer.

That spring of 1955, I knew my job and I enjoyed it. Lying back on the damp nets stacked in the dory after the early morning sets, trundling along the bright white sand in the soft spring light, enjoying the spring breath of the fertile loam that came all the way down to the back of the dunes and blew out over the clean beach—the springtime filled me with well-being despite my drowsiness, despite sore hands, despite the prospect of a long hard day that, if we were lucky, would end long after dark in the cold freezer of Montauk Seafood, hosing down and packing and icing bass.

As a seasonal fisherman, I could afford to romanticize this life, to indulge myself in wondering why a veteran bayman such as Milt Miller would inveigh so vehemently against his lifelong occupation. (Not that this habit was confined to Milt. As an old saying goes, "I'm gonna put this goddamn oar over my shoulder and head west, and the first sonofabitch asks me what it is, that's where I stick it in the ground and settle.") Like most baymen, Milt was a skilled carpenter, boatbuilder, and jack-of-all-trades who could easily have set up his own shop or found well-paid work in the construction industry; no law but his own had told him to be a fisherman. But as he said, it was "in his blood," there was nothing to be done about it.

In spring the net is set from east to west, insuring a hard row into the onshore wind each afternoon, and Milt, behind me at the bow oars, would curse into my ear with every heave. "My boy Mickey ever touches a fishin net, I'll tan his hide! Worked like a donkey all my life and here I am, still workin like a donkey, cause I don't *know* nothin! Not one bit better off than when I started!" Milt would row some, get his breath, and start all over. "Boy, this life here is just one big mess, in case you ain't found that out yet! Best thing Mickey could do would be read up a little, get a job as a psycho-analyst, you know, like that loony I run into over here the other day. What you do, you lay down there on a couch and earn you a day's pay in a hour, just listenin to rich people belly-achin! You and Johnny got a education, Pete, how come *you* ain't psycho-analyzin? Pay you better than bassin, I'll tell you that!" Milt would be winking slyly at Stewart Lester in the stern, I could read it in the grin on Stewart's face, but he was serious, too: he was fighting to make sense of a hard life.

Milt said that in the early thirties, when he had fished Captain Gabe Edwards's set nets on a share basis, both bass and bluefish had been very scarce. "Cap'n Gabe used to talk about acres of bluefish back in the old days, and who was I to disbelieve a captain and deacon of the church who never was known to tell anything but the truth? But if we got four or five bluefish out of eight or ten set nets, we thought we were lucky." He stuck out his left thumb to show the scar. "That was done by a bluefish when I was just a kid. He was slippin out of the net, and because he was so rare, y'know, I wasn't goin to let him go; stuck my hand down quick, right into his mouth, and when I flung him, them teeth opened me up right to the bone."

In 1934—he remembers the year because of the intense cold that winter, the last winter in memory when the salt water froze solid on Gardiners Bay, permitting walking expeditions from Fireplace to Gardiners Island—Milt had hauled seine with his cousin Elisha Ammon "down around Mecox," where his father was caretaker of the Mecox lifeboat station. Their rig was a Model T ford with oversized tires and a platform for a small boat, and the small net was hauled by a winch built by Elisha from parts of an old potato digger, turned by the drive shaft at the front end of the car. So far as Milt knows, this was the first winch ever used for hauling on the beach. "And Model T's were the first real beach vehicles," he remembers. "Before that they'd row down the beach to where they spotted fish, set net and haul, and bury the catch up in the sand, pickin 'em up later with the dory; then they'd row 'em back and hand-barrow 'em up to the roads at the beach landin."

Elisha Ammon, born in Springs in 1911, had spent most of his life out on Montauk, where he can recall killing five deer in a day for winter meat. His grandfather, born at sea and landing at Sag Harbor when what was then known as "the Port" was a port of entry, became a crewman on "the bony boats"—the early steamers fishing for the bony fish, menhaden. Later he worked on the traps and draggers for the Jake Wells and Parsons fish companies on Fort Pond Bay. Elisha's father had done the same, and Elisha did it, too; as he says himself, "I was never brang up to do anything else." With his Uncle Royce, he ran a string of 750 lobster pots, using dabs (daylight flounder) for bait, and for two

years he worked in the Parsons garage to save up money
before he got "brave enough to buy a boat"; it was here that
he assembled the prototype winch used for hauling seine
with the Model T at Mecox.

Elisha became a successful draggerman and swordfisherman, which meant that he was mostly away from home.
"You'd just say 'Good-bye' when you leave and 'Here I am'
when you get back. I'd never say when I was getting back;
better just to say, You'll see me when I get home. Get up
three o'clock, get home ten, eleven; children never even
knew who I was until they was twelve–fourteen years old."
Like many fishermen's sons in recent decades, Elisha's son
quit fishing to become a carpenter when he got married,
and although Elisha understands this, he is wistful. "Might
still have a boat today," he says, "if he just stayed with me."

When he was fishing with Elisha, Milt had already married Etta Midgett, and in 1934 he moved to her home state
of North Carolina. But his wife missed East Hampton,
where her uncle and father[2] had already established themselves as fishermen, and after three or four months the Millers returned to the South Fork. It was now the Depression,
the fishing families were selling off land that they had held
for generations, and even the Gardiners were forced to get
rid of most of their property on Three Mile Harbor; they
gave the present commercial dock site to the Town rather
than let it go for tax sale. "Times was so hard," Milt sighs
today, "that what I done was row at night from Bonac Creek
across to Gardiners and around to the east shore and sneak
across the beach into Great Pond when there was no moon
and scratch up maybe four bushel of clams, then lug them
four bushel back over the beach out to my sharpie. And I
couldn't afford them nice wire baskets, I used wood produce baskets with sharp wire handles, nearly cut my hands
off. Then I'd row all the way back, and a couple of times I
damn near swamped, comin around out of the lee at Cartwright Shoal. And when I was done, I got fifty cents a

bushel for them clams, and was glad to have it; I had kids cryin at home, and I had no choice.

"Independence costs you a lot of money," he told me quietly. "I starved myself to death for independence when I could have made good money at a trade. You ever seen anybody yet get fired from fishin? No, no! You're just glad to find somebody stupid enough to go fishin *with* you."

# 10.

# Sportsmen
# and Politicians

E very year since 1951, a bill designed to curtail or eliminate the net fishery of striped bass had been submitted to the New York State Legislature, accompanied by a great amount of paper-waving, fist-shaking, and shouting, and a pervasive outrage not unlike the crackling sputter of a basket of blue crabs. These perennial "bass bills" were the violent concern of the thousands of New York anglers who were said to support them and the few hundred commercial fishermen who were opposed; they also concerned marine biologists and conservationists, most of whom had never endorsed such legislation, first because, despite strenuous claims that these bills were conservation measures, the real benefits to the bass itself were not apparent, and second because their one consistent feature had been dogged insistence that the recreational fisherman be permitted to sell his catch on the commercial market, in direct competition with a handful of men who still earn a hard livelihood from the sea. From the start, these anglers had been encouraged by their allies in Massachusetts, which prohibited netting in 1945, yet remained one of the leading states in commercial landings of striped bass; all Massachusetts fish sold on the market are caught on hook and line.

On February 29, 1956, I went to Albany with a delegation of commercial men led by Captain Ted Lester of Amagansett to attend the Joint Public Hearing on Striped Bass Legislation; we were there to fight the latest bass bill, known as the Hook-and-Line Amendment, which proposed to follow Massachusetts's lead in reserving the capture (and sale) of the species to those who fished with rod and reel, thereby eliminating the commercial netters at a single blow. With self-serving statistics and conservation propaganda, the sportsmen's lobbies were establishing sly tactics that would harass the netters for the next twenty-five years.

The New York State Assembly chamber, ornate and heavy in the style of a cathedral, was brightened that day by the cold bright light of winter afternoon in the high windows. The small group of commercial men, squashed into one wedge of benches far around to the Speaker's left, seemed almost excluded from the chamber by a noisy crowd of anglers, who were passing about a stuffed striped bass for the edification of the Conservation Committee. After five years of debate, the legislators showed small interest in this plastic fish, and the bass, a large browning specimen with a stricken gaze, was probably more helpful to the delegates from the bird and garden clubs, who otherwise might not have known what manner of beast they had been mustered to defend.

Observing the horseplay from their corner, the baymen spoke little among themselves. They did not feel comfortable in sports jackets, much less in the assembly, and with their livelihood on the line, they did not share the jocularity of these "sports" who were so anxious to put them out of business. For the most part, they fidgeted in silence, like children instructed not to speak in church. Staring upward and about at the vast stone monument to their state taxes that enclosed them, they waited grimly for the business to proceed.

Shortly after 2 P.M., the Speaker (Leo Lawrence) called

the hearing to order. Welcoming the delegates on behalf
of his committee, he expressed the hope that this year
things might go more peaceably than in the past. He then
introduced various personages in the legislature, the Conservation Department, and the Sportsmen's Council, Marine District of New York, an organization of one hundred
or more fishing clubs that coordinated the anglers' political
lobbies. Finally he introduced the secretary of the Long
Island Fishermen's Association (Nick Griek), an urbane,
sad-eyed, soft-spoken man whose crestfallen air at the very
mention of the Hook-and-Line Amendment conveyed deep
sorrow that such rank hypocrisy could be presented as a
conservation measure to the honest lawmakers of New York
State.

Presently the sportsmen and their affiliates rose one by
one to identify themselves, and to read off the names of
their fishing clubs and kindred organizations, all of which
had organized behind a lobbying outfit called the Sportsmen's Council, and all of which pledged undying support
to the high principles of the Hook-and-Line Amendment.
The idea was to confront the legislators with a whole army
of earnest voters whose main concern in life was the rescue
of *Morone saxatilis*.

The Speaker had earlier announced that all speakers on
both sides, in any number, would be limited to five minutes
apiece, and the anglers elected to turn over their collective
time to a Howie Fink of Montauk, whose smile of greeting
faded quickly as he got at the meat of his dissertation. At
what one must suppose was the top of his voice, Mr. Fink
portrayed the migration of unsuspecting Chesapeake
stripers, venturing north along the coast until, in all inno-
cence, they fell afoul of the treacherous shores of eastern
Long Island. "There," cried Fink, red in the face, so outraged was he by his own revelations, "up pops the DEVIL!"—
he whirled to stab a big thick finger at the small diabolical
delegation in the corner—"and MASSACRES those fish!" De-

scribing such infernal machines as the beach truck, seine, and dory, Fink invited the assembled politicians to contemplate the sad fate of those voters—hotel and motel keepers, restaurateurs, garage owners, tackle shop operators, tavern keepers, and liquor store owners—who were being forsaken by the empty-handed anglers, and the suffering caused by the seiners' unholy greed. In effect, he accused the fishermen of cruelty to the rich, since the victims were far more prosperous than their oppressors.

The baymen stared at Mr. Fink in sincere astonishment, then laughed, and their amusement was shared uneasily by some of Fink's own cohorts, who looked taken aback by the vehemence of their champion and no doubt feared that his violent speech would come back to haunt them.

When Fink had subsided, the Speaker turned over the floor to the bill's opponents. The first of these, a young surf caster, said he was ashamed of his fellow anglers, who were being selfish, since there were plenty of bass to go around. He ignored Fink's address, and so did the Suffolk County Supervisor (Stewart Topping); representing the region whose small businesses would theoretically benefit the most by the legislation, the supervisor had come to Albany to state that Suffolk County was squarely behind the netters. Nick Griek, nodding sadly at Mr. Fink, sighed as he rose, "Up pops the Devil," and stood there smiling diabolically until the laughter had subsided; then he coldly dissected the true purposes of the "phony sports" and "commercial sportsmen" who wished to have the sale of bass all to themselves. A fish trucker (Rodman Pell), who was familiar with Fink's sales slips, said that Mr. Fink was cleaning up as a commercial sportsman; in his opinion, Mr. Fink's Montauk residence had been constructed at the expense of the striped bass. The mayor of Greenport (Otis Burke) pointed out that the year-round economy of a fishing town depended a great deal upon the commercial men, whose welfare was at least as important, from a municipal point of view, as that of the seasonal anglers. A manufacturer of fish boxes (Jack Scheres) called the New York State pressure on the striper insignificant by comparison to the commercial landings in Maryland and Virginia, and a spokesman for the Fulton Fish Market (Joe Monani) denounced the bass bill as a dishonest conservation measure. A representative of the Wholesale Fish Producers and Dealers (Bob Johnson) reminded the committee that a great number of jobs—drivers, packers, countermen and the like—were dependent on the commercial men, and Captain Ted Lester wondered aloud why Mr. Fink, a self-proclaimed expert on the commercial bass fishery and a resident of the seining area, was unaware that two beach trucks were invariably used and not one, as he had stated.

When the sporting faction had recovered its wind, a number of protesting voices asked to be heard. The Speaker limited the right of rebuttal to just one, a delegate from a Long Island fishing club not affiliated with the Sportsmen's Council. This young man, speaking for "true" sportsmen, said that the anglers of his acquaintance had no interest in profiting from their catch, and did not feel that the right to do so had any business in the Hook-and-Line Amendment: they supported the bill because, as serious students of conservation, they had concluded that the haul-seiners were "decimating" the bass. (This conclusion spoke poorly for the conservation studies of his club, but his misgivings about the sportsmen's right to sell their catch while denying that right to the netters were shared by many other anglers, the great majority of whom do not catch fish in commercial quantities and would not consider themselves sportsmen if they did.) In conclusion, Perry B. Duryea of Montauk, minority leader and lobster dealer, who would lead the political opposition to the bass bills for many years to come, extolled the heritage of the East End baymen and their right to continue in their traditional livelihood.

From the beginning, the Montauk charter captains had

played an ambivalent role in the bass bill disputes. These captains, whose own livelihood in spring and fall depends in great part on the bass, could have told their clients that the fish were plentiful but unresponsive, and that lack of success when conditions are not perfect rarely stems from a depleted bass supply. It stems, as they cannot point out, from the anglers' own lack of experience and skill with a phlegmatic creature not easily captivated by jigs, spoons, bucktails, plugs and poppers, swimmers, or rigged eels except during the rare "blitz" when the fish will take almost anything that moves. Sometimes big bass have been observed lying like logs on sandy bottoms, and it seems, at times, that the lure must bounce from fish to fish in its quest for a susceptible and energetic specimen. Of those fish caught from charter boats, many are actually jigged[1] and hooked by the captain or mate, standing behind the client "checking" his reel as the boat passes over a known hole or rock. Once the fish is well-hooked, the mate hangs on to the jumping line as the rod is returned to the unskilled labor in the cockpit; then he lets go, and the strike—"There he is!"—occurs a moment later. Even with such stratagems as these, few bass are outwitted on the average day by the much greater number of men and boats dedicated to this purpose.

In 1956 Captain Gus Pitts stated at a meeting of charter men that striped bass were plentiful, but his less expert colleagues supported a bill prohibiting the sale of striped bass in New York State, thus making it a game fish. This bill won very small support from the organized sportsmen, who, for all their conservation talk, were not yet ready to give up their own form of commercial fishing.

Once again the Joint Conservation Committee decided against the bass bill, explaining its reasons in a statement issued a week after the hearing. "The striped bass has been the subject of study for a number of years by a number of eminent marine biologists, none of whom recommend such

a law. . . . The Committee is much impressed with the
healthy growth of salt-water angling as a recreational sport,
and the figures which were offered in testimony to show
that the sale of tackle, bait and other goods and services
purchased by salt water anglers represent an important economic consideration. . . . At the same time, the Committee
feels that the residents of Long Island who, like their forebears, have engaged in commercial fishing, are entitled to
consideration in view of the lack of any showing that their
fishing operations are endangering or even depleting the
striped bass population."

With their defeat in Albany that year, the anglers' lobbies put aside the discredited conservation argument, producing instead a ten-page bulletin of economic statistics,
copies of which were delivered to the Conservation Committee and the newspapers. The bulletin's purpose, to quote
from its introduction, was to "present certain statistical data
and economic analysis heretofore overlooked in considering
the proposed Hook-and-Line Amendment for Striped Bass
in the Conservation Laws of New York State." Under the
heading, STRIPED BASS IS NOT AN IMPORTANT FOOD FISH IN
THE COMMERCIAL NEW YORK METROPOLITAN MARKET, the bulletin asserted that "striped bass, expressed in terms of 'fish
meal preference' served to the public, amounted to only
one-tenth of 1 percent of all fish meals served!" The excla-
mation mark was characteristic of the astounded tone of the
bulletin, which also arrived by ingenious means at the figure
of 22.5 million dollars as the annual sum expended by
striper anglers for the direct benefit of the "real solid citizens" of Nassau and Suffolk Counties (further identified, in
capitals, as *VOTERS*). This amazing sum was favorably compared to the less than one million earned in the bass fishery
by the commercial men, whose support of the businesses of
the "real solid citizens" was not worthy of mention.

The qualifications of the sportsmen's statistician[2] were
listed in imposing array on the final page. He was a member

of five statistical and trade organizations, and he was also
the delegate to Albany of the Matinecock Rod & Gun Club
of Glen Cove, Long Island, and a director of the Sportsmen's Council, Marine District of New York, at that time
the main lobbying organization. His bulletin supported the
first of its two main points with an eye-catching pink chart
portraying two diagrammatic columns, side by side. One
column, running nearly the length of the page, claimed to
represent the consumption of all marine fish other than
striped bass in terms of "fish meal preference," or f.m.p.;
the adjoining column, dwarfed and pathetic, represented
the f.m.p. consumption of striped bass. But his chart did
not bother to indicate that over thirty-five species were represented in the first column, nor did it reveal that cod, butterfish, fluke, whiting, and porgy accounted for over 80
percent of all fish consumed, and the porgy alone for nearly
half; on close inspection, it turned out that the great majority of popular food fish were in far worse "fish meal preference" condition than the striped bass. That year, among
the remaining thirty species, the bass ranked fourth in
pounds landed, third in total value, and second only to the
swordfish in wholesale price per pound, plain figures that—
to people ignorant of sportsmen's statistics—might encour-
age the idea that we like to eat it. In all of these categories
the bass exceeded the bluefish, a poor f.m.p. fish if ever
there was one, and it also exceeded in value as well as
poundage the combined contribution to the New York
markets of the shad, weakfish, sturgeon, and mackerel, all
heretofore desirable species whose f.m.p. rating on the
sportsmen's chart was simply terrible.

Under the heading, HAUL-SEINERS CAN EARN MORE MONEY
ELSEWHERE, the sportsmen's dishonest bulletin went on to
state that in "Printing and Publishing, the Apparel Business,
and other industries," the fisherman could improve upon
the ninety-four cents an hour that was his meager lot in
1956. Unmentioned was the likelihood that the fisherman

would prefer a free and modest subsistence in the beautiful ocean landscape where his family has lived for hundreds of years to industrial labor in the cities as a wage-earner in the Apparel Business; that he might enjoy his way of life every bit as much as these sportsmen enjoyed the manipulation of statistics; that he should not be deprived of his traditional living so that a more powerful group could make money on its sport.

It is true that most fishermen are poor, but they are proud of their work and proud of their independence. Working on shares rather than on salary, they are no man's employees, choosing fishing as a way of life in the full knowledge that they could make more money elsewhere. Because striped bass are essential to their livelihood, they are at least as concerned about this fish as are the sportsmen; they dislike the destructive seining of immature fish in southern waters and the ruin of the many rivers that formerly harbored bass. As Dr. Edward Raney, the striped bass biologist, once observed of the campaigns against commercial men by anglers, "If the sportsman would put equal energy into correction of known contributing causes to scarcity of stripers, the future of the species would be far brighter."

# 11.

# Swordfish, Fish Flour, and Bunker Boats

O ne day in the late spring of 1956, on the *Merlin's* radio, I picked up the wild shouts of a draggerman up around Noman's, south of Martha's Vineyard, beaming the news to anyone who cared that he was rich. Apparently his dragger had hove to overnight in the thick fog so prevalent in June, when the sea is still cold and the air much warmer, and at daybreak had found herself surrounded by a company of migrating swordfish, which lay dull as logs on the smooth surface. The striker harpooned thirty of the weary fish before the rest took alarm, and the dragger was now on her way into New Bedford to celebrate her extraordinary good fortune.

In those days most swordfish were taken by big draggers, which were fitted out with a spotting tower and a long harpoon stand, or pulpit, extending forward from the boat's bow. The "finning" fish with its dorsal and caudal fins like black curved knives slitting the surface was struck by a detachable brass dart or lily with tandem barbs, fitted to an eighteen–twenty inch iron rod inserted in the tip of a long wood harpoon pole perhaps fourteen feet long. The lily, which pulls free of the iron when it is struck into the fish, remains fastened to several hundred feet of line coiled in a tub; this line is secured to a wood keg that is thrown over the side to mark the location of the fish and also tire it. The wild "green" fish cannot be horsed into the boat but must be tended carefully by hand, to be sure that the dart is not pulled free.

In previous summers, swordfish had been scarce, and I wanted a chance to strike one from the *Merlin*. On a certain slick calm day of June, Stewart Lester recalls, "We made a haul down Napeague and didn't do nothin, but the ocean was dead calm, so we decided to take your boat, go get us a swordfish. I think Richard was with us; anyways, we went off southwest of the Point, and it wasn't too long before I seen a fin. Ol' Pete here"—he nudged my arm—"was at the wheel, but when I seen that fin and started forward to the pulpit, Pete hollers, 'Hell, no, Stewart, this is my boat and I'm gonna stick the first one!'"

Among the draggermen, there were a number of great swordfish "strikers." Stewart's cousin, draggerman John Erickson, Jr., says that the best of them rarely or never missed with the harpoon, even when the fish was well below the surface. One miss out of ten might be accounted for by the fish flaring off at the last second, but as Elisha Ammon liked to say, "If you miss two out of ten, you get off the pulpit, let somebody else try it." Even men like these, who made a mystique of swordfishing (Johnnie Erickson's record for these waters was nine in a single day, although he has taken twice that number off Nova Scotia), were very nervous on the boat's approach, which required as much skill and precision as the strike itself.

And so I was wound tight with expectation as I ran forward to the pulpit, freed the long harpoon lashed across its rails, and stared ahead at the two curved blades tracing a thin slit on the water. The beautiful fish was of moderate size, less than two hundred pounds, a swift and graceful distillation of blue-silver sea (larger fish are darker, and look brown). Its round eye, a few inches beneath the shining surface, appeared huge. I was still staring when the night-blue fish shivered and shot away, leaving only the deep sun rays in the sea.

Years later, recalling this bad moment, Stewart grinned. "If that had been my old man, now, you would have got nowhere near that pulpit. That time with my Uncle Bill when my dad beat somebody to the harpoon by sliding down the guy wire from the spotting tower, there was a turnbuckle at the bottom where the cable wasn't spliced, and he ran four or five of them wires right through them burned hands. Blood all over the boat, I heard, but he never noticed, not until after he had struck that fish. Anyway, I took the wheel, put you right on that fish, too, but you never struck him, never even let go of the pole; you just stared at him, and you know why? You seen the eye. My old man taught me never to look at the eye, just at the dorsal fin, because right alongside the fin is where you strike him. That fish rolled his eye out and he fixed you, and you ain't the first. Nobody believes how big that eye is, and by the time they get over the surprise, the bow is past him and that fish is gone."

By 1956, Pete Scott and John Cole had despaired of making a living as commercial fishermen; both departed the South Fork for jobs that might take better advantage of their education. That spring I hauled seine with Ted, Stewart, and Milt, and sometimes Capt. Frank's son Lewis Lester, or whoever else might fill in on the crew. When there was no weather on the beach, I sailed an occasional charter out of Three Mile Harbor, and that summer, rather than hunt up a new mate, I avoided the dog fight at Montauk, where too many boats, fouling one another's lines around the Point, had taken most of the fun out of the fishing. I sailed out of Montauk only once, in late July, when the *Merlin* was hired by a man named Peter Gimbel, who did not show up. I took his friends out anyway, and upon returning, we learned that

Gimbel had left for Nantucket the night before. He was the first diver on the wreck of the *Andrea Doria,* which had just been sunk by another ship on the Nantucket Shoals.

Running without a mate out of Three Mile Harbor, I worked the rip over the sunken sand spit between Gardiners Island and the Ruin, which in those days was still used for bombing practice. More than once, the amateur airmen of the National Guard scared hell out of my unsuspecting clients, missing their target by a mile. That year the blowfish and the kingfish (a small relative of the weakfish) were still thick—both would disappear a few years later—and sometimes I ran bottom-fishing parties to Crow Shoal and Pigeon Reef, using skimmers that I harvested with tongs from the west side of the Three Mile Harbor breakwater. Most of my parties came aboard at the Town Commercial Dock near the harbor inlet, and coming up the channel from the head of the harbor, I sometimes picked up small striped bass by trolling a white bucktail in my wake.

On occasion I ferried workmen out to Gardiners Island, or ornithologists who wished to band the ospreys. The great sea hawks were so numerous in those days that their huge stick nests, built higher every year, were constructed all along the upper beach along the southwest shore and across the channel on Cartwright Shoal as well. The first black skimmers that I ever saw on the South Fork were already established on the little island across from the Commercial Dock, and the first oystercatchers were nesting on Gardiners Island. (The last-known Labrador duck, or sand-shoal duck, pied black and white like the swift old squaw, was shot down here on Gardiners Bay in 1874).

Out on the bay, even in summer, a few solitary loons and gun-shot sea ducks left behind by the northward migrations would be scattered among the gulls and terns that nested on Cartwright and on Gardiners Point. Among the white birds dipping on the fish were the roseate terns that hunted out over the tides from their nesting place in the old gun emplacements on Gull Island. One day, bluefishing in the Race, I saw a big ice-colored glaucous gull that had wandered down out of the Arctic.

In midsummer, the snapper blues would invade the channel, attracting summer children with long bamboo poles and red bobbers who fished in small excited flocks from the Commercial Dock. The snappers reminded me of Cap'n Posey, an old barnacle of local legend, who was popularly supposed to say at this soft, misty time of year, "Some foine day, bub! Yis, yis, bubby! Goin out, goin citch m'silf a miss o' snop-uhs!" Not until many years later did Bill Lester tell me that Cap'n Posey was his father, Nathan Lester. "In the old days, now, all the Lesters was fishermen, and farmers, too, but I guess the Amagansett bunch was the only ones that never stopped—kind of the offsprings of the family, don't you know. And they called us the Posey Boys or Posey Lesters because Father used to wear a rose in his lapel goin to church. So they called him Cap'n Posey, and all around here near the old homestead, they named that Poseyville."

I loved the quiet of the summer bay, the blue water and the hot sand shores with their acrid horsefoot smell and windrows of stout quarterdecks and light gold jingle shell that in other days was gathered up for oyster cultch; the gulls plucking scallops from the shallows, swooping upward, and dropping them on the old erratic boulders carried down out of the north by the great glaciers that formed the high moraines of "fish-shaped Pommanocc"; the ospreys lugging glinting fish across the sky, the bright lobster buoys and white sails, the yelp and crying of the nesting gulls, the screech of terns; the dull red shadow in the sea made by myriad gills of flat oily menhaden that turned that red purplish, so the bunker captains said, when the school was thick; the phosphorus from the plankton in the night water that thickened in the boat's wake as it entered the warmer water of the harbor; the rising of the bow wave as the shallows neared, in warning to the boatman (baymen say that the boat has a natural pull toward the deep of the channel). On every shore were the long silhouettes of pounds, or fish traps, with their weed-hung mesh, looped up on the stakes for drying in the August dog days, on every stake a tattered shag perched spreading its ancient wings to dry.

Off Gardiners Island I sometimes glimpsed Milt Miller, on whose boat Pete Scott's place would be taken by William Havens's young son Benny (and later, despite all Milt's precautions, by his own boy, Milton Jr., known as Mickey). Mostly he used a run-around net—essentially a gill net, heavily weighted to sink fast, which is run quickly around bunker slicks, terns diving on popping bait, or other sign of bluefish feeding in the open water. Although he had no use for traps ("Went trappin three times in my life, and went broke three times; wouldn't pay me nothin for what I caught") he did pretty well with dragging, power-seining (setting a seine by power boat, then hauling from shore), and set nets. Milt had spent half his life out around Gardiners. Often he slept on the island overnight in order to make an early morning set, dining on oddments of marine fare for which a market might one day be developed; he would try anything out of the sea, including scallop guts and gull eggs, and he swore that the black roe found in horseshoe crabs was as good as caviar.

A swift run-around boat that the *Merlin* sometimes passed off Gardiners Island was a trim Jersey skiff belonging to a fisherman named Dick Hamilton, who never waved when our boats passed. Hamilton was an up-Islander, fierce loner, and hard drinker who turned up with the migrating fish schools in the spring and disappeared again when the bluefish left the bay in the late fall; for years he rented a small shack that used to sit in the corner of Ted Lester's yard in Poseyville. By habit Dick was a man of few words, and those words, it was said, were likely to be abrupt and rude. I had never met him face to face until one windy day close to Thanksgiving, the year before, when a tight-faced stranger accosted me on Newtown Lane. "For many years," this stranger growled, "I had the prettiest boat on the east end of Long Island. Now she's the second prettiest." That was all he said, and he walked away before I realized who it was. I wanted to call after him, but I wonder if Dick Hamilton would have turned. Within a few years I would sell the *Merlin* to my brother, who took her back to Massachusetts, and once again Dick Hamilton's sea skiff was the prettiest boat on the east end of Long Island.

"In the days when I used to go fishin with Milt Miller," Benny Havens told me some years later, "Dick Hamilton was out there, too, and he outfished me and Milt every time; never done nothin but run-aroundin all his life, I guess. I used to fish with Dick a little, and he'd talk to me some but not much. Dead now, from what I hear—drink got to him, I guess."

By far the largest boats on the summer bay were the "bony boats," or bunker steamers that sailed in summer from the Smith Meal Company and Edwards Brothers docks at Promised Land. The bunker boats used large purse seines of 250 fathoms, set from the sterns of two circling seine boats thirty-six feet long; the seine boats met and passed each other in order to close the net, doing their best to avoid bluefish, which bit holes in the netting with their razor teeth. The bunker fishery was (and is) the largest commercial fishery in North America.

The ship dispatched in 1633 by Governor Winthrop of Connecticut to explore the East End fisheries had observed huge schools, many acres in extent, of a fish known to the Indians as *munnohquohteau*, "that which restores the earth," but not for many years did the settlers adopt the custom (popularly attributed to the Indians) of burying a moss-bunker, as the Dutch called it, in each hill of corn, and spreading these bunkers on their fields. By the end of the eighteenth century, after the trees were gone, and the bare land worn down to old-field pasture, the farmer-fishermen harvested this fertilizer in a systematic way, using large seines and round-bottomed lapstrake[1] skiffs, fifteen to twenty feet long, hauled down to the sea on horse-drawn carts. In 1822, the Reverend Timothy Dwight, in his travels through the region, described "the immense shoals of whitefish [menhaden] with which in the beginning of summer its waters are replenished" and which—together with "the fish called horsefoots [horseshoe crabs], the remains of which yield a smell still less supportable"—were being used to restore the exhausted soils. Eight thousand bunkers, it was estimated, would "dress" one acre. By 1840, there were thirty full-time seine gangs, or seines, with a main summer occupation of harvesting menhaden for the farmers. Each small community owned a seine about 2,500 feet long that required hauling by forty or fifty men.

In 1847, at Jessups Neck, Marcus Osborn used whale try pots to process oil from the menhaden. As a new substitute for whale oil, this bunker oil was reserved for paints and tanning; only the dried scrap was used for fertilizer. A new industry was under way, and improved potworks, or bunker factories, twenty or more, were built at Northwest, Shelter Island, Greenport, Cape Gardiner, Napeague, and various locations on Peconic Bay. With the growing demand for fish oil, the community seine boats had given way to large commercial vessels. By 1880, 232 sailing boats and 24 steam vessels were purse-seining bunkers in Gardiners Bay; one wonders how they found room to maneuver.

With the advent of the purse seine,[2] which could be fished offshore in open water, a large coastal fishery had been born. In May 1876, Oliver Osborn was noting in his journals the presence of bunker steamers[3] off the beach: "The first steamers that I ever knew to do anything fishing off here came along last week. They did well." With such a steamer, in the single season of 1888, Captain Josh Edwards of Amagansett caught an estimated eleven million bunkers. Cap'n Josh, his brothers, and their sons—the Edwards Brothers—built docks on the bay shore at Napeague where fish factories were already in operation, and where deep water for steamers came in close to shore. This location, known as Bunker City, was judged the most remote from the new summer visitors to East Hampton, who protested from the start the strong aroma that came their way on an east wind. (The bunker men, who were now plying the coastal waters, and who lived for long periods with large cargoes of rotting fish on unrefrigerated ships, were not sympathetic.) Later this smelly place was known as Promised Land, the proposed name for a proposed post office to be situated near George Conklin's general store, established there in 1879.

In 1909 the Gardiners Bay Company, developing a summer colony at Devon, sought in vain to prohibit by law the malodorous pall being cast over its genteel community by the "fish factories" on the low shores of Napeague and at Deep Hole on Cape Gardiner. The factories were consolidated about 1920, when the coal-burning wood steamers were still running, and workers from Nova Scotia came as summer help, but they were shut down throughout most of the twenties as the menhaden became scarce. (The Edwards Brothers ran a curtailed operation, with the crews of two small steamers also serving to process the fish ashore.) In 1931 and again in 1933, the main buildings of the factory, closed for a decade, were destroyed by fire, but the fish had already started to return, and the old factory site adjoining the Edwards Brothers dock was acquired by Smith Meal, which brought in crews of black fishermen from the South and took on the Edwardses as captains.

"The younger generation, my uncles and my father, they all went on bunker steamers sometime during the days of their life . . . and I took a likin to bunker fishin," says

Joshua (Jack) Edwards, grandson and namesake of the old whaler, Cap'n Josh; he recalls being sent down to Virginia and bringing back a whole truckload of black fishermen, who were now replacing the Nova Scotian crews on the steamers that tended the ocean traps in spring and seined menhaden for the fish factory in summer. Jack's father, Cap'n Sam, and his uncle, Cap'n Bert, were concerned about his poor hearing and poor eyesight, saying he would never make a bunker captain—"You gotta have a pretty quick eye sometimes to see them bunkers playin," Jack admits—but his Uncle Evvie (Cap'n Everett, or E.J.) encouraged him to pay them no attention. Jack Edwards did well in his first season, in 1938, and "stayed at the top of the fleet for many years."

With the advent of World War II, and the big sea-going draggers that came after, the ocean trapping operations of the Edwards Brothers were dissolved for good, and the trap anchors and barrel nets were sold to Rhode Island fish companies for use in Narragansett Bay. But Smith Meal resumed operations when its requisitioned steamers were returned after the war, and the Edwardses stayed on as captains of new steel ships up to 175 feet long. The factory crew numbered 125 men, with 290 more as crew on ten big boats. Eventually some 1,500 boats were working the continental shelf, from the Gulf of Mexico to the Gulf of Maine.

In the 1950s, Cap'n Jack's 151-foot *Shinnecock* was one of the swift steamers working Gardiners Bay; I passed her often on the way out to Crow Shoal and the Ruin, or when I put into Promised Land for fuel. Her huge black crewmen, lonely and far from home, became a part of local legend with the wonderful chanting heard across the water as the big steamers drew close to the seine boats and the nets were lifted; the chant insured that all pulled together, since the net was so heavy. "Oh God yes, they were strong, they were really strong men, the whole gang of them," Jack Edwards says. "There wasn't many of those colored fellas that lived to be too old, because they were such hard, hard workers."

In the 1960s the picturesque high crow's nests on the raked steamer masts would give way to spotter planes and electric scanners that tracked down the last enormous shoals of this oily herring whose great numbers shivered the broad reaches of the sea. Inevitably the fish became so scattered that local factories were no longer efficient. Residents and real estate speculators, unable to develop the Napeague Stretch because of the smell, had been pressuring the town for years to close the fish factory, and in 1968 the old Bunker City closed down for good. A few steamers still tied up on weekends at Smith Meal's shipyard in Greenport, but the center of operations was moved to New Jersey. In recent years, the bunker fleet has been based still farther south, in Reedville, Virginia, and Cameron, Louisiana.

When the Smith Meal factory closed, the Edwards Brothers fish company, founded before the turn of the century when the family patriarchs were going off after their last whales, "died right out, too," Jack Edwards says. His brother, Captain Norman Edwards, went south with the bunker fleet (though his home is still in Amagansett) and Cap'n Jack became master of one of the big ferries between Orient Point and New London until he retired with heart trouble just a few years ago. (His old ship *Shinnecock* was converted to deep-water clamming for the fried clam and canned chowder market, using jet dredges in water as deep as eighty fathoms.) Today the bunker fleet consists of six large refrigerator ships, each with its own spotter plane, and capable of carrying up to 2.5 million pounds. Captain Norman Edwards, locating a huge school in 1980 in the Gulf of Maine, took 750 thousand pounds, or over three hundred tons, in a single haul. "Fish are not so plentiful all over the place, just here, there, and everywhere," says his brother Jack, "but eventually them fish are coming back."

The local menhaden fishery might well have been replaced by a commerce in the so-called trash fish that the commercial men heaved over by the ton. In a new plant set up in Greenport, sea robins, skates, dogfish, daylights, and other unmarketable denizens of the deep were trundled on conveyor belts from boat hold to dockside factory, emerging presently as "fish protein concentrate" or FPC, a pristine white flour with long storage life, perhaps the most economical source of pure protein yet devised. (FPC could also be made from bunkers, and tollhouse cookies made with fish flour were well received at a promotional meeting for this product, Jack Edwards says.) One day in Greenport I visited the new factory and tasted FPC, which could be baked into long-lasting bread: the flour was bone white, with no odor or fishy taste of any kind. Inevitably this wonderful new product was seen as a threat by bread and dairy interests, which maintained powerful lobbying groups in Washington. These lobbies saw to it that government agencies banned the distribution of fish flour as "unsanitary" because of those processed spines and guts and eyes; certain solvents used in the manufacturing process were also attacked. As a result, the Third World leaders whose countries were in desperate need of a cheap protein source were unable to advocate its use, knowing that their political opponents would accuse them of foisting on their countrymen an unclean product that Yankee capitalists were trying to dump on poorer nations. Meanwhile the fishermen themselves could not or would not bring into the factory sufficient tonnage to make the operation viable, according to Dick Nelson, the plant manager. And so a safe, healthy, and remarkably economical source of protein was denied the world's poor, a new fishing industry was destroyed, and the new fish flour factory at Greenport was closed. Once again, tons of wasted fish killed in trawls and traps and nets were dumped over the side by the commercial men, who were finding it more and more difficult to make ends meet.

In August of 1956 I was approached by Lewis Lester,

who had been picked as the new captain of a rig owned by
Reggie Bassett and was putting together a new crew. "Got
most of 'em, I guess," Lewis said, "but I'm still looking for
a good, experienced man." I shook my head; my days as a
commercial fisherman were over. My marriage had disin-
tegrated, my old fishing partners were scattering, and my
friend Jackson, driving drunk, had destroyed himself and
a young woman passenger when he lost control on the
Springs-Fireplace Road. I had lost all heart for charter fishing, which meant that I could not afford to keep the *Merlin*,
and I soon sold to Jimmy Reutershan a beautiful piece of
woods high on Stony Hill, in Amagansett, where I had once
planned to build a house.

It was time to move on, but Lewis's words sent me on
my way feeling much better. I would never be a Bonacker,
not if I lived here for a century, but apparently I was accepted as a fisherman. The three years spent with the commercial men were among the most rewarding of my life,
and those hard seasons on the water had not been wasted.

# MODERN
# TIMES

# 12.

# Changes

For the next four years I was traveling to remote corners of the Americas, from Alaska and the Yukon to Tierra del Fuego, and I rarely visited the South Fork. The *Vop-Vop* had already gone to a charity summer camp on Three Mile Harbor, and I sold a half-interest in the *Merlin* to my brother Carey, who was now a marine biologist on Martha's Vineyard. In the late fifties I took the *Merlin* to the Vineyard, where Carey showed me his boat-casting spots on the ocean shoals south of Chappaquiddick. Here striped bass and blues, on the right tide, could be taken with almost every cast into the breaking seas. Like many Massachusetts sportsmen, he was taking big bass in such numbers that he sold commercially what he could not use.

One day on the way to Noman's Land, looking for swordfish, we came upon a dead humpback whale under Gay Head. The huge black body lay awash in the heavy swells, which rode ashore and boomed under the cliffs, the echo riding back in the soft mist. That summer I had a phone call from a charter boatman who sailed out of Provincetown. Knowing of my interest in whales, he told me that orcas, or killer whales, had appeared on Stellwagen Bank, between Cape Race and Boston, together with finbacks, humpbacks, and pilot whales. I left next morning for Provincetown, and found all four species on the surface in a slick August calm.

Then in the summer of 1960 I visited for a while at a friend's house in Sagaponack, an old farming community in the potato fields between Wainscott and Bridgehampton, in Southampton Town. From these farm communities, a road led over the scrub oak moraine to Sag Harbor (originally Sagaponack Harbor) where the South Shore farmers had once kept their boats. In the old days, these fields were "dressed" after the Indian fashion with the tons of menhaden seined out of the bays. As the American Midwest became planted in wheat, the local wheat crop was replaced by diversified crops of potatoes, strawberries, and cabbage, and potatoes emerged as the main crop when, in the first part of this century, a number of Polish clans arrived to join the founding families.

"Sagaponack" is another form of "Accabonac," an Indian word for an edible tuber that was gathered in both places.[1] Like all of the earliest settlements, it was still organized in the European way, with the house lots within shouting distance up and down Sagg Main Street as a protection against Indians, wolves, and pirates, and the unbroken fields stretching east to the next farm village at Wainscott. Westward lay Sagaponack Pond, in country so opened up by farming that the bone white steeples in Bridgehampton[2] could be seen against dark hills of the high moraine off to the north. This little-known farm hamlet south of the highway had one of the last "little red schoolhouses" in the Northeast, and a small spare general store owned by Lee Hildreth, who was also postmaster and gas pump operator. The schoolhouse and store, together with an excellent summer boarding house run by Mrs. Sczepankowski on the family farm (the first summer people in the

Hamptons found lodgings in farm homesteads such as these) comprised the whole of downtown Sagaponack. All but a few of the old houses belonged to Toppings and Hildreths, Whites and Fosters, who had been here for many generations; one piece of Topping land between the cemetery and the sea was the oldest piece of land in the United States farmed continuously by the same white family.

No houses were available in Sagaponack, and that fall I lived in a small cabin in the Springs by the Green River cemetery where Pollock had been buried four years before. Toward the end of that year, I was offered a fine property in Sagaponack, part of a tract, still called Smith Corner, inhabited originally by that Richard (Bull) Smith who founded Smithtown after his eviction from Southampton.[3] In 1960 the sudden rise in local land values had not started, and the whole property—six acres, a large decrepit house, an outlying stable and small cottage—cost much less than just one of those overgrown acres would be worth today. The value of the property increased three times in the very first year that I owned it; since then, the selling off of the South Fork has become so frenzied that children of many local families, and the fishermen especially, can no longer afford to live where they were born.

By the early sixties almost all of my old friends were gone. John Cole had settled down in Maine, Pete Scott had died in a car accident in California, and tough "Jimmy Root" would die a few years later of a flawed heart, not long after he had built his house on my former land on Stony Hill in Amagansett. ("Jimmy was a *scientific* fisherman," Milt Miller once observed, "experimental, always looking into different ways of making and hanging nets. Trial and error, mostly error, but since then I have seen different people using his ideas.") Jackson Pollock was dead, and so was Herb Latshaw of the Three Mile Harbor Boatyard, one of my gunning partners on those wintry days stringing for coot at

Cedar Point; the only friend from the old days I saw regularly was the painter Sherry Lord, who moved from the Springs to Sagaponack a few years after I did.

When my neighbors realized that, come the autumn, I would still be there behind my hedge, I was accepted. My friend Bud Topping got me into the local gun club, and sometimes I filled in on the beach with the farmers' haulseine crew led by Bob Tillotson, whose brother Frank had been Ted Lester's original partner in Montauk Seafood. Another crewman—the potato farmer in striped coveralls who would later bring that salmon into my yard (see Preface)—was a namesake and descendant of the John White who appears in the town records within a few years of the first settlement in 1640. Most of these men's ancestors had been farmer-fishermen, and they were still attached to the fishing tradition. Although the farmers were beset by the erosion of poor crop years, heavy inheritance taxes, and the increasing pressure of a summer resort economy, most of the old farm families had held onto their land, which had suddenly become immensely valuable.

The full-time fishermen, struggling to survive, had none of their land left to fall back on. An exception to the rule was Cap'n Ted, who seemed tired, yet more enterprising than ever. On the upper level of Montauk Seafood, near Charlie Lester's old vegetable stand, the fish store run by Jenny Lester and her daughters was doing fine, and so was Lester's Liquors, opposite Brent Bennett's Store, which was now owned and operated by Walter Bennett. But I saw Ted rarely and never saw the other fishermen at all; I lived ten miles away to westward, and was traveling all over the world. I bought a small wood bass boat for the bays, and went clamming and scalloping for my own use and satisfaction out of Sag Harbor; in the fall there was surfcasting for bass and bluefish, as far east as Montauk Light and as far west as Shinnecock Inlet. One winter day with my young daughter Sara, I found a whale skull that emerged from beneath the dunes after a storm. Perhaps this creature had been a drift whale, like that dead humpback rising and falling in the sea under Gay Head, or perhaps it was killed from a small boat by the farmer-fishermen of other days.

In 1958 the Army Corps of Engineers, at the instigation of a rich and influential summer resident who desired to shore up his dune house at Georgica at the public expense, had begun the construction of a series of ocean groins, or jetties, up to 750 feet long, to stabilize the unstable ocean beach. The vast enterprise failed to take into account the very strong set, or current, alongshore, and the sea carved huge scallops in the beach between these rock piles, which had no more place on the open Atlantic coast than that doomed fish pier that broke up at Napeague in 1881. Captain Frank Lester called the engineers "damned fools," and all those with experience of the ocean beach agreed that the jetties had seriously worsened the great damage caused by the line storm[4] of March 1961, with its violent northeasterly gales. The storm picked off some houses built on sand that had no business on the high dunes in the first place, and temporarily laid bare stretches of peat, scored by cart tracks and ox prints of colonial times, that had long since been covered over by the sands. The high dunes at Sagaponack where Bud Topping had a big green summer tent were washed away, and Southampton Town replaced the dunes with a large parking lot, trash cans, and toilets, together with a big poster picture of the politician who wished to take credit for all this progress.

With the sudden rise in value of the land, the peaceful atmosphere of the South Fork began to change. The change developed like faraway massed clouds in the northern sky, the first iron weather of winter storm. Sagaponack was now the closest public beach to Sag Harbor, and traffic down its main street increased quickly. Within a few years the old Hildreth store expanded its services to accommodate the swelling tide of tourists, and the old village's quiet days were over. A new rash of real estate speculators, entreating other newcomers to "share our heritage," discovered Sagaponack, where the smaller local farms, unable to compete with the huge agribusiness in the West, or survive the growing tax on land inheritance, had begun to die. Even that oldest family farm in the United States was sold off by the squabbling heirs, with most of the money, it was said, gone to the lawyers.

The wells and water table had been polluted by chemical pesticides and fertilizers that leached into the earth and were washed by rain into the creeks, where the stunned fish were scavenged by the ospreys. The DDT absorbed by the microorganisms and plankton, and concentrating in the fish tissues on which they fed, weakened the osprey eggs, which broke when incubated. The great fish hawks were once so common here that twenty-five or thirty at a time could be counted over Fort Pond Bay;[5] by the early sixties the huge primitive nests on Gardiners and Cartwright Shoal stood empty. Within the decade, the osprey was so rare that I would call my children out to look when one passed over, for fear that this sighting might be the last. The blue crabs that used to run in streams out of every salt pond when the gut was opened to the sea, and the fiddler crabs, once so thick in the spartina grass of the tidal wetlands that the flow of claw-snapping brown creatures could be channeled into tubs for use as bait, were killed off by DDT in the aerial sprays. Filling, bulkheading, and pollution of the wetlands were eliminating marine life spawning grounds and the last resorts of the wild duck, and even the long strings of sea duck had been much diminished by massive oil spills in the coastal waters. The remnant flocks were harassed by speedboat shooters who cared more about noise than boats and birds, who chased the flocks as they labored off the water and did not bother to pick up what they blasted down.

For a few years I resumed coot shooting at Cedar Point with Alvin and Bud Topping, Cliff Foster, and Ed Hildreth, but as rapidly as the fast plastic boats increased, the birds declined. A few years later, despite some memorable shoots at Sagaponack Pond, I gave up all gunning for good. Occasionally in fall I drove over to Northwest, past white pine woods and hoary orchards and the old fields of the early settlers with their fallen wells and shadowy foundations, to the Alewive Brook landing where our sharpies were once launched for Cedar Point. Here I harvested scallops washed ashore in a northwest blow or forked up a truckload of bleached eel-grass for the garden from the windrows on the quiet stretch of shore known as Kirk's Beach.[6] In winter I went clamming from this shore, stopping every little while to blow on my red hands and watch the strings of coot and old squaw beating north over the chop toward Cedar Point.

One fair October afternoon I was surfcasting in autumn solitude at Mecox, where the gut had just been opened to the sea. The ocean was sparkling and mild, in a mild sun. A thud on my line was the first sign of what turned out to be a school of medium bass, and I had three fine stripers on the beach when Bobby Lester's Southampton seine crew came along and set around me. Bobby was Cap'n Frank's third son; I knew him by the resemblance to his brothers, the pale blue eyes in the hawk-nosed ruddy face. The trailer was backed down at high speed into the wash, the man at the truck wheel hit the brakes, and the big dory shot straight off its rollers through the surf and kept on going. This was the first dory I ever saw that was powered by an outboard motor, which was kept clear of the net in a well toward the bow. The old cotton nets, once six hundred fathoms long, had been replaced by nylon nets three times that length; instead of turning east a hundred yards out, this dory, larger than any I remembered, was going way offshore back of the bar.

On other days I saw the rigs from Amagansett, but except for Bill Lester's steady crew—I recognized his son Billy Lester, and the long-faced Havens boys, and Dom-Dom

Grace—few of the faces seemed familiar; I felt like a
stranger, and I kept my distance. The dark bulk of beach
trucks in the pearly mist was reassuring, it was good to know
that the haul-seiners were still there, yet my heart was struck
each time I saw them by a pang of loss. I missed those
fishing years much more than I cared to admit. I enjoyed
my work and was making a good living, and I came and
went, as independent as any fisherman, yet book royalties
and magazine fees had no reality when compared to a day's
pay earned out of doors. I missed the dawn light and the
sunrise, the suspense of every haul, the calloused hands; I
missed the smell and feel of boats and I missed the water.
Also I missed the rough humor and old stories of such great
events as the time that Lindy Havens and another fisherman, the late Edward (Peebo) Raynor, who lived out back
of Cap'n Posey's house, got their car stuck while jacking
deer in the Hither Hills. Having bent his shotgun barrel
trying to lever out the car—"Hell, *that* don't mean nothin!"
Peebo said—he hacksawed it off short and kept right on
going.

In 1966 I sailed on a commercial Cayman schooner on
a green turtle fishing voyage to the Miskito Cays off Nica-
ragua, and in 1969 I was writer-diver on an oceanic expe-
dition to the Indian Ocean and Australia that obtained the
first undersea film (*Blue Water, White Death*) of the great
white shark. But here at home, living just ten miles west of
Amagansett, I had lost track of "all thim Poseys." One early
spring I bailed a truckload of minnows trapped in Sagg
Pond dreen to spread upon my vegetable garden, and another year I bought his whitebait seine from Bobby Tillotson, thinking to fish it by myself down on Sagg Pond; the
seine lies untouched on the shed rafters with my old clam
tongs, harpoon, and outriggers, and some balsawood black
duck decoys from my gunning days. My scallop dredges had
been "barried" some years ago and never returned, the big
tuna rod that had bested that flying porgy was missing, too,

and so was the old fighting chair that we mounted for the epic voyage of the Shinnecock chiefs to Rosie's Hole, off the New England shore.

Promised Land had closed down in 1968, and the big bunker steamers and swift seine boats, working the menhaden schools off the ocean beach, passed by no longer. Long-range factory stern trawlers from Europe and Japan, often visible on the ocean skyline, were fishing the continental shelf, increasing pressure on the open ocean species even as the fish themselves declined. Overfished by the longliners (a long line is a trawl, up to sixteen miles long, set in deep water, usually along the deep sea canyons), the bluefin tuna so abundant in the fifties had been drastically depleted, necessitating strict quotas, and long-lined swordfish seemed certain to follow. Meanwhile, the expanding dragger fleet worked much closer to shore, roiling the water brown inside the bar.

Weakfish and kingfish, fluke and bottle fish, had vanished, whereas striped bass and bluefish were abundant; despite the doom cries of the sportsmen, the numbers of striped bass had continued to grow. In 1968 Bill Lester's crew made the biggest haul ever recorded on the South Fork, and bass landings in 1973 were the highest ever. The next year the striped bass began a long decline, but demand for these fish kept the price so high that the diminishing fishery maintained its value. Nevertheless, the seine crews dwindled, one by one. Beach ordinances (as well as the bass decline) forced Bobby Lester off the beach, down in Southampton; as Bob Tillotson grew older and the bass harder to find, the farmers' haul-seine crew in Sagaponack disbanded, too. Frank Lester, injured, had long since retired, Bill Lester's strong crew had broken up, and although he fished intermittently until 1970, Cap'n Ted had sold his rig some years before.

"They are all gone now, the Indians and the whalers, the Indian whalers, the part-Indians, the part-whalers, the farmer-fishermen . . . the narrow insular men and women who lived and bred for two and a half centuries in a backwater-corner of the United States, yet sometimes knew Canton or the Sandwich Islands better than they knew New York," wrote Captain Josh Edwards's great-grandson[7] in 1978. There was truth in this, but the statement seemed premature; a few still knew about the old traditions.

One day in December 1964, Stuart Vorpahl, Jr., cod-fishing with Dominick Grace seven miles offshore near the Mecox sea buoy, felt swells begin to rise beneath the dory and headed for shore. (This was Captain Clint Edward's old dory in which Milt Miller had been so sick fifty years before. "She was cedar with hackmatack[8] wood knees, from Nova Scotia," Stuart says. "All I had to do was put a new stern into her; the old one was nail-sick from two hundred Posey nails. That old girl's there back of the fish market yet to-day.") It was snowing hard by the time they neared the coast, the winter day was already growing dark, and Stuart could not make out the landing road or see the truck that he would need to haul the dory out of the surf where he came ashore; if he landed farther down the beach, he might lose the dory. Therefore he was happy to see headlights, shining out to sea from the landing at Beach Lane. The lights were a beacon from Elisha Osborn, an old fisherman-farmer of the Wainscott whaling clan. Like many old surf-men, Cap'n Lisha had the habit of driving down and gazing at the ocean. Coming upon Stuart's truck and trailer, he had known at once that a cod fisherman might be in trouble, trying to regain the shore on a darkening day.

# 13.

# Poseys and Bonackers

Someone had told me that Cap'n Ted had not been well, and I meant to go see him. Not long afterward, in August 1973, he died of a cerebral hemorrhage. Soon I left on a journey to Asia, and neglected to call on Jenny Lester when I got back. A few years later I apologized, and she cleared the air immediately. "Oh hell Pete! You're just like me!" said small, big-hearted Jen in that gravel voice she had acquired in decades of chain-smoking and shouting. "Got all them good intentions, y'know, and never get around to 'em!" Jenny herself died of kidney and liver failure in June 1979. "What they died of," their son Stewart says, "was plain hard work."

Theodore Roosevelt Lester and Jenny Mayes Bennett, both born in 1908, met each other first at age thirteen while out picking blueberries on Montauk. At that time Ted had already quit school to become a fisherman, helping his older brothers support their parents. He met Jenny again three years later at one of the home dances described earlier by bayman Jarvie Wood. "Used to hire a horse and hay wagon, two–three dollars for the night; that was the way we went courtin the girls," Bill Lester says.

After their marriage, in 1926, Ted and Jenny lived on

Abraham's Path, north of the highway, in a three-room cottage with a wood stove. Jenny Bennett's grandmother Mayes had been raised in the old settlement out at Northwest, and her people were mostly carpenters and farmers (plumbers and electricians were as yet unheard of) but Jenny was as energetic as her husband and threw herself wholeheartedly into the fishermen's life. "Mom could hang nets, mend a hole if she had to, but not as good as Dad or my grandfather," says her daughter Jenny, born in 1927, who still remembers the World War II days on the beach when the dory was moved from the landing road down to the sea on rollers, and she helped her father haul his small seine by hand.

The Posey Lesters, young Jenny recalls, were basically religious, though unlike up-street Presbyterians such as the Edwardses, they were apt to take the Lord's name in vain and went to church mostly in the winter. The rest of the time, her father would say, "Well, the Lord give me that good weather to go fishin, and I had to go; if the Lord didn't want me to go fishin on Sunday, He'd have had it rainin." Sometimes in later years, young Jenny recalls, the minister would visit Montauk Seafood and offer to pray, and Ted would say, "Well, okay, so long as you don't mind doing it on the fish boxes." And the wary crews would sit down on the fish boxes while the minister prayed for good health, good weather, and plenty of good fish. The older men, at least, are still religious; most of the families attend church on Sundays, and the men do their best to avoid bad language in the household.

Because of their long and irregular hours, the baymen have small opportunity for social visits. In Ted's family, an annual Fourth of July picnic was celebrated with the Bennetts, while Thanksgiving and Christmas were usually spent with Grandmother Lester and Harold (Happy) at the old homestead across the highway. They did not see much of other Posey families, though five of the six Posey Boys lived within a quarter mile of one another. Frank, Bill, and Ted were ten years apart in age, and all had large families of their own to see to.

Besides Jenny and Stewart (born in 1935), there were four younger daughters in the family—Ruth Ann (after her mother's sister Ruth, who married a fisherman, Elmer Fenelon), Gloria, Lavinia (named for Cap'n Nathan's wife, Mary Lavinia, and much like her grandmother in grouchy temperament, so say her sisters) and Stephanie, called Sally, born in 1951. Sal was three when I first went fishing with her father, and was much underfoot as her mother struggled to expand the seafood shop. Eventually the shop occupied the whole top floor of the packing house and freezer, which was built like a potato storage barn into the bank north of the house.

Of all the children, only Jenny is old enough to remember Nathan Lester, who died in 1937, when she was ten; she recalls a big, broad-shouldered man with no belly and "white white" hair, mustache, and whiskers. "I can see him setting there on his little stool, mendin net for the men to go fishin, cause he couldn't do much fishin no more, he was too old and his legs wasn't very good. He'd call my mother and say, 'Jenny, I got no puff.' And she'd say, 'What's the matter, Pop? Where's your tobacco?' She would hunt up a dime, warning him not to give it away to his grandchildren for candy, which he always did unless she went for the tobacco herself. 'Okay Jennie!' When he came back, she'd ask why he didn't have any tobacco in his pipe, and he'd say, 'Oh, I saw the kids!' "

Sally remembers her grandfather from family stories. "He always had his high water pants on: in other words, he couldn't get pants long enough, tightened his suspenders too much, I think. Had those funny shoes that came up high, and his socks showed: high-boots shoes and high water pants!" She also speaks of the flower in his buttonhole, which led to the name Cap'n Posey and came to distinguish these 'Gansett Lesters from the Pantigo and Round Swamp Lesters, very few of whom still fish today. (According to Stewart's daughter Gail, young Nathan Lester was wearing a flower given to him by his sweetheart when his boat capsized in the surf; he won the name Posey Lester because the flower was still flying when he came ashore.)

"Grandma Lester was a crotchety old thing, you threw a hat in before you walked into her kitchen," Jenny says. "One day somebody come to her house asking for Mr. Posey, and she said that nobody by that name lived there, and he said, 'Oh, I'm sorry, Mr. *Lester.*' That's how Grandma found out he was called that, and to the day she died, she didn't like it."

"She thought it was degrading," Sally says. "People back in those days were very proud, there was etiquette and proper ways of talking. Today everything is so lax, really. In them days you had so much love for your husband that anything he does, he could never do wrong. I know that my own husband, nothing he could do would be no sin to me because I worship the ground he walks on, and that's the way I feel about him today. And my grandmother did, too. And that extends to family. You argue with your own, but if an outsider comes in. . . ."

Jenny scarcely recalls her Uncle Harry, who hung himself in May 1951. The reason for the eldest brother's suicide is unclear, but it is felt that the trouble might have started when he moved away to "the other end of town," a disruption that was blamed upon his wife. ("Henpecked was his sickness," Jenny says. "She mentally disturbed him.") But her brother Stewart, who remembers Harry as a man handy at everything, and a superb carver of weather vanes, believes that his uncle was "happy enough; he killed himself because he was crazy with pain with what we call Posey disease, a lot of little strokes. Got so he couldn't drive no more, and that's no good; lost his independence, and he couldn't handle that. My old man died of the same disease, at the same age, in his early sixties. He had got pretty heavy after he got sick and left the beach, and he went from two-forty to fifty-eight pounds in just three months."

Their Uncle Harold, called Harlin or Hollin by his mother and Happy by everybody else, was the brother closest in age to their own father. ("They called him Happy because he was happy-go-lucky, always good with children and everything," Francis Lester explains.) Happy Lester was regarded as an alcoholic, and sometimes he exasperated his brothers; although she says Ted took good care of him, Jenny remembers her father yelling at him on the beach. Nevertheless, Happy did his work, and is remembered by the family with affection. Jenny says, "I thought a lot of him; he was a nice man." Until his death in 1953 he lived with his mother in the old homestead across the highway. "What it was, nobody wanted him," says Stewart, who like most Poseys is unflinchingly forthright. "Everybody thought my grandmother was dyin, and Uncle Happy was just scared that if she did, they was goin to put him away for good in a old-age home. That's why he hung hisself, or choked hisself with a rope—typical fisherman! And my grandmother went on livin for another six years!"

Charlie Lester had also died; the last of the six Posey Boys were Frank and Bill. Cap'n Frank and his wife, the former Sadie Eames, were "foinest koind," as the fishermen say of anything that is good, but especially of anything worn that keeps on going. Cap'n Bill's first wife had died in 1949, and a few years later Bill married Lottie Wood, whose older brother Jarvis is a full-time bayman, and whose younger brothers John and Dick have fooled with fishing all their lives (Dick Wood worked for a few years on Ted's haul-seine crew) and still tend fish traps before going to work.

John Wood, who keeps what he believes is the last cow in the former farm community of Springs, recalls attending East Hampton High School in the forties and being called "just a clam digger from Bonac." In those days anyone from the Springs District was a clam digger. It was only when outside people moved to Bonac, and their kids came to East Hampton High School, that the name Bonacker came into general use. Native-born people of the outlying communities are sometimes identified as "bubbies," a term used freely among themselves—"Bub" or "Bubby," like "Cap" or "Cappy," simply means "Friend." But these terms are much disliked when carelessly applied by "people from away," who tend to equate bubbies with Bonackers and have no clear understanding of either one.

Strictly speaking, Bonacker describes any local person whose ancestors were born and bred in Accabonac, which has retained longer than most local communities the Elizabethan usages of the first settlers, including the old Dorsetshire inflection called the Bonac accent.[1] (There are also old Kentish usages, such as the word "dreen" for drain—a stream, creek, or outlet—as in, "Thing of it is, 'at dreen's terrible clugged up, ain't no bait gittin in ner gittin out.") As Bill Lester says, "You can always tell a Bonacker by the way he talks. Whether we don't know how to talk or whether we talk better, I don't know."

Poseys regard themselves as Bonackers, and increasingly the name is used to include not only those born in the Springs District but all natives of East Hampton and Amagansett. But Sally's husband, who came here and attended school at an early age, can never be a Bonacker, having been born in Vermont, and it annoys Sally that the East Hampton High School athletic teams now call themselves "the Bonackers," when three-fourths of the kids are outsiders who have no idea what the term means, and no acquaintance with a scallop dredge or clam rake, far less a haul-seine crew. No doubt because of exposure to outsiders, most young Bonackers of the present generation are losing the strong Bonac accent; this is most noticeable in girls (Stewart's daughter Gail has almost none). What remains of the

Bonac accent is perpetuated by the young men who give up school at an early age and work with older baymen on the water.

As for Poseys, Lester daughters remain Poseys until they marry. Jenny says that her daughter is no Posey; even if she had a son who fished, he could not be a Posey unless his name was Lester. On the other hand, Stewart's son Teddy would be a Posey even if he gave up fishing, and the same is true of their cousins' sons, most of whom wish to be fishermen, despite the dark outlook for the future. "Really a Posey is through the boy. Girls kind of fade out, so there aren't many Poseys left." Among the original Posey Boys, Harry and Harold had no children, and Charlie had just one child, a daughter; Ted had one son, and only one of Bill's four sons survived. But Frank's five sons are all alive, and all of them are fishermen. Some of Frank's grandsons are also fishermen, although whether fishing will survive is another matter.

Ted Lester's children were aware in school that fishermen were looked down upon in the community. When an up-streeter told her child not to play with Jenny any more, Jenny said, "You needn't ought to worry!"[2] They were also aware that in other days the fishermen had been respected, so long as they held on to some land. These days, the prosperous Parsons and Dominys, Osborns and Fithians, were no longer fishermen. The only wealthy fishing families left were Edwardses, and they, too, had expanded from the fisheries into other enterprises. With all their property, with all their big boats, docks, and gear, they had never been thought of as baymen. "The Edwardses bought land out here when it was cheap," Jenny Syvertsen says. "They were high-class, they were up-streeters, they were educated. Doc Dave Edwards got to be educated, but his father [Cap'n Josh] was a fisherman. Other fishermen were considered a lower class of people, but not as poor as clammers."

The clam diggers often squatted on poor land near the

harbor edges, especially at Lazy Point, Napeague, where they lived mostly in shanties "with the stove in the living room and a small bedroom to the side, and an outhouse." By up-streeters (and by some outsiders, too) they were apt to be dismissed as seaside hillbillies, beset by shiftlessness and drink, but their worst offense in a comfortable community was chronic poverty.[3]

To this day, among East Hampton's middle-class, there lingers an idea of most Poseys and Bonackers as hidebound and procrastinating people, lacking ambition; very few of their townsmen understand what the fishermen bring to the community. Robert Vetault, a liberal up-streeter who worked in the town government during the sixties, says that most of his neighbors perceived the baymen (and especially those clam diggers who peddled clams and scallops from door to door) as "semicomic figures." East Hampton, he says, became very snobbish when it turned into a resort in the 1890s; his own grandmother, leaving the Springs to live in East Hampton, "thought she was entering a whole new wonderful world." Yet as late as World War II, most up-streeters were exceptionally provincial, still identifying with New England and suspicious of New York, still traveling to New Haven or New London for their shopping. There were scarcely any Jews in town, Catholics were identified as lower-class servants, and fishermen were totally disreputable. "I don't think that the up-streeters ever understood what these fishermen go through, what it was like to cut holes in the ice and spear eels, to go out and tong when it was so cold that your fingers froze off. Most of the up-streeters had total ignorance of what was happening within ten miles of town." Vetault understood that the fishermen were not inferior, far less semicomic, but "a whole different and fiercely proud and independent group, some of the most extraordinary people I've ever known. Milton Miller, Ted Lester typified that sort of fierceness."

After her marriage, Jenny moved up-Island for some

years, returning now and then with her husband and child
to visit. One day Sally pointed at her, demanding to know
"How come that woman and that man and that kid come
here all the time?" And Sally's mother said, astonished,
"That's your *sister!*" Subsequently Jenny returned to Amagansett, and her husband fished for a year or two with Ted
while getting himself established as a carpenter. By then the
family's life had changed. Using the money made from
swordfish, Jenny says, Ted had gone into partnership with
Frank Tillotson in Montauk Seafood. By the time Sally went
to school, her father had bought Tillotson out. He was already prospering as a businessman, had joined the Masons
and was attending Legion dances, and so, for Sally, the local
prejudice against men without regular jobs was a lot less
marked.

Young people of fishing families are much more likely
to marry outsiders than to marry townspeople, and every
one of the Lester children has done so. Their parents—and
all the older generations—almost always married within
the community. Over the decades the Posey Lesters have
intermarried with almost all the baymen families except the
Havenses, who first came to Bonac from Sag Harbor and
Shelter Island at the turn of the century. Ted's daughters
remember Henry Havens as "a sweet old man," and they
also approved of his son Billy (now known as William, to
distinguish him from his own son) who was often at Uncle
Bill's, across the street. "But some of William's brothers,
they sowed some wild oats! Lindy, Gump, and Fred raised
hell since they was born, and the girls ain't much better."

Sally recalls her early days hanging around down at the
packing room when the haul-seine crews came in with fish.
"With Daddy's own crew I could go down there when they
were packing out, cause he would tell them to watch their
language, but Uncle Bill had a crew and he had a lot of the
Havenses on it, and there was young Lindy and young
Gump, and they were flopping it around, and Daddy used

to shoo me out. When two big trucks got in there side by side, it was no place for a child anyway."

Although two other Amagansett fish markets had been established in the fifties—Stuart's Seafood, run by Stuart Vorpahl, Sr., at his place on Oak Lane, and Scotty's Market, established on Schellinger Lane by Cap'n Frank's brother-in-law, Scotty Eames—Montauk seafood continued to do well, and Jenny's fish shop expanded to include such Bonac specialties as deviled clams, clam chowder, and clam pie. Next came homemade potato salad, coleslaw, cakes, and fresh fruit pies (the favorite was strawberry-rhubarb), frozen in season and stored with the bait fish in the room below. In 1967 Ted opened a liquor store out on the highway. "You could buy a whole meal," remembers Jenny, who with most of her sisters worked in their mother's store, "then go down the street to Lester's Liquors. Daddy had quite a monopoly, we did quite, quite well!"

Despite snide nicknames such as Cap'n Seagull, no one who ever worked with Ted denied that this fiercely energetic man was a skilled fisherman. Alone among the crew captains, he traveled to Albany each year to defend their way of life from the threat of the recurrent bass bills (in the early years he was accompanied by Ellis Tuthill, whose family had been in the forefront of this fight since 1924). He also became the main spokesman for the fishermen against the groins, or jetties, on the ocean beach. Later in life, when he went to Florida in winter, he spent most of his time with local fishermen, thereby looking for small tricks of the trade that fishermen at home might put to use. Because of his eager curiosity about life, Ted was one of the few fishermen on the beach who would take the trouble to send away for identification any strange species of fish that turned up in the nets, proving to the biologists that stray bonefish and other tropical species wandered northward in the summer Gulf Stream.

"Ted put me onto erosion control," Robert Vetault says.

"His views were instinctive, based on generations of observation. The baymen couldn't explain it in terms of forces and all the rest, they just knew if you put something in the water that interrupted the flow, a certain scouring action is bound to happen; I've been hostile to groins and jetties ever since. With Ted's help, and the help of fishermen who were by then really getting organized, we wrote some legislation that kept other legislation from happening, we did our bit to keep the striped bass bill out of Albany."

At the time I left the beach, in the mid-fifties, the conflict between seiners and surfcasters was still increasing. One year Bill Lester was "down Montauk, dragging Shagwong Point, and I left my net back up on the hill, and evidently some of them playboys or whatever you might call 'em cut my bag off my net. And they had different things they tried, you know. Stay awake all night thinkin about ways they can hurt the fishermen. They catch one hundred to us one, and they don't want us to catch that one." In 1959 the haul-seiners agreed to cede the anglers the whole Point, from Shagwong all the way around to Ditch Plains, down near Montauk Village, with the understanding that the anglers would not go to Albany again with a new bass bill. They have never forgotten that the sportsmen went to Albany the very next winter, and they have mistrusted them ever since.[4]

In the same period Ted Lester was involved in a conflict between the haul-seiners and the Montauk Boatmen's Association. The charter men wanted restrictions on the scuba divers, who were tying up whole stretches of good bass and bluefish ground around the Point. The baymen—with long memories of the days when private oyster companies, gaining control of public grounds, all but ended oystering in open waters ("Ain't that terrible what they done to us?" Bill Lester says) and leery of aquaculture projects ever since—resisted any restriction on freedom of access, fearing that the netters might be next. The situation, complicated by the fact that the Indian land acquired by the Bensons did not come under the town ordinances, was finally solved when the divers agreed to avoid the Elbow, from Rocky Point south around the Light to the cove called Frisbees on the ocean shore.

As Amagansett became fashionable in the late fifties, this outgoing dory fisherman and his lively family were an easily accessible element of local color, and Ted was sought out in his store and on the beach by such movie stars as Bette Davis and Marilyn Monroe, to name only those celebrated visitors best remembered by his children. "Daddy just never treated anybody any different," Sally says. "Everybody was his friend, you know? He didn't make any big fuss over them, and they used to love it, they used to come down to the beach just to talk to him! Just to *talk!*" But his older, more conservative brothers thought that Ted and Jenny were leading a fast life as they grew prosperous, and drinking too much with their rich customers; it was concluded that Ted's illness had somehow been brought on by unhealthy exposure to outside influences.

"He was never really a big man like people remember him before he died," says Jenny, who like her sister Vinnie would fill in now and then with the crews on the beach. "He was always a very thin man, you know. My grandmother used to say to my mother, 'Jenny, I don't know, Ted's not a very well man.' He was a strong man in his own way, but the beach killed him. Starting at twelve years old, working straight through, just wore his body out.

"They used to always ride the beach, and he would say, 'I guess we better stop here, boys, and have a look.' Gas was way up, and they couldn't keep riding. So after they sit there two or three hours, the men said, 'Well, Ted, you better go home.' And he said, 'You ain't goin home. You want to go home, you go home, and I'll get a new gang. I'm sitting. I smell some fish out there.'

"The guys today have it darn easy; they don't work now like my father worked, they ride around. Fishing is fishing when you go on that beach and fish, not going down fly-by-nights."

Ted sold the liquor store in 1971, after a dispute with the son-in-law who kept its books. He died in 1973, and for the next two years his daughter ran the seafood shop, which his wife then leased to a fishermen's co-op. Eventually the co-op failed, and four years after Jenny's death in 1971, the whole place was sold off to the developers.

Both Jenny and Sally miss the fun and banter of waiting on the summer people and giggling at some of what they saw. They also miss the fish shop atmosphere, including filleting and dressing fish, and in recent years have been happy to open scallops in a small shop that their brother Stewart has set up in his garage near Three Mile Harbor.

Much more than their parents and grandparents, who took it for granted, the younger Lesters are aware of the fragility of this ocean land. "The east end of Long Island is beautiful because of what we have here," Jenny Syvertsen says, "the fish and scallops and clams, the land that people could come out and see. But what's it going to be like ten years from now? It's going! Your regular fisherman is going to go, which is a sin. These people from the city are coming out here and pushing us right out. They say it's so beautiful, they want it, and they're pushing us right out. It's never going to be stopped."

"You're here every year, and you see this goin up and that goin up, and you don't really notice," says her cousin Calvin, who is Bill Lester's son by his second marriage. "But say you wasn't here for two years, three years, you come back and look, you'd say, Jesus Christ, where the hell am I *at!*"

Since the fish factory closed, land values have soared at Napeague, and Beach Hampton, a development in the barrier dunes at the east end of Amagansett, is spreading eastward all the way to Hither Hills. "I hadn't gone down on the Napeague stretch at night in a year or two. The condos and motels, I was appalled!" Sally exclaims. "Holy shit! Lights after lights after lights!" Her Uncle Frank had said that he would be "tickled pink" by a good hurricane, and she agrees. "I've been praying for a hurricane for two years; I want one so darn bad it isn't funny! The 1938 hurricane would straighten this town right about out straight. Cause there will be no more Beach Hampton, no more of those hotels along the stretch. Look at Westhampton Beach, all that erosion, all those people: *you cannot build on top of dunes!* And the farming industry on Long Island is almost shot, right in the backseat, because these poor farmers, they can't afford the taxes. What do the people in New York City think they're gonna eat if they keep pushing? The fishermen don't *have* anything. They can't tax the water on us, but if they could tax that water on us, they would."

"This is God's country!" Stewart says. "It's nice out here! I've been up and down this coast from Maine to Florida, and this is the only place like this." Stewart is worried about the decline of the fisheries as the pressure on them constantly increases, and also about such formerly abundant elements as good fresh water. "You talk to some of these old-timers, they used to go down about forty-five feet and get beautiful water; now they're going deeper and deeper. Too many people, throwing out too much. In the summertime we had summer people, but after Labor Day they was gone. Now they don't go, they stay and stay and stay, till Christmas, even, first of the year."

Like Milt Miller, Ben Havens, and many other fishermen, Stewart has moved away from Amagansett, where he can no longer afford a house, but he also disliked the contamination of soil, air, and water by farm poisons that, in his opinion, make it dangerous to live in farm communities. Today he lives in an oak woods development off the Three Mile Harbor road in a ranch house that I recognized on my first visit by the ship's anchor that used to sit in front of

Montauk Seafood, and also the boats, decrepit cars, tubs, fishing gear, nets, pots, and buoys that characterize all baymen's yards on the South Fork.

At forty-seven, Stewart is a powerful man with heavy arms and a hard belly whose face looks tougher than it is because of the scar on the left side of his mouth. "Dad was chasin me, and I fell in a wood pile, cedar stakes," he explains with a wry grin. Ted's children agree that when Ted was working the long haul-seiner's day, sometimes four in the morning until eleven at night, and the kids woke him during his quick rests, he could "get ugly and get the belt out." Yet despite the fights between the two, Stewart's sisters feel that their father spoiled the only boy.

Stewart was not spoiled, but he was confident. Having tried early and without success to tell his father how to do things, he made certain that any new men on the crew— and outsiders especially—deferred to his own superior experience; and sometimes this way of compensating for his youth came across as stubbornness and arrogance, especially out in the dory where his father could not yell at his mistakes. As the man setting the net, he was dory captain, and no one disputed him except the "captain's captain," as Stewart called him, the man in the long-billed cap and checked wool shirt waving his arms and yelling from the beach.

One day of big rolling swells, with the net set and the dory headed back toward shore, Stewart realized he had left behind the gloves he needed to hold the jack line that would slow the dory and hold her stern into the seas as she entered the surf. "Hell, that's nothin," Stewart said, as if this was the way that he had planned it. Since there is no cleat on a dory—it would foul the net—he took a turn around his leg to snub the line, then jerked his stubborn chin toward the white beach that rose and disappeared again behind the wave crests.

That day I was stroke oar and John Cole was in the bow.

Watching Stewart's set face and the seas looming behind him, John cleared his throat in comic alarm and I grinned an uneasy grin. Big swells lifted and fell beneath the dory as we pulled toward shore, all set to "put our back in it" to catch the first small wave, yet being careful not to move too fast in case the boat was picked up by a sea too big for us to handle. At the best of times, the man on the jack line needs strength to hold the dory on the back of the wave, behind the crest; not until this wave collapses does he ease off a little on the line so that the dory settles on the broken wave and coasts ashore. When the beach is flat, the trick is a lot easier. This day the tide was high and the beach was steep, and it seemed to the unhappy oarsmen that the seas were growing.

The wave that finally caught us was too big; it lifted up our stern and pitched us forward. Stewart was strong, he did his best to haul us back bare-handed, but even with that dangerous turn around his leg, the yellow dory was too heavy; the line sizzled through the transom notch as she gathered speed. Our dory captain wore a strange expression. To this day, I can see the white scar standing out on his stiff face as the pain hit him, and the shrill warning cry from shore, like the voice of a far gull across the wind. Stewart, grunting, let go of the line—he had no choice— and the dory shot forward, stern rising to the sky as she cascaded wildly down the wave face.

Yanking the oars in, we spun on our seats, prepared to jump. In the corner of my eye I saw Ted Lester, scuttling over the sand much faster than a man in waders was ever meant to run. Seeing that dory careen toward the steep beach, he knew just what was going to happen, and it did.

I was starting my jump when the bow stem struck the sand, and the breaking wave pitchpoled the dory in a violent forward somersault. John and Stewart, bow and stern, were flung aside into the wash, but I was catapulted straight ahead onto the sand. That boat was coming down out of the sky as I tried to roll out to one side: Ted arrived at the last instant to squat and catch and hold the falling stern. He was already shrieking at poor Stewart as I scrambled free.

Hearing us talk of that bad day, Madge Lester called out from the other room, "Stewart was always a devil; he still is." Her husband cocked his head in the Posey way and grunted. "Burned right through my waders, that line did. I still got notches on my leg where I tried to hold it."

Madge Lester is one of the lucky baymen's wives who love the water. Nowadays a number of women go out on the boats, even crew on draggers, but this is recent. Tom Lester's mother, Ruth, back in the fifties, was the first woman to crew regularly to help her husband, and received a good deal of foul language and abuse ("You left your dishes in the sink?") before winning the men's respect; she later became the first woman to run for bay constable (the second was Gail Lester, and both lost). Ruth Lester was also a conservation-minded town trustee who fought the developers' road that closed off the north entrance to Bonac Creek. Tom's wife, Cathy, who also loves the water, is active in the fight to save Northwest Harbor, "the finest scallop ground on the East Coast," and she, too, has recently become a town official.

Jarvie Wood's wife, on the other hand, does not go fishing ("She don't even want to go down to the shore," Jarvie says), but despite a loss of income, she went along with her husband's need to give up their store and return to the water. Ann Havens (wife of William) and the late Kathi Lester (wife of Jimmy, Cap'n Bill's grandson) were leaders in the Baymen's Ladies Auxiliary, which organized benefits and other events and put out an excellent public relations newsletter in the mid-seventies.

To some fishermen, such as Fred Havens, women are Jonahs, and until one day when Francis Lester invited her along, Fred would not permit his wife, Carol, on the beach during the haul-seining. Fred, who is Stewart Lester's age, left the water to try mowing, carpentry, even highway work to support his new family, becoming "very quiet and withdrawn," says Carol, until her father, who hated to see his son-in-law work on the road, told his daughter that her husband was a fisherman and belonged on the water. She said she was afraid they'd starve, and he told her to go out and get a job, which Carol did. These days most fishermen's wives must go to work if the family is to survive as a fishing family.

Carol Havens, who still works to make ends meet, is philosophical. She believes that a fisherman's wife must accept being a single parent during the fishing season, that she must be as independent as her husband, and learn to lead two wholly separate lives. Fishing, she says, "is not a livelihood but a way of living, because we live different than everybody else."

My own last season—1956—was a good year on the beach, but in 1957, Stewart says, he made just $2,200 haul-seining, and a good deal less than that in 1958. "Didn't catch nothin. Made just one good haul in that whole year, and the damned market dropped the price on us overnight from fifty cents to eight cents a pound!" Stewart shook his head, disgusted still: "That was my last year on the beach." That winter Stewart and his father, with Milt Miller and Ted's nephew Johnnie Erickson, went codfishing with Elisha Ammon on the *Russell S,* setting their trawls east of Shagwong Reef on the last of the ebb and lifting them after the slack tides, on the first of the flood. Because of bad currents and strong tides, setting cod trawls on these grounds was tricky work, but they benefited from a strong and experienced crew. They landed about six thousand pounds a day, Stewart recalls, which split six ways—there was one share for the boat—worked out to about three hundred dollars a man.

By 1960 the codfish had declined, but Stewart crewed

again on the *Russell S,* dragging on the Backside for yellow-tail flounder. That spring he bought an old twenty-seven-foot lobster boat, and that summer he tended three hundred pots southwest of the Point. Then, in 1963, Stewart acquired the forty-foot *Driftwood,* which he used for dragging. The spring run of fluke, or summer flounder[5]—as much as two thousand pounds a day for ten days or two weeks—was very profitable; he dragged on the Backside, half a mile to three miles off the coast. In early June he removed the dragging gear, loaded up his lobster pots, and set them about three miles southwest of the Point, in from sixty to ninety feet of water.

The lobster fishery, which began in the late 1700s, still extends from Long Island north to Nova Scotia, and while lobsters are intermittently plentiful along the coast—they fell off sharply in the 1920s—increasing pressure has moved the main fishery offshore to the submarine canyons south of Georges Bank. Lobstermen are supposed to release juveniles[6] and also egg-bearing females, but many take "shorts" for black market sale and scrape the "berries" off the bellies of the females, tossing them into the well after the rest. A lobsterman whom I saw do this in the early sixties shook his head at my plea for conservation and just laughed.

Lobstering was profitable until mid-October, Stewart says, when some of the pots were taken out "before the real bad blows. Along in the middle of November, first of December it's getting rugged, an awful lot of nor'westers and a lot of blows. I'd lost a hundred and fifty, two hundred pots, just trying to fish half my gang; just couldn't find the buoys, and no time out there, no fuel left, to spend looking. So then we'd rig up some long-line gear, try tilefishing, maybe two trips a month is all we'd get for January. And February, mid-February through March, six or seven weeks, we'd get a spring run of codfish in 120–180 foot of water, maybe an hour from the Point. Meanwhile you'd be working on your lobster gear, and the first week of April you take the first load of pots offshore, forty pots to a trawl. Had to check 'em every four–five days, and I was fishing almost eight hundred, so we'd haul about half every other day and get ready in between."

For a while, Stewart unloaded so many lobsters—1,500 to 2,500 pounds a day—that the same sort of people who prey upon the haul-seiners on the beach would come up to him on the dock and ask for one, ignoring all the hard work and risk represented by each lobster. At last he would take a ten-dollar bill out of his pocket, saying, "Here, I may as well give you this." Nevertheless, he made very good money, declaring about $45,000 a year; he bought a new car and new truck, and also his new ranch house in the woods.

In 1968 Ted and Stewart commissioned the pretty forty-three-foot *Posey*, built in Camden, Maine, but that same year the lobstering fell off, and for the next two years the *Posey* was limited to dragging. Ted rigged a trawl that would work inside the bar, and as these were great years for striped bass, she did very well. "Used to knock down surfcasters, that's how close I was," Stewart says. "Put her high and dry twice." Like most draggers, the *Posey* carried a harpoon stand, and Stewart would take from three to eight swordfish a year on the runs back and forth from Montauk Point. In 1970 he set 580 lobster pots at the sixty-fathom line, almost halfway to the edge of the continental shelf, but two years later he was still losing; not only were the lobsters scarce but many were soft-shelled, and died in transit. Stewart sold the *Posey* with regret and bought a big fifty-nine-foot steel boat that made twenty knots and cut the return trip from six hours to three. "First year we done all right, but the second, the lobsters started dropping off bad, and we moved off as far as 120 fathoms. I hung on for the next three years and that was the end of it—forget it!"

Nearly broke, Stewart sold his boat and quit the lobster business; he gave up ocean fishing and went back to the bay. Today he is content with an open boat and outboard motor. With part-time help from his son Teddy, he tends two traps at Water Fence, east of Napeague, goes clamming and scalloping, and runs a scallop-opening shop here at his house.

In my scalloping days, the openers gathered at a long outdoor table under the trees, in a kind of community event like a house raising or corn husking. In the thick of the gossip and laughter, the shells flew, and an eye was separated each few seconds from an organic tangle that the novice might take half a minute to unravel. Like so many small freedoms of East End life, from burning leaves to sleeping on the beach, opening scallops on outdoor tables under the oaks has now been regulated out of existence by busy bureaucrats. Scallops today must be opened indoors, under certified conditions; even the old wood-handled knives have been replaced by hygienic plastic implements. Yet opening remains an exhilarating social event, a lot of fun, according to Madge Lester. Madge believes that the skilled twist of the wrist in speedy work comes easier to women, and speaks in awe of Henry Havens's granddaughter, Carol Nation, who has drastically speeded the usual technique (Pop the top shell off, go back to the hinge and scoop the gut up and over the top of the adductor muscle, or eye, clean the top shell on the way forward and flip it off, finish removing gut, cut eye, and flip it into the container); this inspired woman holds two scallops at once, flicking the eyes free without troubling the guts. Some openers "cut" a gallon an hour, at a present rate of nearly ten dollars a gallon, which, added to the bayman's own time, labor, and overhead, accounts for the high price of bay scallops.[7] (Similarly, the high price of flounder fillets—pronounced *fill*-its—is accounted for by labor and lost poundage: 1.5 pounds of fluke, 2–2.5 of black-backed flounder, and 3 of yellowtail are required for a pound of flatfish fillet, and a good filleter may take a year to learn the job.)

"After I quit the beach," Stewart says, "my dad took on Pete Kromer, who married one of Francis's daughters. Milt Miller, Jimmy Reutershan, Jens Lester, Benny Havens, Dick Wood, J.P. Fenelon—that's my Aunt Ruth's son—hell, just about everyone fished with my dad at one time or another, though most of 'em didn't last too long. Long about '62, they went over to outboards, Uncle Bill or Bobby Lester in Southampton was probably first. Old-timers was suspicious, of course, said them motors would scare the fish off to deep water, but in a year or two, why, everybody had 'em. And with that power, they began usin a lot more net, three times the size, they were goin way out back of the bar, and so the dories had to be five or six foot longer, too.

"But it seems like they got lazy or somethin, in them years after the motors come—never fished hard no more, not the way we done. One year before my dad sold the rig, he got sick there, had a fish bone in his hand or somethin, asked me to run the rig for him. That day down off Hither Plains, it was a little sea runnin but not too bad, not with the motor, but them fellas just didn't want to go, so I got disgusted, cause we could *see* the bass, right close inshore. I said, Well, shit, if we ain't goin bassin, I'm goin home. No, no, they said, wait a little while, sea might go down a little. So J.P. Fenelon goes along a little way, lookin for a better place to set, drives right by as many bass as you ever seen in your whole life, right in the surf, and never even notices. I know that Uncle Bill is into fish back to the west'rd, had 280 boxes that same mornin, and I'm goin crazy here, because they're *still* not interested; I'm in charge of the rig but there's nothin I can do. So I drive straight off the beach and go on home, tell the old man he ought to fire that whole gang, and that was the last time in my life I ever went haul-seinin.

"In the sixties, everything got complicated—withholding tax, unemployment insurance, liability, licenses, I don't know what—and it just didn't pay for one man to own the rig, so eventually Pete Kromer bought in. Today one man may be captain, but the rig is owned by two or three; one guy owns the net and a truck, another the dory, and so on. Anyway, the crews started catching bass again about 1960, and it just seemed to get better and better. My dad fished with Pete Kromer right up until he got sick, about 1970."

Despite his famous fights with "the captain's captain," Stewart is proud of his father to this day. A portrait of Ted by a summer artist is prominent on his living room wall, and he keeps a large file of Ted Lester documents and photographs. Like his sister Jenny, Stewart feels that Ted was worn out by his own energy. "My dad was one of those guys so fired up most of the time that he never really stopped to take a rest. Even when he got sick, you know, still had to jump into the car every damn mornin, run down and make sure that ocean was still there."

# 14.

# The East Hampton
# Town Baymen's Association

On a September day four or five years ago, coming ashore at Montauk Lake from a day's fishing, I saw a familiar figure in black waders unloading scallops from his battered sharpie. Milt Miller's stiff black brush was silvered now, and he was heavier, but he cocked his head and grinned in a certain way, and I recognized him the same instant he recognized me. Milt set down his burlap sack with a solid crunch that brought back in an instant those scallop seasons of a quarter century before and came stomping across the shallow water to shake hands. "B'god, bub, I *thought* that was you! How *you* been doin?" And we just stood there for awhile, shaking our heads and grinning, glad to meet again without having or needing very much to say; the twenty-five years in between seemed unimportant. We asked after the men we knew in common, and inevitably arrived at Pete Scott's death.

"Pete only fished with me five years," Milt said, "but after he left here I really missed him. Took my boy Mickey after that, and Benny Havens, good fishermen, too, but I never run across anyone like Pete. That fella really loved to fish; you tell him you're sailing at 3 A.M., he's there at 2. I never had to wait for him, not even once. No, sir, I don't know how anyone could ever get mad at Pete." Milt's voice was quiet, and his eyes had softened; he glanced at me quickly, saw that I saw, then looked away. Impatient with his own feelings, he admitted gruffly, "Guess I miss him still.

"I tried to keep my boy there from goin on the water, keep him from making the same mistake I did—it's just a hell of a hard life, you know that? For a long time I never took him with me. But soon's Mickey come back from the Korean War, he took it up, and he ain't never looked back.

"Seems to me I spent most of my life out around Gardiners, can't stay away from it. Used to take all these young fellas out there and teach 'em. Used to spend the night out there, make lean-tos, and go back fishin before daylight. I know that island better'n any Gardiner, I'll tell you that, and I feel kind of protective about that place. Always let 'em know when I see campfires of people that come in there off of boats, because a fire out there would destroy all them old woods, destroy everything. Not long ago, I seen a fire there and I went over and warned the people: They got no fire equipment here, I said, so if that fire gets away, it'll burn this island flat. Well, damn if the lady I was speakin to wasn't a Gardiner herself, turned out she owned the island! And she was so pleased by my attitude, and the care I took, that since then I can't do no wrong out there."

I asked Milt if you could still tong surf clams west of Three Mile Harbor breakwater, and he shook his head. "Them clams is gone; gone from the channel, too. Don't know what become of 'em. But they'll be back. Everything comes back."

When I knew Milt, he lived on Meeting House Lane in Amagansett. Since then, he had moved away to Accabonac, and later to Olympic Heights at Three Mile Harbor, where he found a small house with a big fisherman's yard out in the back. "Don't need that land, but my boy Mickey will, way land is goin. See the way this place has changed, do ya?" Milt jerked his chin at the littered shores of Montauk Lake, which in the fifties had been mostly moorland. "Already closed the south end to clammin with all the people and pollution; gettin like that everywhere. The fishermen can't afford to live here in East Hampton Town no more, and the fish neither; won't be nothin left here but developers!"

In the late nineteenth century, Milt said, the baymen had organized a delegation to Riverhead to protest the appropriation of the oyster bottoms by private corporations. Ignored, they resorted to their own measures, plying the company warden with liquor, then raiding the oyster beds at night; the oyster-poaching enterprise became so well organized that a special truck came regularly from New York to pick up deliveries for the market. (Eventually the markets colluded with the oyster companies and refused to accept these moonlight shipments. Since then, the few wild oysters harvested by baymen are sold to the companies for planting.)

Resourceful men such as the oyster poachers took to rum-running with flair and dedication, and some of them later found ways to evade size limits and other regulations that the sportsmen were sponsoring in the state legislatures. From the beginning they had felt beleaguered by wealthy outsiders—not only sportsmen but bureaucrats, developers, city people buying up the land—and they felt obliged to flout the law for their own survival. In the early fifties, as the sportsmen's campaign for a bass bill got under way, a formal baymen's association was discussed, but it got nowhere; while a few baymen understood what was at stake, most were unwilling to cooperate for the common good. Year after year it was left to people like Ted Lester to defend their livelihood while the rest of the men went on about their business.

But as the bass increased and the threat of a bass bill diminished, interest in a baymen's organization diminished, too. Not until the late sixties was there real concern about fisheries conservation. Ironically, the first species that needed help was the faithful hard clam, the only important marine resource that had never been known to suffer a drastic decline. Hard clams, though never a leading fishery on the East End, gave most apprentice fishermen their start, and were always out there on the flats in hard times and in winter.

By the late sixties the oysters had all but disappeared from Accabonac, Montauk Lake, and Three Mile Harbor, where they had been common after World War II. ("Too much salinity," Milt believes. "Oysters need brackish water for good spawnin. Water table was lowered by all this development, and dredgin the channels brought in too much salt water, that's my opinion.") As for Accabonac's clams, they had been reduced to an estimated one tenth of their former numbers. Development of the sand spit called Cape Gardiner—now Gerard Park—had closed the northern channel of Accabonac, cutting down tidal circulation and the flow of tide-borne nutrients from the spartina bogs; the stagnant shallows, once an important marine nursery and reservoir of shellfish, eels, diamondback terrapin, and other life, were invaded by an alga called enteromorpha. Fed by farm fertilizers and accumulating sewage, the algae formed a thick mat over the bottom. Decomposing, this hairy mat bred swarms of bacteria that used up too much of the scarce oxygen, suffocating not only quahogs but also steamer clams, horseshoe crabs, sea cucumbers, and winkles, as well as the young of such valuable species as flounder and blowfish.

Milt and I could remember how, back in the fifties, blowfish had been so abundant that the haul seine sometimes came ashore like a downed dirigible. The panicked fish filled themselves with air and sand, packing the bag tight with white squeaky bellies and chafing the twine with their abrasive skin, and the crew had to attack the bag with icepicks, to deflate it enough to winch the haul ashore. The puffer had been one of the first trash fish to find a market, and when they showed up in sufficient numbers, we would set up long tables on the beach for "skunning off" the froggish green-eyed creatures; the delicious meat in one shrimplike piece on the extracted backbone had become popular as chicken-of-the-sea. In the sixties the blowfish swarm was a plague to pin-hookers, taking every bait. Then, in the early seventies, it disappeared throughout its range, from Massachusetts south to the Carolinas. The kingfish had all but vanished, too, and both sea bass and porgies were way down. As for the weakfish, it had disappeared entirely after '52, despite the huge numbers of small fish seen that year; when it reappeared again, in 1974, the first weakfish caught were very big ones. Where had they come from? More than any fish cycle in recent decades, the curious history of the weakfish persuaded the baymen that the ways of fish were still a mystery, not only to fishermen but to biologists as well.

In the 1950s, when Bill Lester had been "clam king" here on Montauk Lake, the decline of the hard clam had already begun, and in 1957 Milt Miller, William Havens, and Francis and Billy Lester met in Billy Lester's basement to discuss what would develop two years later as the East Hampton Baymen's Association. "Billy Lester was conservation-minded, Francis, too—most people ain't—and William Havens was always a good, conscientious person, didn't waste nothin, threw back small scallops. Remember how Old Bill, and Ted, too, used to take their garbage down to the beach, dump it out into the slews, get the tourists hollerin? Anyways, we wanted a few sincere people to help educate the baymen, and we ended up educatin the whole town. Wouldn't be any wetlands left here in the harbors if it wasn't for the association, and that's a fact. But most of the baymen never helped. Them fellas seemed to think it rained clams every time it rained, they'd just cull out the small clams, dump 'em on their driveway for gravel. There was always a-plenty in the old days, so the older generation didn't care, and some of them younger ones still think that way, they just don't give a damn: cull out small steamers, white perch, and such, throw 'em away, instead of puttin 'em back where they belong." Milt Miller sighed. "If you want any future as a fisherman, you got to take care of things, that's all."

The sixties had been good years, though few baymen would admit it. Traditionally, times had been hard, and they had learned to be close-mouthed, careful with money. Many talked poor as a matter of habit, knowing that one-third of their income must be put aside for maintenance and gear, that their costs were rising steadily, that the town would sacrifice their interests whenever they interfered with the resort economy. They were also convinced that the fish stocks were being dangerously depleted by boats from other states and from abroad—"Fishermen get all stirred up when anyone tries to take somethin' away from them," Milt says—that no matter how high fish prices rose, there would be no future in fishing unless they organized to defend their interests. Enthusiastically supporting the new association, they elected a popular part-time fisherman named Howard Miller as first president, with Milt vice-president; a few years later Milt succeeded to the presidency. A membership of well over one hundred included an encouraging number of townspeople who had realized that, in many ways, an end to its fishing industry would be a great loss to the town.

The Baymen's Association fought the pollution and destruction by fill, bulkheads, and marinas of the precious wetlands all around the bays. It also promoted the planting of seed clams and denounced the sportsmen's efforts to reserve for themselves the striped bass, which had been more numerous in recent decades than at any other time in the past century. In 1976 some association members set up a co-op in Jenny Lester's former fish shop, providing gear at wholesale cost and guaranteeing five more cents a pound than the Fulton Market (which was giving the fishermen "a rookin," said co-op sponsor John Collins. "They know you gotta get rid of the stuff, and that's it."), "I'm not gonna get much out of it," Francis Lester said, "but maybe my son will, and my grandson."

But the co-op, despite the sincere efforts of many baymen,[1] collapsed from debt a few years later due to bad management, unauthorized payments and appropriations, and other abuses, including a tendency among certain members to undercut it by continuing to buy gear from their customary sources, selling fish to their own customers, and refusing to help in crucial co-op expenses such as the repair costs of Ted Lester's old freezers. An ornery, opportunistic attitude is the destructive side of the fishermen's hard-nosed independence, and most baymen recognize today that the failure of the co-op, which attracted, then lost, the strong support of many people in the town, was a self-inflicted wound that lessened their long-term chances of survival.

"Some of 'em came out of that co-op with flyin colors," Milt says wryly. "You don't see them people around too much no more. But other fellas, the ones that was sincere, like Francis and his boy Jens, Benny Havens and them, they lost their shirt. Fisherman ain't cut out to run a business. What the up-streeters never realized was that a lot of baymen, myself included, never believed in that co-op and never joined, and we never approved of the way that it was managed, neither. But to the public it was all hooked up with the Baymen's Association, and that done us a lot of damage." After the co-op fell apart, Milt was reelected president of the association, which recovered some of its prestige with the establishment of a volunteer dory rescue squad for beach emergencies and also a new clam-seeding program,[2] still in progress today. Its close attention to environmental issues has made it a strong and respected force in the politics of the town.

We sat in the Indian summer sun on Montauk Lake and talked a while.

"The Lester boys was the best there was after the old whalers went," Milt was saying. "Old Frank, he was some fisherman, that fella! Never in a rush like Bill and Ted, y'know, always lightin up that pipe, and if you was buntin up when he come along, he'd always stop and lend a hand, no matter if fish was breakin out all over the place. Never try to beat you to a set, the way his brothers done; Ted was the worst that way, but Bill was lingerin not far behind.

"One day down Erdmann's, fish was showin and Frank was there first, but that old Model A of his, one had the platform on back for the dory, she got stuck in that wet sand right to the axle. So we come along, and Ted backs down right alongside. He ain't there to help his brother out, y'know, he wants the set: 'Better try 'em, boys! Let's go! Let's go!' So I said, 'Looks like Frank's set to me,' and Ted is hollerin, 'He ain't gonna make no goddam set, bogged down like that!' Well, I was the stroke oar, and I said, 'Ted, if you want to set this net that bad, you're gonna have to row it out yourself.' I was some mad, and I wasn't the only one. We left Ted shoutin in his truck and our crew went over and helped Frank go off and make that set. Got about two fish out of it, as I recall. But day in, day out, Frank caught some fish with that wore-out old gear of his, and when the end of the season come, he always done good as the others.

"Another time there I come into Montauk Seafood with a pretty good load of bass from Gardiners Island, and Ted said, 'Where'd you get them fish?' and so I told him; he was fishin the ocean and I was fishin the bay, and I didn't think nothin about it. But by Jesus, that evenin, when I went out there from Bonac Creek, I found Ted on my spot with some of his haul-seine crew, and when I said somethin about it, Ted let me know I never owned the bay. Well, I told him to hell with him, knowin he planned to make his set at sunset; to get those bass, you had to fish the tides. So he makes his set, don't get a single fish, and the next mornin I come in with a thousand pounds. Old Ted had a fit: said I had told him the wrong place to go, said I had lied to him!" Milt laughed. "But most of the time, Cap'n Ted and me, we got on good.

"Ted was a good surfman; he was quick. Some of 'em was overcautious, waitin' for a good slatch, but Ted could see slatches where nobody else could. Cap'n Frank would take his time, make sure you got out there, and Bill was somewhere in between, but Ted would push you off into damn near anything, when others would say it wasn't fit to go. And you had to *row!* If you didn't pull when Ted hollered *Pull!*, you were gonna get wet! But you had to have confidence in the captain, and I did; when Ted said Go! I'd go."

Remembering how Ted's quickness saved my hide, I said I missed him, and Milt Miller nodded. "A lot of people was jealous of Ted; he had too much drive. Said he didn't whack up fair and things like that. I always trusted him; wouldn't have fished with him if I didn't. And even if I didn't, I'd never have questioned him like that, I'd just go away. After you left, one of Ted's relatives come on the crew, used to yell at him, accuse him of sellin on the side them few flounders that come in with the bass—well, even if he did, what of it? He had to clean up that damn freezer after we got done packin out and went on home, and by God, he earned them few flounder! You know the fella I'm talkin about; we won't say his name because he's bigger'n us. But anyway, it was embarrassin. I walked right out, couldn't listen to it, and that's why I finally quit Ted's crew."

Milt grinned that sad-eyed, sly, and kindly grin that I remembered so well from the old days; I noticed he had lost his sight in his right eye. "Course I ain't saying now that Ted weren't thrifty! If that fella seen a bass loose in the net, he'd drop everything, run right down and wrassle with it in the water; you'd think that bass was the last fish in the world!" Recalling Ted's frenzy at such moments, we burst out laughing, but already Milt was serious again. "Well, that's the spirit he took up to Albany. Once Ted got up to talk, he'd never sit down; you'd have to knock him down. Talk to them people about makin a livin, payin off bills, and he'd talk from the heart; that's how you get people to hear. Who wants to listen to a guy who stands up and rustles a lot of papers?" Milt shook his head. "There's nobody like Ted around here now, nobody who'll get up on his hind legs and holler. And without that, the bass fishin is goin to go." Milt lifted his brown hand to the Indian summer day, and the gesture seemed to wave away all the once-bountiful waters, all of the harmonious ocean landscape, all of the slow serenity of South Fork tradition. "All of it is going to go," Milt Miller said.

# 15.

# A Dying Fishery

In 1978 a study by the University of Rhode Island discovered that rod-and-reel fishermen harvested 93 percent of the striped bass taken that year in the state, and that most of these fish were sold commercially. In all the Atlantic states, commercial netters take only one tenth of the striped bass landed, according to long-term Interior Department figures; in New York, the Department of Environmental Conservation (D.E.C.) estimates that as many as half the bass sold at New York City's Fulton Fish Market during the past decade were taken on rod-and-reel—these in addition to the great numbers of fish given away or consumed at home. Yet the recreational fishermen had never offered to limit the size of their own catch. Instead they continued to attack a small, traditional livelihood that does far less damage to the fish stocks than they do themselves, and almost none when compared to the real enemy of the striped bass, which is the sickening destruction of its breeding grounds in the fouled waterways of the Atlantic coast.

Until recently, at least, the tidal rivers of Chesapeake Bay were thought to supply nine out of ten of the striped bass that migrate up and down the Atlantic coast. Since

1970 the accumulating pollution by sewage and sewage chlorines, industrial and agricultural chemicals, and toxic metals in the bay mud have poisoned the water, depleted its oxygen, and dimmed the necessary sunlight, wiping out most of the aquatic vegetation in the food chain;[1] inevitably, this pollution has destroyed the vulnerable eggs and larvae, not only of the striped bass but of six species of anadromous perches and herrings of commercial value, reducing the surviving fingerlings to a scattered remnant. In the ten years after 1969, herring catches in Virginia waters dropped from more than 30 million to one and one-half million pounds; in the same period, there was an 80 percent drop in landings of American shad in Maryland, which finally prohibited shad fishing in 1980.

A small number of female bass can restore the species even in years when the population is low; the problem is that a viable percentage of the young can no longer survive. Robert Pond, inventor of the "atom popper" lure (Cap'n Bill's Bluefish Flash Bass Atom Popper #5 was my first and favorite), has invested his earnings in a research outfit called Stripers Unlimited, and has shown convincingly that, in Chesapeake headwaters, the buoyant striper eggs and larvae are devastatated by chemical assault. But Pond is convinced that federal biologists are slighting his research, in apparent deference to the chemical and agricultural industries, which (like the dairy and bread lobbies that undermined fish protein concentrate) strongly influence the federal bureaucracy.[2]

In consequence—and despite massive and evil-smelling evidence to the contrary—an absurd share of the blame for striped bass scarcity was still being ascribed to overfishing. This argument has some merit in the Chesapeake itself, where immature fish are taken in great quantity and adults are netted on the spawning grounds, but when applied to migrating fish along the coast, there is scarcely a reputable biologist who takes it seriously. In fact, few if any are convinced that management laws in effect since the 1930s have had any measurable effect.

"The existing sixteen-inch and eighteen-inch size limits and laws prohibiting netting in the Middle Atlantic and New England states do not appear to be of any benefit to the striped bass population, and it is quite evident that further restrictions in these states will have little or no effect on the abundance of the fish," wrote John C. Poole of New York's Department of Environmental Conservation in 1965,[3] an opinion affirmed a few years later by the D.E.C.'s Dr. Richard Schaefer: "It seems extremely doubtful that New York fishermen have any measurable influence on the abundance of striped bass which occur seasonally along Long Island's south shore. It also appears that effective management must be centered largely at the geographical source of the stocks. . . ."[4]

These opinions were written in the late sixties, when bass were plentiful, yet there seems small reason to quarrel with them now that bass are few, since it is clear that the drastic Chesapeake decline that recurred in the early seventies was caused less by fishing pressure on its migratory populations than by gross contamination of its tributaries.[5] The larger tributaries include the bay's ancestral river, the great Susquehanna (which descends from New York's Finger Lakes and Mohawk Valley through Pennsylvania with half the Chesapeake's supply of fresh water and a sour burden of both states' industrial filth) as well as the seriously befouled James, Rappahannock, and Potomac. In the Hudson River, the bass population seemed more stable, yet the Hudson, too, had become so contaminated that in 1976 the sale of bass caught in the river was prohibited, because of the high level of polychlorinated biphenyls (PCBs) found in these fish. New Jersey, too, forbade the sale of bass from Hudson waters. But efforts to clean up the Hudson were succeeding. The bass were increasing and the level of PCBs was going down, and it appeared that a healthy fishery could be restored.

Today spawning salmon are returning to the Connecticut River, ascending the river by fish ladders installed to carry them past the dams, and the adaptable striped bass, uninvited, is also ascending these salmon ladders, and has been observed in increasing numbers as far inland as the Vermont–New Hampshire border. It is thought that all the New England rivers once harbored *Morone saxatilis*, which could return to the Northeast, and prosper, with even the smallest encouragement from man. Yet in the crucial Chesapeake region, despite the pleas of Maryland biologists, the bureaucrats continued to avoid the issue, paying lip service to conservation while doing nothing to offend the local watermen.

Refusal to deal with the underlying problem was not confined to tidewater politicians. Even when the extent of mortality in bass eggs, larvae, and fingerlings became well known, the sportsmen's lobbies paid little attention. Under one banner or another, in every coastal state from Maine to Texas, they were waging their crusades against "commercials," thereby encouraging the impression that their actual intent was to reserve the more desirable fishes for themselves. In New York State, claiming to represent untold thousands of anguished voters, they continued to seek exclusive access to the disappearing bass without relinquishing the right to make money on their sport, soliciting endorsement from authentic conservation groups, as well as from bird and garden clubs, freshwater anglers, and others susceptible to the claim that the last of these beautiful striped silver fish would soon be dragged out of the sea by the horny hands of the insatiable netters. (The lobbies received very limited support from South Fork sportsmen who had seen commercial netting at first hand; from the start, the stronghold of the anti-netting lobbies has been up-Island, in the environs of Babylon.)

Throughout the late fifties and the sixties, good spawnings occurred every few years and bass were plentiful, and one bass bill after another was discredited as a conservation measure; in 1973 bass landings reached an all-time high because of the dominant year-class in the Chesapeake three years before. Therefore New York's D.E.C. could not support the bass bills, which got nowhere, and biologists in the Chesapeake region generally agreed with the D.E.C. that restrictive legislation on the coastal fisheries was beside the point. The Natural Resources Institute of the University of Maryland observed in 1963 that "man's fishing at the present intensity seems to have little effect on the long-range production of striped bass in Chesapeake Bay. The most essential long-range management measure to insure high spawning success is the protection, maintenance, and in some cases rehabilitation of the favorable environmental conditions in the important breeding and nursery areas."[6] Another biologist in the same institution drew attention in 1970 to the curious fact (cited earlier by Dr. Merriman) that as in the great year of 1934, "dominant year-classes often appear to be produced by smaller parental stocks. . . . That there is an inverse relationship between size of parent stock and recruitment (number of new fish produced by parent stock) is hardly to be questioned in the case of the Chesapeake Bay striped bass."[7] As late as 1978 Benjamin Florence of Maryland's Division of Natural Resources, who would advocate a twenty-four-inch size limit for New York, acknowledged that "contrary to popular belief, prevention of overfishing will not guarantee increased reproduction or even necessarily benefit recruitment at all. . . . Remember that the failure of striped bass to produce a dominant year-class since 1970 is not a function of fishing, so how could the mere act of altering fishing practices solve the recruitment problem? It cannot, so fishermen must not be misled into believing that whatever restrictions they must endure will somehow automatically restore an abundance of stripers."[8]

In 1978, in a good book called *Striper,* John Cole documented the destruction of the estuaries and predicted the immediate doom of the striped bass; and as it happened, a mediocre year-class that same year was the sole spawning after 1970 that slowed the decline of the Chesapeake race. Maryland biologists, finding one fingerling where in other years there had been thirty, advised all the Atlantic states that the 1978 hatch represented the last chance to restore the Chesapeake population, and a New York group called S.O.S. (Save our Stripers) lobbied for a bill to raise the size limit on bass from eighteen to twenty-six inches. Meanwhile, Perry Duryea, Montauk assemblyman and Republican minority leader, heretofore a staunch defender of the baymen, abandoned their cause in pursuit of his own ambition to be governor, and with Duryea abstaining from the fray, a bass bill won its first victory in the legislature. However, it was not endorsed by the D.E.C.'s Anthony Taormina, who had studied the bass since the 1950s and agreed with his colleagues that there was no biological justification for raising the limit above sixteen inches. When this fact was drawn to Governor Hugh Carey's attention by an aide from East Hampton,[9] the bill was vetoed and returned to the arena. However, the end of the half-century struggle was now in sight.

Meanwhile, the 1973 peak of fifteen million pounds in commercial landings had fallen steadily each year, to one third that amount by 1980. The market value of the much-diminished catch had nearly doubled between 1970 and 1980, and the retail price soared from about one dollar to at least six dollars a pound as bass grew scarcer. In New York State, the 820,250 pounds taken in 1981 fell to 469,100 the following year, a "record low"; no attention was paid to the inconvenient fact that this record low was nearly four times higher than the highest figure in seventeen straight years between 1921 and 1938.

Predictably, sportsmen foresaw the "extinction" of an exceptionally tolerant species already successfully transplanted to the Pacific Coast and well established in freshwater habitats; and in response to this pumped-up emergency, a state-federal Striped Bass Management Plan, issued in 1981 by the Atlantic States Marine Fisheries Commission, recommended an all-state twenty-four-inch limit, which, it was said, would enable adult females to return to the Chesapeake and spawn at least once before meeting their doom. (The question of how all this spawn would fare in a bath of poison was again ignored.) Biologists knew that an eighteen-inch limit, and probably a sixteen-inch limit, would accomplish the same purpose, and that an increase in numbers of adult fish would guarantee neither good spawning nor a good "recruitment," which depended almost entirely on favorable conditions in the estuaries. However, the pressure to *do something* seemed insurmountable, so long as what was being done evaded the political consequences of a real solution to striped bass decline. Despite accumulating evidence that the last few netters on the migration route were probably the very least of the bass's problems, the sportsmen showed little interest in a hard campaign to clean up the spawning rivers. Intent on winning their long feud with the commercial men, they pressed for restrictive legislation up and down the coast.

As Putnam McLean of the Sea Bright Fishing Company wrote in a letter to *National Fisherman* in August 1984: "The problems besetting striped bass: pollution, pollution, and pollution. The quick and easy solution is closure or limiting catches, but there is so much energy and publicity going into these solutions that the real culprit, destruction of spawning habitat, gets screened out. A lot of big toes are going to get stepped on when the real villain in the story finally emerges. Closures will help, but they should not be the major focus in solving the problem."

The one point on which both sides could agree was that existing striped bass laws were self-defeating and unfair. Though laws vary widely throughout the Atlantic states, most northeastern states endorsed the twenty-four-inch rule, which was also in effect in coastal waters of all the Middle Atlantic states except Delaware and North Carolina, both of which permitted twelve-inch fish. But Maryland and Virginia, while supporting the twenty-four-inch rule along their ocean coasts (where there was no fishery) refused to admit that the thousands of miles of saltwater shoreline on the Chesapeake were "coast" as well; here the size limit was fourteen inches, despite widespread agreement among biologists that in taking fish of less than sixteen inches, the year of their fastest growth in weight was lost. In the period between 1954 and 1981, Maryland and Virginia accounted for more than 60 percent of the commercial catch on the entire Atlantic coast; an estimated 74 percent of this Chesapeake catch were immature fish of about fourteen inches. Yet neither state was doing anything of significance to reduce the harvest of immature and breeding bass, or to slow the destruction of the Chesapeake. Since small fish in New York and Rhode Island were apparently being saved to go back to the mid-Atlantic states to be netted, the last two northeastern states that permitted net fisheries for bass saw no point whatever in adopting the twenty-four-inch recommendation, despite the great pressure on their legislators from indignant sportsmen's lobbies in Connecticut and Massachusetts.

The twenty-four-inch limit "would result in reductions of 33 to 82 percent in number and 9 to 42 percent by weight of commercial harvest and would have a major impact on the fishery," the D.E.C.'s Taormina concluded in a staff report of February 1, 1982.[10] (New York's pound trap fishermen and gill netters catch small school bass up to twenty inches almost exclusively, and this is true also in Rhode Island, where in 1981, 92 percent of the bass taken were between sixteen and twenty-four inches; a Rhode Island gill netter reports that small bass bring in 80 percent of his income. As in New York, the netters believe that the striped bass wax and wane in cycles, and are not endangered. In the fall of 1981, Tallman and Mack, the Newport ocean pound trap firm that years ago bought their ocean traps and anchors from the Edwards Brothers, landed 130,000 pounds of bass—the third highest figure since the firm was established in 1910.) Nevertheless, in a recommendation issued just prior to his retirement from the D.E.C. in July 1982, Taormina endorsed a proposed raise in the size limit from sixteen to eighteen inches in recognition of low bass populations, noting in passing that his Marine Fisheries Division was under pressure to pay attention to "social and political, not just biological issues." An eighteen-inch limit was officially endorsed by the D.E.C. at a hearing in Babylon in January 1983, and a bass bill favoring this limit was prepared for submission to the state senate in the spring.

But S.O.S. was still lobbying hard for the twenty-four-inch limit, and so was the New York Sportfishermen's Federation, a noisy newcomer that claimed 35,000 members in its affiliated clubs. (This number is questioned, to put it politely, by the baymen, who believe that the federation actually represents that small group of commercial anglers who regularly make money on their catch.) These people also claimed the backing of sportsmen's lobbies from all over New England, as well as motels, restaurants, tackle shops and manufacturers, garages, saloons, and other angler service operations, all of which, as the federation advised the politicians, would register their gratitude at the ballot box. This latest campaign, made more persuasive by the unquestionable decline of the striped bass, seems to have worked.

Assured by the sportsmen of support (that was not forthcoming) for a new saltwater sport-fishing license to fund their conservation operations—provided a new bass bill became law—the D.E.C. fell into line. On April 18, 1983, it officially endorsed a twenty-four-inch bill sponsored by a Babylon assemblyman named Patrick Halpin, who knew nothing at all about striped bass but needed some issues for his election campaign against Suffolk County Supervisor Peter Cohalan. The sudden D.E.C. decision to ignore Taormina's long experience was ascribed to his young successor, Gordon Colvin, who blamed it in turn on poor bass landings in 1982 as well as his personal eagerness to comply with the state-federal recommendation. No one consulted with the baymen, although the D.E.C. admitted that the twenty-four-inch law would have about five times more impact on the netters than on the sportsmen; the small striped bass between sixteen and twenty inches, used for fillets by markets and restaurants, is the "money fish" of gill-netters, trap fisherman, and haul-seiners alike, without which a bass fishery could not survive.

In a letter to the East Hampton Baymen's Association after the D.E.C. decision, Mr. Taormina declared that the poor landings of the year before were "still well within the historical norm" (again, the highest yield of bass for any year between 1921 and 1938 was about one fourth of the 1982 "low") and a leading bass biologist, Dr. J. L. McHugh of the Marine Sciences Research Center of New York State University at Stony Brook, agreed with him. Dr. McHugh, who has made a study of bass population dynamics for the half century since 1933, believes that the general level of abundance of bass in New York State has decidedly increased over that period, despite the evident deterioration of the Chesapeake spawning grounds and despite the present low point in its cycles. Similarly, D.E.C. biologist Byron Young, who has been sampling the small bass taken in the East End nets and traps for over a decade, has indicated to the netters from the start that the twenty-four-inch limit would accomplish almost nothing. (Young knows as well as anyone what a small harvest of the coastal schools the haul seines take. A few years ago at Montauk,[11] when he released twenty tagged bass into a net already set by the Havens crew, all but three of the enclosed fish escaped during the hauling.)

Not surprisingly, the Fulton Fish Market (which controls 80 percent of the eastern sales of striped bass) denounced the bill, inspiring *Salt Water Sportsman* (May 1983) to warn state legislators not to be intimidated by "mob pressure." The Montauk Boatmen's Association, which represents the charter men, called the ruling unfair and unenforceable— there was nothing to stop boat anglers from coming ashore with bass fillets instead of bass. Also, the ruling was very bad for business: about four million dollars worth of boat-caught bass are shipped to market in an average year from Montauk, in addition to all the stripers taken home. But the politicians perceived a sportsmen's constituency for the 1983 elections, and Halpin dutifully repeated the sportsmen's notion that the striped bass was "facing extinction." To harassed Long Island legislators, sick of the controversy and ever alert to the next election, it must have seemed quicker and easier to turn their backs on a hundred-odd baymen than to take on the powerful sportsmen's lobbies, not to speak of big industries on the Susquehanna and the Hudson, which were protected by the legislators from upstate.

In May 1983, at an antinuclear rally on East Hampton Green, I discussed the latest bass bill with Baymen's Association officers Dan King, Don Eames, Jr., and Arnold Leo. The men felt frustrated and uneasy. Early this year they had been persuaded by friendly legislators in Albany that the baymen had better go along with an eighteen-inch bill if they wanted to avoid something worse. At a baymen's meeting, the membership had accepted this advice, all but two trappers who insisted that an eighteen-inch law was unacceptable, that a bass bill had never passed before and would not pass this time either. Their stubbornness had turned the vote, said Donnie Eames, disgusted. "What's the sense of sendin us to Albany if they don't listen to us when we get back?"

Standing beside Dan's big steel dory with the American flag painted on the side, we received assurances from Peter Cohalan, Suffolk County Supervisor, whose job was being sought by the bass bill sponsor, that his sympathies were entirely with the baymen. But a month later, on June 25, the bass bill passed easily in the state senate, and Babylon Republican Owen Johnson, citing the rich tourist economy of the Hamptons, jeered at baymen King and Eames with the suggestion that fishermen put out of business by the bass bill could always find work "changing sheets in motel rooms"; as Eames said angrily, "They were just laughing at us." The Babylon boys clearly smelled victory, and Cohalan lost heart when his opponent's bill rode easily through the assembly. In July, while Governor Mario Cuomo wondered whether he dared veto a bill that (so his associates said) he recognized as unsound and discriminatory, Cohalan endorsed it after all, and this turnabout by the ranking politician in the baymen's county gave Cuomo the political excuse that might be needed.

For most of the summer the disheartened fishermen awaited the decision of the governor, who was said to be increasingly troubled by the barrage of letters opposing the bass bill that began to appear in his mailbox and in the newspapers. A *New York Times* editorial of July 27 pointed out that "the wiser course would be to make any law wait until 1985. The Federal Government is funding an emergency study of striped bass.[12] It aims to determine what is happening to the bass population . . . and how best to increase it. By rushing to make life impossible for commercial fishermen on Long Island before the facts of bass life are fully known, the sports fishermen and their friends in the Legislature create the impression they are as interested in getting rid of rivals as they are in saving the bass."

But in the end, political expedience prevailed over the best opinion of those who knew most about striped bass, and on August 8, only hours before the deadline, Mario Cuomo signed the bass bill into law. In a two-page attempt to justify his decision, the governor cited "poor reproduction and intensive fishing." There was no mention of the gross pollution in New York's stretch of the Susquehanna or in the Hudson, far less in the Chesapeake Bay.

Almost immediately the bill's chief sponsors in the D.E.C. began backing away from the strong statements issued in support of the bill, and confessed doubt about long-term results. Gordon Colvin admitted there was no "gilt-edged guarantee" that it would help: "Nobody really knows," he said, "what factors, man-made or natural, influence the spawning."[13] His superior, Herbert Doig, Assistant Commissioner of Natural Resources and a long-time ally of the sportsmen's lobbies, claimed, "We never indicated this was a sure cure solution to the spawning problems in the Chesapeake Bay." In short, the bass bill's sponsors now acknowledged that even a ban on the taking of this species at any place at any time would not insure its eventual survival. Unless the state and federal agencies stood up to the industrialists and politicians, unless the streams and estuaries were restored, the great silver bass, like the Atlantic salmon and the shad, would vanish from the gray and silent rivers.

In February 1984, the head biologists on the Emergency Striped Bass Research Study[14] would report gingerly to Congress that chemical pollutants "may be" a factor in the destruction of eggs, larvae, and fingerlings of bass, and that fishing "may be" inhibiting reproduction. In effect, the federal biologists were still protesting that the causes of the bass decline were not well understood, and one had to agree that a relatively successful spawning in 1982 was hard to explain, since the cumulative pollution in the Chesapeake had not lessened.

An explanation was soon forthcoming, however. Studies of the Chesapeake's Choptank River, where only a decade ago a boat might pass "through ten to fifteen miles of breaking fish"[15] had related poor bass reproduction to heavy spring rains, though no one was quite certain why this was so. Apparently the mystery had been solved by strong new evidence that the critical factor was acid rain (nitrogen and sulfur oxides produced by the burning of fossil fuels and transformed to acid rain by contact with moisture in the atmosphere), the impact of which has been well established by the death of innumerable lakes and forests of eastern North America and Europe.

In the flat coastal plain, in the swift runoff after heavy rainfall, the waters are poisoned in lethal "acid pulses," intensified through chemical action as they draw from the bottom the aluminum and other toxins already present. In most years such rainstorms are frequent in April and May when bass are spawning in the streams and the millions of eggs and larvae are most vulnerable; the spring of 1982 was unusually dry. The new evidence suggests that lowland streams as far apart as the Rhode River in Maryland and the Annapolis River in Nova Scotia—and many poisoned water courses in between—have been destroyed as bass spawning grounds largely as a consequence of acid rain, which is also blamed for the serious decline of a half dozen anadromous perches and herrings, including the valuable American shad. The deep Hudson, where bass are increasing, has apparently been spared because its river limestones buffer the acid.[16]

Meanwhile, the Chafee study endorsed the Atlantic

States Marine Fisheries Commission's recommendation of a
55 percent reduction of the bass harvest in coastal states
from Maine to North Carolina. Senator Chafee was in favor
of a moratorium until a federal management plan could be
put into effect, and his associate in the House, Claudine
Snyder of Rhode Island, submitted a bill authorizing a
three-year federal ban on the sale of bass at any place at
any time. This bill was supported by Stripers Unlimited,
Save Our Stripers, and various concerned individuals. A
House bill submitted in late summer by Representative
Gerry Studds of Massachusetts, authorizing a moratorium
in any state not abiding by the 55 percent reduction, was
passed in the early fall of 1984 and signed into law by the
President in late October.

On August 30, 1984, Governor Mario Cuomo would
turn up in East Hampton at a reception for a congressional
candidate who had endorsed a by-catch bill acceptable to
the commercial men. I was talking with Bill Lester when
the governor walked into the gathering, and I watched
Cap'n Bill with admiration as he stepped right up to the
startled politician, just as Ted might have done, ignoring
the aides who tried to head him off. "I been a fisherman all
my life," Bill said, "and I know that twenty-four-inch bill is
a bad bill." He looked his man over. "Why, *you* know that's
a bad bill, governor, same as I do!" Cuomo, smiling, did not
deny this, and after his speech took an hour to listen to the
fishermen, who made it clear that what they wanted was fair
treatment, not charity or welfare. The governor said that
he assumed that few of the men voted, and that those who
did would vote Republican; he was not interested in votes,
he said, but what was right. He told the men that the bass
bill decision the year before was the most difficult he had
had to make among all the ten thousand-odd bills that he
had signed. He promised to support a by-catch bill and to
remain informed on the situation.

A fortnight later the Maryland Tidewater Administration (part of the Department of Natural Resources), after years of ignoring the best judgment of its own frustrated biologists, gave in to increasing public pressure to restore the Chesapeake.[17] Abandoning its long-time political commitment to the watermen, it announced that the striped bass had been designated a threatened species in Maryland, on the basis of an "alarmingly low" survival rate in the spring hatch, and that as of January 1985, this valuable fish would be fully protected by a moratorium that was expected to last for at least four years. (As one estuarine biologist remarked, "Maryland has taken a drastic step with the best of hopes, but we have no assurances it will work. Pollution in the bay may have gone too far.")[18] Since the Maryland bass population was all but gone, most sportsmen strongly supported the new ruling, which was bound to increase political pressure for similar legislation the whole length of the Atlantic Coast. Already the National Marine Fisheries Service was considering placing the bass under the Endangered Species Act, which would lead to a federal moratorium of indefinite length.

Years ago, the Marine Fisheries Commission, which now supports the twenty-four-inch bill, listed four consequences of "social" legislation in the fisheries. The consequences of such legislation still apply:

1. The legislation may damage one type of fishery without any measurable gain to the faction responsible for the legislation.
2. The legislation may tend to be nullified—indeed its intended effect reversed—by the laws of other states.
3. The fishes are unable to read the law books and therefore cannot comply with the legislation.
4. It may result in needless waste—social, economic, and biological.

Meanwhile the strong and ancient bass continued to wend its stolid way in and out of the estuaries and bays and north and south along the coasts, serenely at peace in its ability to fathom the hearts of its well-wishers, and secure in the dim intuition that, whatever *Homo sapiens* decides about his own destruction, *Morone saxatilis*, a much older and more tolerant species, will prevail.

# 16.
# Summer of 1983:
# The Havens Crew

In mid-July of 1983, returning to Amagansett to find out who was still fishing on the beach, I met Ben Havens at Stuart's Market. We rode down to the Napeague stretch where Benny's father, William Havens, and the rest of the Havens crew had already arrived with the dory and second truck. It was just past daybreak, and the daybreak set was best, but the ocean toiled with big thick seas from the day before. The men sat quietly in the truck cab staring out at the Atlantic, hoping the waves would subside enough to permit a haul. In summer the crews must make one or two sets early and get off the beach, to avoid excited protests from the tourists.

"I remember Pete," William Havens said, sticking his hand out of the window of his red pickup, "but I don't guess he remembers me, now do ya?" Although we had not met in twenty-seven years, I recalled Billy Havens as a handsome, private, quiet man not much like his hell-raising and boisterous brothers. In the late fifties, when the bass were scarce, he had left the beach to hang menhaden nets in the seine house at Promised Land; he returned to haul-seining when the bass came back strong in the early sixties, joining his brothers Gump and Lindy on Bill Lester's crew. He was later a founder of the Baymen's Association. "Never used to fish in summer then, remember, Pete? Just six weeks in spring and six weeks in the fall."

The first William Havens came from Rhode Island to Shelter Island in the seventeenth century, and his clan would acquire considerable property in North Haven and Sag Harbor. On Shelter Island, the James Havens house (1743) is now a historical monument, and on North Haven (where the family had a British land grant), the beautiful northwest region of the island, called the Stock Farm, was once Havens farmland. The Sag Harbor Havenses were shipbuilders and whalers, and Benny says that in the Revolutionary War a Havens whaleboat helped sink a British battleship in Long Island Sound.

In the 1890s William's grandfather settled in the Springs, and since that time almost all the men in this East Hampton branch of the family have been baymen. His father, William Henry Havens, moved to Amagansett in the twenties, and fished on the beach for many years with all three crews of the Posey Lesters; I remembered him as an enormous strong old man with a gentle face who used to fill in now and then on Bill Lester's crew. Henry used to say it was bad luck to whistle while fishing, which would brew a storm, and other fishermen seem to agree, since one never hears whistling on the beach. (Some fishermen won't shave during a poor stretch of fishing: "If we can't catch nothin, we can't afford no razor blade.") The Havens house on the old Montauk Highway at the east end of Amagansett overlooked the ocean, and according to Benny, who liked to keep him company, the old man in his final years—he died in 1965—would sit with a long brass spyglass up in the scuttlehole[1] when his sons set gill nets or cod trawls off the shore.

All five of Henry Havens's sons—William, Sidney (Lindy), Orie (Hipboots), Floyd (Gump), and Fred—have been fishermen at one time or another. Fred, Lindy, and

William are still fishing—Lindy lives in the old Havens
house—and William's sons Ben and Billy and Fred's son
Fred fish on this crew.

As a teen-ager in the early sixties, Benny Havens had
gone haul-seining with Ted Lester, like his father before
him, and his grandfather, too. He had also helped Cap'n
Frank set his old sturgeon nets, and he recalls how excited
he was by his first experience with big whiptail rays and
sharks. While in high school, Benny fished mostly with Milt
Miller, gill-netting and power-seining in the bay, but the
adventure of surf fishing had already hooked him, and Milt
was angry when Benny rejoined Ted's crew after finishing
school in 1964. "Spent a lot of time teachin me, I guess,"
Benny says. He was very upset a few weeks later when Milt
blinded himself in his right eye in an accident off Cartwright
Shoal, where he was found lying in his boat by Jimmy Reutershan. "You always think if you was there, that might not
have happened."

Talking of Ted reminded Benny and his father of all
the patches in that old yellow dory. "Ted there, he'd just
wrap something around a hole and keep right on goin;
never had much use for nothin new," said William, laughing. "I recall one time there, he got hung up, tore a V-piece
right out of his net, lost four hundred boxes. Most fellas
would be out of business two–three days, but not Ted. He
was a good net man, Ted was, and he run right home,
found some old nettin in the rafters and hung her in there.
Goddamn it, them Poseys caught some fish with them old
rags! You wouldn't believe it! Ted was back on the beach
and got a hundred more boxes that same day. Oh yes, he
was a live wire, Ted was, a real piss-cutter."

Benny says he "enjoyed fishin with Ted, cause I always
worked on Ted's end once the net was set. He would work
the inshore end [where the dory is launched], and I went
back down there when the dory came ashore. He worked
me hard, but I never let him bother me: I thought a lot of

Ted, you know. I pulled the truck ahead, jumped out, pulled the net out of the sand, tied on, ran the line up and down, and he would just stand up there hollerin, tendin the winch."

After two years on the beach, Benny went into the service; by the time he returned, Ted had sold his rig. Benny fished with Francis Lester for a year before starting a new crew with his Uncle Fred, Bill Leland, and Danny King (whose father, Virgil King, was another veteran of the Ted Lester crews). They fished hard and did well, but he and Danny could not agree on methods. "Once you've fished long enough and you get good at it, well, I don't know about 'good,' but you always think you can fish better than someone else. So you start tellin guys on the crew what to do, and they get arguin, and one guy will quit, start his own crew and that's how it's been goin." When Bill Lester's crew broke up in the early seventies, William and Lindy joined Benny's new crew, and he and his father have worked together ever since.

Bill Lester's rig had been taken over and a new crew formed by his son Calvin, and Bill helped Calvin out for a few seasons, but the day of the old Posey Boys was over. The rig once run by Cap'n Frank, then his son Francis, passed along to Francis's son Jens, who was several years older than his Uncle Calvin. Both had fished with Ted for a few years, and they fished together for a while in the early seventies. "When Ted got sick there, Stewart didn't want his father's rig," William explained. "He was already draggin and lobsterin. So Ted sold it to Pete Kromer, who still has it. Lindy's fishin some with that crew now."

"Not long after Ted quit the beach," Ben told me when his father was out of earshot, "Lindy and Dom-Dom [Dominick Grace] decided that Cap'n Bill was gettin too old for this work—well, they were wrong. Why hell, it must have been '68, when the bass was at its height, Bill and his crew hit 367 boxes right down here to Hither Plains!" Benny

Havens pointed. "And Ted's crew come along and got one hundred boxes more from the same bunch. That was September 1968, because I was with Francis, and we had been fishin every day on that same set, but that day we stayed home: it was Francis's birthday! Francis ain't *never* goin to forget *that* birthday! Bill's haul was the record around here, and it still is. That crew was Old Bill and my dad there, Lindy, Gump, and Dom-Dom, probably the best crew was ever on this beach. Anyway, Bill's crew started in to fightin amongst themselves once Bill was gone, and the drinkin caught up with Lindy, and finally that crew broke up for good."

Ben Havens and his father ("We used to fight like cats and dogs, just like Ted and Stewart") have been fishing together now for fifteen years and get on well, running the crew from opposite ends of the beach. Although Benny put this rig together, he respects his father's long experience and regards him as the leader of the crew. He did not work well with his younger brother Nick, who eventually left the beach to work on the draggers, but gets on fine with his brother Billy and young cousin Fred who, with Doug Kuntz, made up the present crew.

The Havens, Calvin Lester, and Danny King crews, with their big dories, are the strongest crews left on the beach. Jens and Francis, with a smaller rig, haul seine less regularly, spending more time over on the bay. "Pete Kromer has a big rig, too, but the guys on that crew now are older, and they don't fish that hard," Benny Havens says. "The older you get, the leerier you get with the ocean. The young guys will fish harder weather, but eventually it will get you, the boat will roll over or something. I don't think you should be out there if you're scared. I've been leery of it myself a lot of times when it's a heavy sea. You want everything workin for you, you know; if you break one shear pin in the surf, you're done. Them big heavy motor dories, solid full of net, you just can't row 'em; you can hold them, maybe, if you get back of the surf, but it's almost impossible to row 'em. Nineteen eighty, I broke a shear pin, and my brother Nick made it to shore to get another, but I watched him pretty nearly drown, tryin to swim back; he was in too much of a rush, got tired out, and Sammy Merritt had to go in after him." (Stuart Vorpahl, Jr., haul-seining with his father and his brother Billy in the mid-sixties, was going off in the dory when the motor stalled, the pull-cord broke, and the dory filled up and rolled over; the sand roil filled his waders as he washed along, he could not find his footing, and might have drowned if Tommy Bennett had not caught up with him and grabbed him by the hair.)

We drove along the beach a ways, looking for fish sign. "Used to make our first set in the dark," Benny said. "Now we have to hunt 'em. Can't just slap her in anywhere no more. With four–five real calm days like this, them god-damn sand crabs move inshore so thick you get 'em strung out all along the wings and maybe eighty boxes in the bunt. Got to wait till they move off again, at daylight. Day in, day out, the daybreak set is best." He pointed at the terns and gulls working offshore, like night spirits in the soft half-light. The horizon softened, took on color, and behind the birds, here and there on the horizon, moved the dark slow silhouettes of draggers. "Anyway, them fish is wider'n they was yesterday. Looks like them draggers pushed 'em out. That one close in, that's Scottie Bennett's *Seafarer;* Nick's on there as crew. They done good squiddin for a while, but now the squid are fallin off, they're down to flukin."

Another big dragger was working just behind the bar, and the Havenses discussed the damage done to the inshore fishing grounds in recent years by all these boats, and the pressure on fish stocks offshore from the long-range factory stern trawlers that had turned up from Europe and Japan in the 1950s. "Twenty-six draggers out here the other day, all in sight at once," William Havens said, "and some of them foreign boats got their nets in night and day. That big one you see there, farthest off, that's the Spanish squid boat took the place of them Japanese was here last year. For them boats there ain't no such thing as trash fish, they don't throw nothin back at all, save every fish, and I guess there's nothin wrong with that. But they ain't doin us one bit of good, tearin up the ground the way they do. And now the bass bill hangin over our heads, and all them new gill-netters, them part-timers, on Montauk, gettin the sportsmen down on us by setting net between the rocks; and all these city people hollerin like hell if one crab gets left behind after a haul. They're squeezin us right off the beach, the way they done to Bobby Lester down Southampton."

The crews are beset by upset anglers and sunbathers, and also by people who come up and take fish, saying they'll come back with the money; sometimes they just take the fish and run, knowing that busy men in heavy waders cannot chase them. ("If we get a big bunch of fish, we lose quite a few, but there's only so much we can do," says Danny King, a big man with a kind and open face, red cheeks, and an old-fashioned chin beard. "I don't mind if they come up and ask for a fish, I'd more than gladly give it to them, but if they steal it, you know—I just got my principles against stealing.")

Two years ago Danny King's crew was approached on Flying Point, down in Southampton, by the bay constable, who said that the village police had ordered him off the beach. As it turned out, two surfcasters had filed a complaint that the fishing trucks had no beach permit stickers. Danny ignored the order, telling the bay constable that if the village police wanted him off the beach, they had better come down and tell him so themselves. The police never came, and he fished there the rest of that autumn. But Bobby Lester, tired of the pressure, finally gave up haul-seining to go lobstering.

"Ain't hardly a crew down west no more," William was saying. "Roger White and Sonny Schellinger, is all. Not even a farmer crew in Sagaponack! Poseys and Bonackers are the last fishermen on the beach, and we got no business here neither, cause there ain't no fish—not this year, by Jesus! It ain't just the bass. There wasn't enough fish anywhere all spring to pay our gas, although the traps done pretty good, over on the bay; one day they come in with two truckloads of weakfish when we couldn't scrape up one damn carton."

Benny recalled a nine-week period in the fall of 1981 when each man in the crew made just two hundred dollars. Long ago his father had advised him that there was no future in fishing, just as Milt Miller had advised his son, just as all their fathers had advised almost every fisherman on the beach. Today Benny was saying the same to his boy, Michael, despite his own lifelong commitment. "I don't know what I would do if I didn't fish. Cause that's all I've done. I enjoy it. I love it. It's my life, really. It's like huntin, I love to hunt, but it's vanishin out here; even huntin is goin. There's no land left, you know."

"Well, them bass are going to come back, just like they always done," William said. "For the last four–five years we been gettin plenty of short bass, lots of them real little ones, just slip like spearin through the mesh. Somebody was tellin me there's plenty of them little bass up the Peconic River, thinks maybe they're spawnin up there, and over in Connecticut, too. Them biologists tell us all our bass come from the Chesapeake, but we don't believe it; they been taggin bass down there for twenty years, and not one of them tagged fish has ever showed up in the thousands and thousands of fish in our nets and traps, not even one."

We discussed the fact that on Long Island the striped bass was scarce for over a half century, from the 1880s until the 1940s. In our own lifetimes, such common commercial species as bluefish, sea bass, weakfish, kingfish, yellowtail, fluke, porgies, butterfish, and blowfish had all declined seriously, or disappeared, for years at a time. The deepwater tilefish vanished so completely near the turn of the century that for several decades it was thought to have gone extinct: for the last five years, commercial tilefish landings have approached three million pounds, nearly twice the harvest of blues, weaks, fluke, and both black-backed and yellowtail flounders, and exceeded only by porgy and whiting.

"Water's chippin up there now—was slick a minute ago," Benny Havens said, sniffing the wind. "See that black at the edge of the slick, do ya? Ain't no fish under that bait; we'd seen 'em. Just four–five bluefish gulls[2] dippin, is all; them little-gulls[3] got their bellyful, comin ashore now. But all that bait is a good sign, maybe got pushed down here from the east'rd by them weakfish that must be comin round the Point, lookin for cold water. Bass will be herdin up now, too, maybe they can feel that autumn comin." Adjusting his black cap on his balding head, Benny, a shy, sand-colored man, made a wry grin, as if surprised that he had talked so much. "Heck, I don't know nothin any more, not a damn thing. Everythin's changin on us, too damn fast to keep up with. Other day here, had three–four weakfish with roe, middle of July! How can that be? And them shitepokes don't belong here neither, not in midsummer." He pointed at four loons swimming along just behind the first wave. Classified 'em as song birds now, ain't allowed to shoot 'em way we used to. Milton George, he's ate them damned things, but I could never. Can't eat striped bass neither: don't like the taste of it."

His father nodded in agreement: "Bass just ain't a eatin fish," William Havens said. "Can't understand the high price that they put on it. Back when you was fishin with us, there was times when bass was like bluefish is today, remember? You wouldn't get ten cents a pound." Apparently the public had gotten used to eating bass when they were plentiful and cheap, and as soon as they were scarce again, they became a delicacy.

"In the days when I used to go with Milt, out around Gardiners in the sixties," Benny said, "we'd take our ice and food, we had little huts to stay in out there, never come in much. And Milt'd eat them young gulls out of the nest; before they started in to eatin fish, Milt said, they tasted like chicken!" Milt Miller was famous for trying out everything in the natural world that might be edible; I mentioned his discovery that the roe of horseshoe crabs looked and tasted like good sturgeon caviar, and we all laughed.

Remembering the sturgeon in Ted's nets, I asked if sturgeon still showed up in the spring, and William said that old Cap'n Frank, who was ninety-three this year, had been the last man to set nets for sturgeon. A few were still taken by the draggers, and Cap'n Bill still liked to fix the roe, but the haul-seiners rarely saw one. "Don't pay you to set net for 'em no more, nor codfish neither.

"Old Bill was a good fisherman, all right, Ted and Frank, too," William recalled. "Frank never let nothin bother him, you know, just took things as they come, and Bill always acted pretty calm, but I guess he wasn't. One time there, goin off in rough weather, he was hollerin at us, 'Pull! Pull!'; he was clenchin his teeth so hard on that first sea that he bit his pipe stem off! He was always spittin, all them Lesters done that, but Bill used to actually get sick sometimes before the first set in the mornin, and he told me he never did that on days when there weren't no fishin, so I guess you might say that Bill was nervous, too.

"I recall one mornin it were blowin a livin gale, and Happy Lester, he were the youngest next to Ted, he spit to windward, hit me right in the face with one of them big oysters—goddamn, I was mad!" William Havens laughed, looking around for his dog, Cap, which rides with him wherever he goes. "Where's my dog," he muttered, genuinely uneasy; he grunted when he saw the small white dog running through the dunes. "Cap'n Slime! That fella never give a damn about nothin! Bachelor, you know, lived with his mother there in the old homestead, never had no car, I don't believe, lost all his teeth. All he cared about was drinkin beer, which is why his brothers was so down on him. Called him Happy, and sometimes it seems to me his mother called him Harlin, somethin like that, but I believe that his real name was Harold.

"I was there that mornin up Georgica Coast Guard when Jenny Lester come to the beach, said Happy had hung hisself; they found him on his knees there in that old shed back of where the Lester homestead used to be. And Bill and Ted looked at each other and both of 'em said at the same time, 'Well, I expected it.' I don't know how a fella could bring himself to do that, hang himself on his knees! And Harry Lester, who was the oldest brother, the one turned to house paintin and moved away to the east end of Amagansett, he hung himself, too, but that was long ago. He was named Harry and Happy was Harold. Harry and Harold."

That morning it was too rough to set, and after a while I returned to Stuart's Seafood. Montauk Seafood was going strong when Stuart Vorpahl, Sr., opened his own market across the highway, off Oak Street. That spring of 1955, Stuart Junior had signed up with the East Hampton high school team as pitcher, but the same afternoon, arriving home, he was told by his father to get to work digging out a foundation. The night before, Stuart Senior had arrived late at Montauk Seafood with a good catch of spearing, and Ted would not open up for him; furious, he swore then and there that he would establish his own packing house. Young Stuart spent the rest of that spring working on the new building after school—"the end of my baseball career," he says. With one thousand dollars—borrowed with great difficulty from the bank—and credit extended by the men who brought him fish, Old Stuart got his start, and kept on going. Not long thereafter, profiting from his example, Scotty Eames opened Scotty's Fish Market on Schellinger Road.

These days Stuart's, run by Billy Vorpahl, is the only fish market in Amagansett, and most of the baymen of the region pack out their fish there.[4] The catch is unloaded from trucks into large tubs in which sand and blood and gurry are washed off, after which the fish are weighed, packed into the cardboard cartons that have replaced the wood boxes of thirty years ago, then iced and tagged. Every evening from Sunday to Thursday the fish are picked up by trucks from the Fulton Fish Market, and the ice, cartons, utilities, and freight (about seven cents per pound of fish) are deducted from the checks returned by the wholesale fish dealers. Because the abuse has continued for so long, the fishermen routinely expect that the dealers will deduct 10 percent of the real weight of every shipment; protest as they will, they are told their scales are wrong, and they must take what they get. And this graft is routine, not only at the Fulton Market but also in Greenport, New Bedford, and other places where their fish might be sold. The one exception in recent years has been the market in Newport, Rhode Island, famous among fishermen as the only honest market in the region.

At Stuart's, I ran into Frank Lester's youngest son, Richard. "Been fishin all my life," he told me, "and this is the worst year I ever seen—the worst!" At forty-seven, he is the same age that his Uncle Ted was when we all fished together thirty years ago, and he has the same ruddy face, pale ice-blue eyes, and big Posey nose. Richard is known as a good surfman and good fisherman, though inconsistent. "He's always flutterin around, watchin to see how other fishermen are makin out," one man told me. "He's always changin, and he's always a day late. If you want to make a livin as a fisherman, you got to stick to one thing, you got to grind it." But Richard has always been cheerful and likable, and despite his frustration, he was cheerful still.

A few days later I met Richard at Louse Point, at the

mouth of Accabonac Creek, where he moors a small, home-rigged dragger named the *Rainbow*. Like many of the older baymen, he is an able carpenter and welder, and the cabin, boom, dragging frame, and drum on this thirty-six-foot one-time bunker seine boat were all of his own manufacture.

In the late afternoon of a long summer day, we ran out of Bonac Creek into Gardiners Bay, where the *Rainbow* made two drags of an hour each. "Been fishin since I was twelve years old, y'know, quit school at sixteen. I can write a little but I don't read too good. What the hell do I need with readin them old books"—Richard nudged me—"when I got this life on the water here to keep me busy?"

Richard, born in 1935, can remember hauling seine on Frank's one-truck crew; he also accompanied his father pin-hooking for sea bass on the wreck of the old *Catherine* off Amagansett Beach.[5] But his first years as a haul-seiner were with his Uncle Ted "because I was havin some kind of a mix-up with my brothers back in them days." Grinning, Richard imitated Ted: "Let's go! Let's go! Let's go!" He shook his head, recalling the time Ted lost his fingertip when the rope jumped on the winch; Ted had gone right on, unheeding, until the bag was on the beach. "Blood all over the truck!" Richard exclaimed, rearing his head back before squinting at me, just as his uncle might have done.

According to Richard, the younger men who ran the crews had mostly been trained by himself and William Havens; though he started with Ted, he says he was taught fishing by his father, who had also taught many other fishermen who are still on the water. I was still with Ted when Richard returned to his father's crew, and it was Richard and Ding-Ding (his brother Harry) and young Walter Bennett who were in Frank's dory on that day in '55 when we saw its backward somersault from down the beach.

"Didn't have no weather to go off," Richard admitted. "Guess my dad was against it, and my brother Francis, too, but we never give them much to say about it. We was young and broke, so we tried her anyway. Ding-Ding was settin net, and he got thrown clear when she went over, but I was under that boat a while, and Walter, seemed like he was under three–four minutes before you fellas found him. Had a lot of crews there by the end, helpin get everything straightened out; that net was some hell of a mess, washin around like that! But I don't guess old Walter ever went back in the boat again; I believe that was the last time he ever climbed into a dory, and I ain't surprised.

"There's a lot of fellas that you knew ain't around no more. On Uncle Bill's old fifties crew, Dingie Schellinger died of a heart attack, I believe, Roney Marasca, too, and Billy Lester died of emphysema. Old Bill lost both boys from his first family; Kenny went before Billy did, tendin his gill net at Napeague in April. Water was some cold and rough that mornin, and I told him not to go setting no damn net in that old boat, she'd open up on him, but Kenny said Hell, there was only the one net, he'd just keep bailin. Well, the boat filled and he swum ashore, but then he died; had one of them fits in the shallow water. Tongue-tied, you know. He was still warm when we laid him in the truck."

"I remember that day," Stewart Lester says, "cause I was goin down to get me some wood, make squirrel cages. I had found a nest of 'em, and I seen my Cousin Billy go tearin by and knew somethin was wrong. What Kenny done, he took Uncle Charlie's old sharpie that had cedar plankin, and cedar gets dry, you know, have to soak it good for a few days to let her swell. But Kenny wanted them mackerel nets set, just wouldn't listen, and that boat filled up on him. Got ashore, too, before he had his fit; that fella died in six inches of water."

The *Rainbow*'s first drag was completely dry, not a single porgy, but Richard assured me that the first tow after sunset, when the fish on the bottom could not make out the oncoming trawl, would be much better. This second tow

produced twenty pounds of porgies and a single weakfish—
scarcely enough to pay his gas. Richard shrugged, uncom-
plaining, and headed back toward Accabonac. "Money ain't
everythin, you know. Made seven hundred dollars in April,
shared up one hundred dollars on May 10, and got off the
beach. They ain't nothin I ain't tried this year, and I ain't
done nothin; I made five hundred dollars in the past two
months! My wife tells me to slow down, but what do I want
to slow down for? Can't rest anyways if there's somethin to
be done." Shaking his head a little, Richard grinned. "It's a
great life if you don't weaken, ain't that right?"

Before daylight next morning, using his sharpie, we
tended the gill nets that Richard sets behind Gardiners Island, in Tobacco Lot Bay. Since the days when we used to
go gunning there on Cartwright Shoal, the sandbar had
disappeared under the surface, but the bar is still too shoal
to cross, even in a sharpie, and we had to swing way wide,
out to the southward. Across the soft morning water I could
see Abraham's Landing, where Abraham Schellinger had
landed cargos from his sailing ships nearly three centuries
before. The Devon summer colony started here about 1910,
and this sheltered corner of the bay is still the site of a
private yacht club, where white sailing craft as elegant as
swans turned slowly in the early summer light. Farther east
stood the old rust-streaked buildings of the dead fish factory
at Promised Land, and the brick stacks on which ospreys
used to nest, and the stubble of black creosoted pilings
where the docks of the old Edwards Brothers fish company
were sagging down into the bay.

Off Napeague, we swung northeast, heading up along
the back side of the island; along the shoal, long narrow
splashes were sign of a feeding squadron of bonita. Richard
waved to his cousin Brentford Bennett, with whom he
set nets for about five years after the bass declined, in the
early seventies; young Brent had lifted and was on his way
inshore.

In Tobacco Lot Bay, the latest fish sign was shouted across the water by Tom Knobel, who was setting a run-around net on a school of bluefish; hearing him speak, it seemed surprising that Knobel had come from the city just a few years before. He had married a Parsons, Richard said, and settled at Lazy Point, picking up his new trade mostly from Brent Bennett. When I remarked that this young outsider spoke better Bonac than the Bonackers, Richard squinted at me, then laughed, leaning out of the skiff to grab the flag buoy on the first net.

At sunrise, a breeze from the northeast caused the oily slick on the summer sea to glisten, and terns were dipping on a school of fish, and the day was fine. I took the cork line and Richard the leads, and Richard became his old exhilarated self as a day's pay in big porgies and weakfish came flapping in over the side. Gill nets average about one thousand feet long, and are set in various depths and currents. For bass, they are set close to the beach, but bass are sedentary in summer, and these were well out in the open water. "We're havin some fun this mornin, ain't we? With the price of porgies the way it is, they pay better than weaks! I got fifty dollars here, I guess, with them four big weaks— that's good enough to keep *me* happy!" And helping him haul, I felt exhilarated myself. Handling net, talking boats and gear, gave me the illusion that I still knew what I was doing.

Asked how his brother Lewis was getting along, Richard raised his eyebrows and said, "Same as ever." Lewis had hauled seine on the beach until the bass decline in the late fifties. By the time the bass came back strong a few years later, he was running a dragger for Norman Edwards, who was away in southern waters much of the year as captain on a bunker steamer. When I last heard of Lewis, he was "fil-litin" and shucking shellfish for the new seafood shop in Wainscott, but since then, Richard said, he had gone back to the bay. Harry was also on the bay; Bobby was ocean lobstering out of Montauk; Francis was still setting fykes and gill nets and working with his son Jens on the family crew.

Back in '75–'76, Richard and Harry had made their last attempt to set their father's sturgeon nets, but the draggers, working ever closer to the beach, had damaged the nets and driven both bass and sturgeon way offshore. These days the draggers were picking up striped bass four or five miles out, where in Richard's opinion they did not belong. Like most local fishermen, he resents the foreign boats, particularly the huge Russian trawlers with their fine-mesh nets that permit nothing whatever to escape: they crush the young lobsters, the fishermen say, and they spoil the fishing grounds. "But the government don't bother the draggers none, nor the Russians neither; the ones they come after are the last poor Poseys that ain't got sense enough to quit the beach." Richard himself had put a crew together in 1979 but gave it up after 1982. The fish were too few, and the new men so uncommitted that they walked off the beach if anyone got bossy. "It seems like the crews you get today don't want to fish so hard. Quite a few don't know their job, don't know how to mend."

In the early sixties, Richard said, his father had injured his hip while digging steamers down at Shinnecock, and a few years later had been forced to give up fishing. Although a little senile now, he had lost none of the good spirits that had maintained him all his life. "I had a wonderful wife, just lost her three or four years ago," Cap'n Frank had said in 1978. "We were married sixty-five and a half years. I own this house here. I got all my boys [Francis, Lewis, Bobby, Harry, Richard] and these kids who used to go fishin with me are grown up—the Havens boys—and they all give me anything I want, all the scallops I want to eat and all the fish; I don't have to buy nothing . . ."[6]

Until recently, Cap'n Frank had raised a lot of chickens and vegetables in the backyard, insisting on old-fashioned bunker dressing for the garden. "You put a bunker in each hill when you're planting corn," he used to say, "and the stalks'll be a foot high before you're out of the garden."[7] At ninety-three, he was still lively and liked nothing better than talking about fishing, and Richard said he would be glad to see me; Richard, who lives in a trailer behind Frank's house in Poseyville, offered to take me to visit Cap'n Frank whenever I wanted.

Like most Poseys, Richard quit school at sixteen, and he has always been a fisherman; he says he has never worked at a regular job. He peered across the silvered water of the bay, waving his arm to indicate the bay and islands, all the way north and west toward Orient Point. "Out on the water all day long and nobody to bother you—you can't beat that." Richard cocked his head, the better to squint at me. "You been travelin all over, and I bet you ain't never seen a better place than this one here. I ain't never seen better; I just don't want to be no place else."

# 17.

# Indian Summer

O n August 8, 1983, after a fight of more than thirty years, the latest version of the bass bill became law. Because of all the editorials against the bass bill, and because of the prevailing rumor that Governor Cuomo was troubled by the bill, the baymen had convinced themselves that it would be vetoed. When he signed it, the men were shocked. "No matter what we do, we seem to be going backwards," said Richard Lester, whose bad luck had continued into August.

On the Backside, early in the month, the haul-seiners had been making a day's pay, but the market price on everything but bass was dropping quickly. "Whatever we catch, that's what's cheap," Benny Havens said one morning at Sagaponack, where the Havens and Calvin Lester crews were picking out a few blues and weaks from the red rolling mass of jellyfish in the seines. "Can't set till sunrise in the summer cause you just load up with crabs the way them farmers done"—William pointed down the beach to where John White was kneeling on the sand, picking the pale spotted crabs out of his gill net—"and after sunrise we load up with jellyfish."

William told me that Cap'n Frank had died two nights

before. "Long about one in the mornin, they found him half-sittin up in bed, knees up, you know, a kind of half-smile on his face." William, Ben, and Billy Havens, Milt Miller, Donnie Eames, and Bill Lester's brother-in-law, Dick Wood, had been pallbearers the previous afternoon, when Frank Lester was buried at the Oakwood Cemetery in Amagansett; a large crowd had turned out for the patriarch's funeral, where the following poem, written by his granddaughter, was read:

> *Our kind and gentle father and grandfather*
> *How we thought you would never wear out*
> *Your eyesight faded, your memories dim*
> *He insisted on the silliest whims*
> *Never a complaint had he*
> *Always with a tale of the sea*
> *There is a Special Someone*
> *Willing to give him a place in the sun*
> *Where he won't have to worry, wonder, or doubt*
> *That is what God is all about.*

I remembered Frank Lester as a mild, warm, gaunt-faced man with a soft laugh who had seemed to embody the acceptance and serenity of another epoch, what one person has called a "way back way of living."[1] I was very sorry that I had not talked with him again before he died.

"Even though he was older than you," recalls Frank's grandson Walter Bennett, "it didn't seem like he thought he was any better. We went blue-crabbin one summer up at Georgica and got two bushel, got a check for eight dollars for one of 'em and he handed that over to the kids. If you did the work, he'd give you the money; this was one of the things about the family, everybody loved their children. When we were kids, we used to come down and just curl up on the rug. There was him and maybe Uncle Charlie and Uncle Ted or Uncle Bill. We didn't have no TV and we'd sit there and just listen to them stories; it was well worth it, I'll tell ya that. We used to hear the huntin stories and the fishin stories, and we'd keep him goin, ask about another dog he had, or 'What about the geese?' "

Not long ago, Cap'n Frank told Walter Bennett that "no one should live this old; the hardest part of life is when you're layin around." But everyone agreed he had been fine until the last six weeks. After that, he had gone fast, and somehow his death seemed related to the passage of the bass bill a fortnight earlier.

Two days after the funeral, the last of the Posey Boys, Captain Bill Lester, in black cap, black shirt, and black pants, came to Bridgehampton with the five haul-seine crews, their families, trucks, and dories. The baymen had come to picket the bass bill's sponsor, state assemblyman Patrick Halpin, who was guest of honor at a fund-raising reception. Halpin's hostess, a new summer resident in an elaborate house on Sagaponack Pond, came outside to ask these unfashionable folks not to spoil her party; what the fishermen and their families should do was go away. "I let you fish my pond," she reminded them reproachfully, waving her fingers at the calm reach of Sagaponack Pond, stretching away a half mile or more to the ocean beach. Billy Havens, dark hair flying from beneath his Yankee baseball cap, stared at her, incredulous. "Sagg is *your* pond now? After hundreds of years, we got to have *your* permission to fish here? I don't *think* so, lady!"

Halpin, arriving, offered a dazzling smile, extending both hands to the small crowd like a celebrity, but Billy Havens, outraged, refused to shake either one of them. Arnold Leo, Secretary of the Baymen's Association, informed Halpin that he was wasting his time—"You don't know how these people feel about you!" The politician tried to justify his efforts on behalf of the striped bass, but he did not really know what he was talking about, and his crisp blazer and

blow-dried hair elicited jeers from the wives of the angry
fishermen. When someone addressed him as "Mr. Halpin,"
there were cries of "Don't you call him Mister!" Tom Lester's wife, Cathy, and Stewart Lester's daughter Gail did
most of the talking for the women, and Carol Havens told
Halpin, "If you ever done a day's work fishing, you'd never
survive it! How come you never come out here, went fishing
with us, never learned the truth? This man here"—she
pointed at Captain Bill—"he can tell you more about fishing
than all them people you listen to put together! You're just
out for yourself, out for your own ambitions, you don't care
about the harm you done to families that's been fishin for
three hundred years!" Bill Lester tried to explain matters
to Halpin, but the people were too angry to stop interrupt-
ing, and the politician, sticking it out in the face of much
more hostility and distress than he had expected, could not
concentrate on the mild-spoken old man, and soon beat a
retreat into the house.

Walking back to his car as the demonstration started to
break up, Cap'n Bill remarked that his brother's death had
been a blessing. "Frank couldn't do nothin no more, and
that's no good. I'm gettin the same way, with this arthur-
itis; that stuff's no good, you know, not for men like me
and Frank that liked to work. There's something beautiful
about work; I don't know why these younger fellers are so
afraid of it. Fishin's a hard life, but it's a good 'un; it was
an honest way of life, Frank used to say. All you need is a
little ambition and some drive. Need some intelligence, too,
I guess," Cap'n Bill grunted, shifting himself into the car.
"But not too much."

In Indian summer, with the bass so scarce, most of the haul-
seiners went scalloping. The local bay scallop is far superior
in quality to the big sea scallop and also to the calico pecten,
a deepwater species from the continental shelf off the Carolinas and Florida that was competing for the New York mar-

ket. But the bay scallops were so scattered and the eyes so small that many baymen, such as Stewart Lester, went north to Orient or all the way up Peconic Bay to Flanders in search of enough scallops to make up a day's pay. Others gave up quickly and returned to the beach, where the bass remained scarce, and the abundant bluefish were worth nothing.

On September 27 Jens Lester's crew started a set in marginal conditions, and his steel dory, going off, took a big sea over the bow; the water and two thousand pounds of netting put her down by the stern, and she filled and sank. "Them tin boats don't float too good," one fisherman said.

In 1974 Jens had acquired the first steel dory used on the beach; the dory was built by Tommy Field of Amagansett, who built a larger one two years later for Danny King. Steel dories do not open up like the wood boats, which take a pounding on the trailers; the bottom planks must be kept wet and swollen to avoid leaking, and therefore the weight is approximately the same. "Steel boats sink quick, though, I can testify to that," Jens Lester says. "Thing of it was, the feller drivin the truck hit the brake too quick durin the launchin, dropped us off short in the slosh. Then a freak sea come, and we took that over the bow. We still got off all right, but with that big load of net, she was down by the stern already, and every time the bow went up high on a wave, we were takin more water in over the stern. Other times when we filled up, we was able to bail her, but this time I seen that we weren't goin to make it; I tried to turn her back toward the beach, and I holler at my nephew there [Tim Kromer] to grab the life jackets. Well, just then she goes out from under us, she goes under, quick as that, and here we are maybe halfway to the bar.

"I was the first back to the surface, and the cod-end buoy was close by, and when the boy come up, I told him to grab onto it. Just then one of the life jackets shows up, and we have that, too. That young fella was kind of panicked, but I told him just to take things easy, and pretty soon we was able to kick our waders off; in deep water, with any air in 'em, them waders is liable to turn you upside down. Then I seen my son [Mitchell Lester] tryin to swim out to us, didn't have no life jacket or nothin, and I hollered at him to go back. We were thinkin of swimmin for it ourselves when Calvin shows up comin ninety miles an hour down the beach; the guys on our crew had got him on the CB."

Calvin Lester's crew was "maybe a mile down the beach, gettin ready to set," Calvin told me. "I seen Jens's dory go off, looked like she was ridin all right to me, but when I happened to glance back a moment later, she was gone— just disappeared. So I yelled to Walter [Walter Bennett], 'Where's that dory, Walt?' And he was damned if he could figure it out either. And just then word come in over the CB that the dory was sunk. So we just heaved most of the net out of our boat to make her lighter, all one wing and quarter and the bunt, and cut her off and got the hell down the beach and went off after 'em."

Calvin is a strong, quick man with wild blond hair and glasses; like his Uncle Ted, he never stops moving. At thirty-one, he has already made a reputation as one of the best fishermen on the East End, hard-working, shrewd, and well-endowed with the mysterious gift called Posey smell, which anticipates where the fish are going to be. He is also hotheaded and outspoken, and he was angry that local newspaper accounts of the dory sinking got certain details wrong; it was almost as if he were defending the integrity of his way of life, and doing it fiercely out of frustration that his own stubbornness and dedication might not be enough to prevent that way of life from going under. "One said we was haulin when word come that Jens' dory sunk, and another said we was loadin the net into the dory! Weren't doin neither one! And they said J.P. [James Fenelon] was in the dory, and he don't *never* go into the boat; the only ones that go are me'n Donnie! [Don Eames, Jr.] People *read* this stuff! Why can't they get it right?"

Calvin glared at me because I was a writer, and one of the guilty writers was my friend. "Anyway, I don't see why they make so much of goin after 'em. What're we goin to do now, leave 'em out there? All the crews came up, helped 'em straighten things out, and a dragger, too, and them fellas would have done the same for us. Sure, they was scared, but they're okay, and we got a diver out there, brought the dory up. It's all part of this life, and you have to accept it."

Captain Bill Lester, discussing the episode when I stopped in to visit him next morning, recalled the time that Frank's younger boys and young Walter Bennett had their dory somersault on top of them "down Hither Plains"; he was pleased when I reminded him that I was there that day. "B'god, bub, that's right, you was with us, *you* was! Know what I'm talkin about, *you* do." He reidentified me for the benefit of his wife, Lottie, who offered us coffee at the kitchen table in the small house on Cross Highway in Poseyville where Bill has lived most of his life. On the wall behind him was a photograph of Bill and his son Calvin. Though Bill has five daughters, Calvin is his only surviving son; a younger boy, Paul, died in a car accident about ten years ago. Bill did not mention any daughters' names; it is noticeable, among older fishermen, that even when present, daughters (as well as other women) are apt to be called Sis.

Bill's first wife died of cancer back in 1949, and all four children of that first family are dead, too. "Kenneth drowned—don't remember Kenneth? Girl died of leukemia, other girl never seen life at all, and she was in perfect shape; her mother thought she was such a nice healthy girl. Few years ago, 1979, Billy, my oldest boy, why, he died, too.

"Yep, I had a lot of hard luck and some pretty good luck. After I lost my wife, you know, I didn't care for nothin, give all my land away and all. And then I found another beautiful woman"—he nodded in the direction of Lottie Lester, who had gone out to tend to something in the garden before going to work. "I been called an old miser, y'know, cause I love to save, and she's just the opposite, money burns a hole in her pocket! But she's a worker! Good thing for me, ain't it? Just lucky, I was. That's better'n bein a billionaire, now ain't that right?" Bill got up slowly to answer the telephone. "Damn arthur-itis. If I get any lamer, I'll be lame, won't I?"

Bill smiled as he said this; he has the same cheerful spirit as his late brother. As he says, "We have eels, we have fish, we have clams, we have scallops; probably one eighth of what we eat comes out of the water. Eat a mess of fish, mess of scallops, save five–ten dollars. Them poor people in the city on Social Security ain't got nothin to eat; they can't go out on the water and get clams or eel, so I feel very sorry for them.

"I had a very good life, a very good life. I have got into some awful, awful tight jams, but I come out of it; the good Lord was with me, I guess. Times we had plenty and times we were short, but it was a good, clean, healthy life, a beautiful life. I would do it all over again. Ninety-nine percent of it was workin for myself, that was the beauty of my life."

Returning from the telephone, Cap'n Bill resumed his train of thought. "Course fellers always jumped around from crew to crew, same way they do today, but I had pretty much the same crew for near twenty years, from the time you was fishin with Ted until early seventies. We just got along the best of any of 'em. I was head man, I guess, but if one of the crew suggested somethin, I always went along, agreed with it, we tried it out, and if it didn't work, why, we went back. That way, you know, everybody's happy. Then we broke up, you know, fellers had their own family, wanted their own crew, and I was gettin old; I was stumblin around out there, and had to stop. My boy Calvin was fishin with me, and he took over the rig about ten years ago. But he took me along with him, y'know, right up until year before last, when I was eighty-two."

("He knows what he's doin," Calvin says shortly, in a way that suggests that the same can't be said of everybody on the beach.)

Old Bill gazed fondly at the photograph on the wall. "Oh he's a worker, that boy is, he don't let up; goin eighteen hours a day. But with fishin the way it is, I worry that there ain't no place for him to go. Probably end up poor as me, don't *you* think so?"

Bill sat with both big hands flat on the table. "Gettin old, y'know; I ain't so cocky as I was. All my brothers gone, only my sister Catherine still alive, and she's over there in the hospital after a fall. You remember Charles, I guess?" I nodded: old Charlie Lester was no longer a fisherman in the early fifties, but he was often around Ted's yard, keeping track of what was going on. "Charles was wiser'n the rest of us, got into raisin vegetables and chickens, had a little market and done all right, too. Course my brother Harry and my brother Harold died before your time—both su'cides. One day Harold told us he was hearin this loud roarin in his head, couldn't get it out, and not long after that he hung himself, over there in that shed behind the old homestead."

Out of respect for the dead, it seemed, Bill referred to Charlie, Happy, and Kenny as Charles, Harold, and Kenneth; only Ted was Ted. Thinking about Happy, he gave a sigh, as if still wondering if there hadn't been something that the family might have done. "Sold off the old homestead after Mother died, they took it over west, far as Bridgehampton. Too much hardship there, just wanted to be rid of it. There was a great big elm out in the front; that come down, too. Nothin left over there now but a couple of small buildins. My grandson James—that's Billy's boy, sets traps down Montauk—he's livin there now.

"Ted's place was sold off, too, a few years back. Ted had done good, you know, opened Montauk Seafood, then the fish store, then that liquor store out here on the highway.

Even had a little house down there in Florida. But him and Jenny was livin too hard, got in with them middle-class people, what we call the rich, and tried to live harder yet; that's why they died so young, in my opinion. And after they died, their kids was fightin over their property, and most of what Ted put together went to the lawyers. Stewart sold that good wood boat, the *Posey,* got him a tin one, one of them steel hulls that rusts out quick; used that for lobsterin, but then the lobsters dropped out and he had to sell her. I guess that fella's pret' near back down to nothin. House sold off out of the family, both them shops closed down, nothin but weeds and junk in that big yard over there where we used to spread our nets when you was with us.

"Oh yes, everythin keeps changin. In Pop's day, they used to knit up their own nets, in wintertime; then come store-bought cotton nettin, which was kind of tender, and after that come linen twine, *that* was some strong! But we went over to that plastic, what they call nylon, you know, and right away after that somebody thought to put a motor in the dory. Nets got to be three times the size they were, and dories are so big today that a man can't row 'em."

Cap'n Bill was concerned about the harvest of swordfish seventy miles offshore, in the abrupt temperature differential where warm eddies from the Gulf Stream met cold water at the edge of the continental shelf. These days most swordfish are long-lined in deep water by baited hooks about sixty feet apart; sometimes this trawl line is thirty-five miles long. Fifty years ago, swordfish, like cod, came close inshore off the ocean beach; Bill's nephew, Johnnie Erickson, remembers taking a swordfish "in eight fathoms, and another one next day in twelve, both of 'em right in sight of the Montauk office buildins. Them days you might hit one anywhere southwest of the Point." Since then, the inshore dragging fleet has driven them off into deeper water, all the way to the fifty-fathom line.

Like all commercial species, swordfish vary in abundance from year to year. Despite increasing pressure, the best swordfish year on record was said to be 1982, when Bill saw one long-liner come in with decks awash due to the weight of 350 swordfish. But nine out of ten of the fish caught, he said, were "pups" of sixty pounds or less; how long could the fish sustain that harvest? Anyway, the taste of fish dead on the hook was poor compared to those harpooned and bled aboard the boat; it was a waste. He had also heard that Japanese tuna long-liners were killing swordfish right and left; the speed of the retrieval gear ripped their mouths apart, leaving them prey to sharks and starvation. Yet the commercial men were apprehensive about the proposal of the Mid-Atlantic Fisheries Council to halt swordfishing on the East Coast for an unspecified period, because of the decline in average size of the fish landed; species by species, it appeared, the baymen were being regulated out of business. After thirty years, the bass bill had gone through, and Bill feared that fluke and weakfish would be next. Offshore, yellowtail and squid were both declining, even as the number of boats increased.

"What do you think happened to them bass?" Cap'n Bill demanded, after a silence while he thought about the swordfish. And when I said I thought that the main cause was pollution of their spawning grounds, he nodded doubtfully, sitting dead still, both palms still flat on the kitchen table. Earlier this year the weakfish had turned up in the traps "all sores and pink-eyed and bulged out; them fish must have got into some of them chemical dumps, migratin up here, cause a month later they was comin in clear again. But there's somethin besides pollution is gettin to them bass, and I think it's bluefish. For the past thirty years, I guess, there's been so many that now they're eatin on themselves; you dress most of these bluefish out, you find small bluefish, and maybe they're eatin up them small bass, too.

"Thing of it is, there's no price on 'em no more. Fishermen see a bunch of bluefish, they don't bother to set on 'em, and if they get into the nets, they pull the string on 'em, just let 'em go. Why, dogfish is worth more than bluefish, or mackerel, either! Used to leave them dogfish on the beach, long with daylights and skates; now dressed dogs get twenty-five cents a pound! They give us ten cents for bluefish today, when Harry and Frank and Charles and me used to get fifty cents back in the twenties! Never believe that, would ya? And these people payin six dollars a pound for striped bass, which is hardly fit to eat—poorest fish there is! Now they're puttin through this law, twenty-four inches; can't catch small bass no more, all we can catch now are big spawners. Should be just the other way! It's them *big* fish should be protected!"

Like all of the older fishermen, who have seen almost every species come and go, Bill Lester believes that the bass are going to come back, just as they always have. All sea creatures came in cycles, when one was up the other was down, but the body of fish remained about the same, and this was true long before anyone had thought about pollution. "Scallops disappeared entirely, didn't they, piss clams right with 'em, never thought we'd see another one, and not so long ago, neither: 1927, maybe '28. Course that may seem a good while back to *you*. Bluefish, weakfish, bottle fish—why, they *all* dropped out for years during my lifetime, makin room for somethin else to come in strong. I won't see it, but if you live long enough, you'll see them bass come back thick as they ever was.

"Now yellowtail, they're out there in twenty–thirty fathom, not shallow and not deep, just that one depth, and when they start in to fall off, the draggers go over to sea scallops for five years, and the yellowtail come back; that's happened three–four times in my own life. Salmon disappeared, but now maybe they're comin back a little; was forty or fifty caught in the traps last year. Anchovies showed up around here in '74; never seen 'em before, and we ain't seen

'em since. What's all this got to do with overfishin?" Bill
Lester shook his head, disgusted. "Bet them biologists can't
tell us what happened to the shovel-nose shark;[2] don't never
hear about 'em no more, and they used to be thick here.
And the puffin pig![3] Called it the puffin pig cause of the
sound it made; used to show up in the wintertime, get
snarled up in our codfish gear. Kind of plump, up to sixty
pounds, shape of a tuna but tail like a porpoise if I remember it right; open one up, put your hand in, it was hot! Used
to see one or two a day back in the thirties, but now I ain't
heard of one for years; even the Museum [American Museum of Natural History] ain't got none, from what I hear.
But they got that ribbon fish[4] we caught one time, very
pretty silver thing. Roney Marasca, you remember him, he
took it up there; probably up there yet today, with Roney's
name on it!"

In October I went over to Fishers Island, where I helped
my brother with his harvest of young oysters being shipped
out to Nantucket and Cape Cod. As a marine biologist and
lifelong surfcaster, Carey supported a federal moratorium
on striped bass everywhere; he hoped that taking the bass
away from a million sportsmen would bring the necessary
political pressure on state and federal agencies to clean up
the rivers. My own feeling was that a moratorium, encouraging the illusion that something was being done, might
dissipate that pressure; unless accompanied by the very expensive restoration of bass habitat, the moratorium would
be indefinite. But certainly it was the one clean way to eliminate the inequities of patchwork legislation, state by state.

On October 18, surfcasting at daybreak into a hard east
wind and rain, I hooked a bluefish close to fifteen pounds
that took out line against the white-capped current surging
around the eastern point. The silver fish leapt out of the
sea, shaking its red gills in the early light. In its guts, when
I filleted it, was a whole angler fish, ten inches long, and

seeing this unappetizing morsel, I thought about what Cap'n Bill had said about bluefish eating small striped bass.

A striped bass taken that same morning was a five-pounder, just under the new twenty-four-inch limit that would go into effect a fortnight later. The fish hit the lure close in to the white lace around the rocks, and as its thick tail swirled in the wave, I saw the greenish silver of the dorsal, then the broken stripes. This was probably the last bass I would ever keep; a year later my brother and I tagged and released every bass we caught.

That day the air turned colder, and the sky cleared. Fishing from the same rock, in late afternoon, I watched the cormorants and gulls hurrying and diving at the bait churned up by the swift ranging schools of bluefish off Wicapesset Reef. A flight of crows that headed out across the rough bright sea toward far fire-colored woods between Stonington, Connecticut, and Watch Hill, Rhode Island, was a sign of winter. In the clear light I could see far eastward up the Rhode Island coast toward Rosie's Hole, where the *Merlin* had brought those Shinnecock chiefs in quest of giant tuna. But the bluefish did not come inshore, and no bass whirled from the surging tide to slap my lure.

Earlier in the month, the Rhode Island legislature had passed a three-year moratorium on the taking of striped bass in Rhode Island waters. This legislation was pushed through, not by the sportsmen, but by the commercial fishing representatives on the state Marine Fisheries Council. The commercial men realized that New York's passage of the twenty-four-inch law would redouble the sportsmen's pressure in Rhode Island, where the gill net and ocean pound trap fisheries depend entirely on small bass. Sick and tired of harassment, they elected to protect the bass from these self-styled conservationists who took nine-tenths of all striped bass landed in the state. Inevitably, Rhode Island's action inspired discussion of a similar moratorium in New York State, where the fishermen were discussing drastic action.

# 18.
# Baymen and Bureaucrats: Southampton

T hroughout October, the haul-seining remained poor, and on the first of November Jens Lester brought his young crew west to Sagaponack. The crew had finished a sparse haul and was loading the net when I went up to inspect the blue steel dory that had sunk a few weeks earlier out on the bar and to pay my respects to the last of the old-time fishermen on this crew.

Francis Lester, born in 1909, the year the mysterious oarfish, or doplodocous, appeared in a Montauk trap, is Frank Lester's oldest son, and a contemporary of his late Uncle Ted. Like his father and grandfather (and his son and grandson) he has been a fisherman all his life.

Francis and Ted had often fished together as young boys; they had "a little dory" and a couple of trawls, and were "pretty rugged." Francis remembers a winter morning when they tried to beat the men's crews out to the cod grounds. Picking up old discarded baits from the men's trawls, they went off through the surf in too much of a hurry, took a big winter sea into the boat, and were soaked through. "It's a wonder we didn't sink, but we grabbed a bucket and started bailin as hard as we could, and we tried her again." One cod they took that morning on their old rotten bait was so enormous, recalls Francis, that the two boys, struggling together, could barely haul it up over the gunwales.

In later years, Francis went codfishing with his father from Thanksgiving to mid-April, went dragging with his uncle, Old John Erickson, out of Montauk, in the spring, went swordfishing in summer, and harvested clams and scallops in between. During the Depression, he bought his father's farming acre and built the house where he still lives today. There was poor fishing during the Depression, and no bass at all, and in the late thirties he was reduced to working on the road construction crews for six or eight dollars a day. "Last job I was ever on," Francis declares. Hearing that his brother Harry and his brother-in-law Brent Bennett were making one hundred dollars a day hand-lining sea bass out of Shinnecock, he went back to the water, and despite hard times, has been there ever since.

At seventy-four, Francis seemed as wiry, wry, and worried as ever, but today there was no sign at all of the laconic sense of humor for which he is well known. He looked a lot older, and his quiet, sad-faced manner somehow reminded me of his father, whom he resembles in other ways as well. "Always has a young boy with him, teachin him, just like Old Frank used to do," one fisherman says. "Francis has that same good way with kids. Course, all them Poseys was pretty good at gettin somethin for nothin; never had to pay those kids too much, you know."

This morning there were just four bass in the old net, which was torn all along the wings, under the cork line. Kneeling among the sand crabs and squashed jellyfish and daylights, the herring and some snapper blues that the discouraged crew had not bothered to pick up, Francis looked hunched and a little frail as he mended net, his bony hand following the net needle in graceful loops through the chafed twine. The younger men yelled at him to hurry up (his grandson Mitchell calls him Poppy), although not one of them could mend net the way he could. In the years of bass prosperity, many young men joined the crews who have never learned how to mend net at all.

Francis ignored them. "With all this warm weather, we didn't do nothin on the bass all this past month," he told me, "and next week here, they're gonna put us out of business. Maybe we should do what them Rhode Island fellas done, put an end to the bass fishery entirely. That would give them sports something to think about, I guess, make 'em take responsibility for what they're doin. Ain't no bass to speak of anyway, not no big ones. And maybe by the time them fish come back, we can work out somethin reasonable for everybody." He cocked his head, looking up at me, sensing my doubt. "Oh, they'll be back, all right. When I was a young feller, y'know, there weren't hardly no bass at all, we never bothered to set for 'em in spring and only once in a great while in the fall. I never really seen no bass until the forties; after that, they come back strong for thirty years. So I guess them fish'll be back this time, too."

November 2 was a warm, sad, golden day, with the ocean silver, calm, and shining. Thousands of gulls had gathered from along the coast, for the sea was shimmering with sand eels in unimaginable millions, forming dark shadows in the blue. This bait was penned by the huge bluefish schools moving west along the beach in the last days before the ocean chilled enough to slow the golden-eyed swift squadrons and turn their armies off the shore toward deeper water.

Calvin Lester's crew had made a set west of Town Line Road, in Wainscott. In October this crew's best day for bass had been eight hundred pounds, caught in three sets; they had landed scarcely that amount in the fortnight since. But the price of bluefish had gone up a little, and weakfish were still high, and the men shouted when blues and weaks turned up early in the wings. A few fish were seen finning on the calm surface as the orange bag buoy drew closer to the beach.

Though Calvin is—technically—its only Posey, this is unmistakably a Posey crew. Calvin's partner, Donnie Eames, is his fourth cousin. Donnie's mother and Calvin's wife's mother are sisters; Donnie's wife and young Wally Bennett's wife are also sisters, and Wally is closely related to both Donnie and Calvin. These three are the crew's steady members, and usually the other crewmen are relations, too.

Calvin was born in 1953, my first year as a commercial fisherman, and Donnie in 1956, which was my last. Despite black mustache, glasses, and a short, solid, husky build, Donnie still looks boyish. Like many baymen, he quit fishing and took a job when he first got married, working as a butcher in East Hampton from 1974 to 1976; Tom Lester learned a trade setting tiles, Danny King worked for a few years in his family garage, Stuart Vorpahl is an expert welder. But Calvin, like most Posey Lesters—and most Havenses, too—has never done anything but fish. At Amagansett School, he was well known for staring away out the window toward the ocean beach whenever there was fishing weather. Like Richard, he quit school at sixteen and never looked back. No matter how bad the fishing gets, nor how poor he may be, he is probably too proud of his Posey heritage, and too stubborn, to give it up.

Although they scallop and lift traps in season, Calvin, Wally, and Donnie regard themselves as haul-seiners. The Havenses feel much the same way, and these two crews will probably be the last ones on the beach.

As the trucks drew closer, I helped Donnie Eames load the offshore wing into the dory. The hard mesh felt good in my hands, but Donnie had to show me how to lay this immense net that filled the big motor dory all the way forward to the outboard well. "Don't know if we could pitchpole this dory even if we wanted to," he commented, "not with the weight spread out like that. Last year me and Calvin went right up on end, on a big sea off Mecox; if we didn't pitchpole her that day, don't guess we ever will. When you was fishin, now, you had the whole net in the stern and no weight in the bow, and she could go right up and back over."

An older man tending the winch in the bed of the dory truck looked vaguely familiar, and Donnie asked me if I recognized Walter B. Bennett, whom I last recalled from the spring of '55, when he was hauled out from beneath Frank's pitchpoled dory. "Looked like a drowned rat, I did," Walter Bennett said, "with all that ocean in my waders." I asked him how long he was under that boat; it seemed to me it must have been three minutes. "Don't guess I know," he said. "Never checked my watch."

For a number of years Walter owned Brent's Store, which was founded by his father, but in 1975 he had sold the store and gone back to the water, and now he watched as his son Wally freed the hitch and walked the line back down to the water to tie on again. "No, that ain't somethin a man's liable to forget," he said at last. "Part of the trouble was another crew there helpin us go off, see if we could make it; some was pushin and some was pullin, waitin for a better slatch to go. Well, they never found it; we went off too slow. Richard was at the bow oars, and when we went up on end, I seen him dive out to the side; it's narrow up there in the bow, but there was no chance to make it from the middle. So what I done, I just slid under the thwart, grabbed onto it when the boat fell over; never was knocked out or nothin, had a big air pocket, and I knew I was better off right there then tryin to swim up through that surf in waders. Figured she'd just wash ashore and I'd climb out, but I guess you fellas got to me first. Anyway, that was my second experience of somethin like that, and I decided then and there that that was the last time Walter B. Bennett ever went off in a dory."

The seiners agree that to go off through the surf under

power is less dangerous than going off with oars, but nevertheless, as Calvin says, it "takes some practice. You oughta know what you're doin if you're gonna go through the ocean surf."

Sometimes it is necessary to wait twenty minutes for that one moment when the truck is backed down fast and straight into the wash and the brake hit hard so that the momentum of the heavy boat will carry it past the surf should the motor stall. In rough weather the boat often ships water as it slaps through the first wave, and requires bailing even when it does not come close to filling up or rolling over. Or sometimes the dory goes off safely, then has trouble getting in. Calvin recalls a day in the early seventies, a day of big seas after Hurricane Gerta, when the beach was steep and the waves reached almost to the foot of the dunes, and his dory overturned in the surf as it came ashore. "I just got wet," Calvin says, "but Billy Robinson from Southampton there, he almost drowned."

Donnie yelled to Calvin, who had come within hailing distance as the two trucks joined: "See them weakfish finnin?" And Calvin, tending the winch on the other truck, yelled back; there were weaks on his end, too. We jumped to the sand and ran down to the water to manage the bunt as it came into the surf. In the calm sea, the glistening bag, long as the truck, came ashore easily. Eighty pounds of speckled weaks were scattered among fifty cartons (about 3,500 pounds) of the big swift green-blue fish known to the sportsmen as gorilla blues; a solitary bass, near fifty pounds, stripes paling and head green with middle age, lay quiet among the bluefish, as if thinking over a mistake. For the rest of the season, the haul-seiners would do their best to avoid bluefish, which were not worth handling, and bit holes in the mesh.

A trio of surfcasters, put-putting along the beach crest like huge boys on their fat-tired tricycles, glared resentfully at the big bluefish haul, which after all icing and shipping was deducted would probably be worth less than fifty dollars a man. Watching them pass, Donnie Eames said that the twenty-four-inch law would be ignored by most of the surf-casters whom the crews had talked with on the beach. "Hell, them guys say right out that all they'll do is fillet off them illegal bass, take 'em home anyway. There's no provision in this stupid law for filleted fish! And them boat fishermen will do the same—nothin to stop 'em! That law hurts us, cause we can't ship fillets, but it ain't gonna hurt the sports a single bit!"

On November 3 Herbert Doig and Gordon Colvin of the Department of Environmental Conservation (D.E.C.) attempted to justify the bass law to a gathering of fishermen in Southampton Town Hall. Montauk assemblyman John Behan, who had fought the passage of the twenty-four-inch law, warned the bureaucrats that they were now "in bass country," and Doig's report on Governor Cuomo's untested plan for a committee to assist the fishermen in adjusting to the "adverse impact" of the bass bill[1] was met with hostile silence. The men were desperate, and in need of help, yet they clearly disliked risking their independence by accepting charity from people who—they felt—had done them wrong. Anyway, they were suspicious of committees, not to speak of bureaucrats. "These winters are hard around here," a man said. "We ain't got no regular paychecks like you people. We're willin to go out when it's cold and wet, but when the ice comes, ain't nothin we can do."

Colvin, a pale, bespectacled young man in a mod haircut, chirped the good news that striped bass reproduction had been very promising this year in the Hudson, where an eighteen-inch minimum size was still permitted north of the George Washington Bridge. The men glared at him. Chesapeake reproduction, on the other hand, was the second lowest in thirty years. The situation down there was so desperate that Maryland and Virginia were promising once again to take strong action. Both states, lacking coastal fisheries, were proposing coastal legislation roughly equivalent to that passed in New York; they had also "formulated a compact" with Pennsylvania "to address important pollution and habitat protection problems of the Chesapeake," without, however, giving up the right to continue fishing for fourteen-inch fish in Chesapeake waters. Since the baymen know that the small fish they are forbidden to keep are supposed to migrate southward, this political doubletalk brought a groan of cynicism and disgust. "If it was twenty-four inches everywhere, and no exceptions," Richard Lester told me later, "maybe we could accept it. But here they have eighteen inches up in the Hudson and fourteen in the Chesapeake and twelve in Carolina and Delaware—it don't make sense! When small bass show up in the market, who's to say where them fish come from?" In his anger, Richard's face was even ruddier than usual; he squinted. "A lot of 'em will come from *here*, I'll tell you that."

When Colvin had completed his presentation, he asked the fishermen "to put aside your differences with the department . . . and assist us in developing the best possible data base . . . for management of striped bass." Then he sat down, shuffling his papers. There was no applause. A cold, heavy stillness was broken at last by a cold and heavy voice that said, "We cooperated for years with [D.E.C. biologist] Byron Young, and you used that data to legislate against us. I guess you know you ain't gonna get no hand from *us*."

Like Assemblyman Halpin, Colvin appeared astonished by the bitterness of these men. Avoiding their gaze, he frowned into his papers as if discovering something there that he had not seen before, while his smooth-talking superior, Herb Doig, struggled to defend on biological grounds a bass bill that the fishermen perceived as ignorant, political, and punitive. For example, the new Rhode Island law did not take effect until January 1, allowing the commercial men to finish out their season, whereas the New York law

would go into effect on the day before Election Day to insure votes for the politicians who had sponsored it. Election
Day came right at the start of the best month of the fall bass
run, which trappers, gill-netters and haul-seiners alike had
always counted on to make it through the long hard winter.

Doig's biological report was hollow, and when he sat
down, his D.E.C. statistics were excitedly disputed by Arnold Leo, secretary of the Baymen's Association (the artic-
ulate Leo is a part-time baymen who came here from a
career in New York City, and has since become an effective
spokesman for the fisherman). Then Milt Miller rose to
speak. "I been a poor man all my life," Milt said quietly,
"and I guess I'll die a poor man, and I ain't ashamed of it;
I'm proud of it. I know my work and I know the water, and
I forgot more about striped bass than most people will ever
know, but none of you fellers come around and asked me
nothin. If you did, you would know that the bays are full
of little bass, real little ones, that never come up here from
the Chesapeake. You don't *know* where them fish come
from, and there's a hell of a lot else you don't know, and
until you *do* know what you're doin, you got no business
legislatin away our livelihood."

Last year (Milt told me as his son stood up) Mickey Miller
had not caught one bass in his traps that would be legal
under the new law. Composing himself, Mickey nodded to
the other baymen, then said that he had come here to ex-
press his anger—"You people have reduced me to the shell
of a man; I sometimes think I'm goin crazy"—but had decided to do his best to remain reasonable. "I started out
with a scratch rake, and now I got four traps, and the last
few years here I been doin good. But I depend on striped
bass for 50 percent of my income—that's about six hundred
dollars," he said, trying to smile, and the men laughed—
"and the number of bass out in the bay that's over twenty-
four inches ain't no more than a handful. You're lettin 'em
take small bass up the Hudson—why not us?" Looking

strangely hunched up in his hooded parka, as if he had
taken a chill in the hot room, this husky thirty-seven-year-
old veteran of the Korean War gazed around for a few
moments as the baymen watched him—Ben and Billy Havens, Richard and Calvin Lester, Donnie Eames and Danny
King, Stuart Vorpahl, and a number of older men to whose
faces I could no longer attach a name. And I recalled what
Mickey's father had once said, one May afternoon back in
the fifties, shouting over my shoulder from the bow oars as
we pulled Ted Lester's dory into the onshore wind, in a
gray chop: "If my boy Mickey touches a fishin net, I'll tan
his hide!" But this was no time to remind Milt of that story.

"I ain't no public speaker as I guess you can see," Mickey
Miller was saying, "and I don't mean to just speak about
myself. I think I'm speakin for most of the men here in this
room. But I grew up with striped bass, I lived with striped
bass, and spendin nights out there on Gardiners Island, I
learned how to think like a striped bass. I know my business,
and I know there's a lot of things that the biologists don't
know. I bet I released ten thousand little bass from my traps
this year alone, and I had some in there weren't no bigger
than cigars! Are you tellin us that fish that size come from
the Chesapeake? Well, we know that they ain't, and the biologists know that, too. I called up Byron Young, told him to
come down and have a look, because I was still tryin to
cooperate with the D.E.C. And Byron says, 'Hell, fish that
size ain't supposed to *be* here!' Now, how come *that* ain't in
your reports?"

("Byron Young told us that he wasn't going to take a
position for the bass bill or against it, but it was pretty clear
he was against it because he helped Tony Taormina work
out the D.E.C.'s original rejection of the twenty-four-inch
limit," Arnold Leo of the Baymen's Association told me.
"Later we saw a letter he wrote to Doig, saying he fully
endorsed the bill. I guess he had to keep his job. Cohalan,
he was for us, too, and he also let us down at the last minute,

just when we were sure the governor would veto the bill. The governor's people told me they asked Cohalan whether he favored twenty-four or eighteen inches, and I guess he was running scared against Halpin and figured there were more votes for twenty-four. And Cuomo figured if the county supervisor endorsed the bill, he was safe politically himself, and so he signed it. So much for bureaucrats and politicians.")

"They say ignorance is bliss," Mickey Miller continued. "Well, we hate to give up our livin for the sake of ignorance and politics. And that's what I'm doin, losin my livin. I bought my first house just a few years back, I was sendin my daughters to college—how am I goin to pay the mortgage on that house? Or tell them kids I can't afford tuition? I hate to say it, but I lose faith in my country, seein these things happen."

Donnie Eames, young vice-president of the Baymen's Association, asked why the new law went into effect not only in the best part of the season, without letting the fishermen phase out, but also on a Monday, which cost them an additional half-week. There were no pickups by market trucks between Thursday night and Sunday, so that all fish caught in the three days before the deadline would be illegally "in possession" on November 7, which was Monday morning. "How come nobody thought of *that,* before this stupid law went through? How come nobody thought about us at all?" And a voice from the audience shouted out, "They weren't thinkin about us, and they weren't thinkin about bass, they were thinkin about votes on November 8!"

(When I asked him why the department had imposed that arbitrary November 7 date, a D.E.C. man shrugged his shoulders and said, "Politics." He was clearly sympathetic with the commercial men, and gave the impression that the wardens would not extend themselves to enforce the new law, which they perceive as essentially unenforceable. "One man is covering all the beaches and bays between Southampton and Montauk, and in the bays he has no boat; what's he going to come up with?" Asked why Colvin had thrown out the department's best judgment on the bass, as reflected in the opinions of Anthony Taormina and Byron Young, he shrugged again. "Years ago we had a commissioner who was really hammering hard on General Electric for all the PCBs it was pouring into the Hudson,[2] and G.E. went to the governor and threatened to pull out of the state, taking all those jobs. The next thing you know that commissioner was gone, and the guy who replaced him had his orders; just hang out, look like you're doing something. Well, these people we have now look like they're doing something." He shook his head. "Byron Young never believed this bill would do a damned thing for the bass, and said so, but I guess they told him to shut up and get into line.")

Tom Lester, who has traps in Northwest and Three Mile Harbor and also sets fykes for snapping turtle in fresh ponds and diamondback terrapin in the salt marshes, supported the statements of Mickey Miller and others that the twenty-four-inch limit would cripple the bay fishery. Tom is a big man with a big belly, and he demanded to know with a big growl if any bayman had ever laid eyes on a tagged Chesapeake bass? Although the tagging program was already in effect when Tom was born, in 1940, his question was met with a loud, violent "NO!"[3]

Big Tom—besides his Cousin Albie, the only Round Swamp Lester ("We're the originals," he says) who fishes full-time—has strong feelings about such matters as pollution of the creeks by cesspools, road construction, and marinas; the plague of licenses and permits that the men must apply for; the loss of rights-of-way to town waters such as Three Mile Harbor through the town's own actions. "I think it's a conspiracy, I don't think the town wants us here," he says. "Too much money in tourism. They build a lot of tennis courts—what local people ever use tennis courts?—

but they won't spend a little money for a right-of-way."
Asked if he would ever give up working on the water, he
says gruffly, "Probably, if I didn't have no arms or legs."

Like most baymen, Tom Lester sees a difference between "people who catch fish" and full-time fishermen, who
obviously require something besides money. In certain
years, certain fishermen did very well, but most years a lot
of money and long hours were invested for a very uncertain
return. ("Ever eat black duck for *breakfast?*" Tom says, recalling a hard winter when he and his family subsisted on
wild fowl and flounder.) "However, I got nobody tellin me
what to do, where to go, or how to do it; that's what I like
about fishin." Though he fished with Francis for seven
years, and enjoyed his Posey cousins, Tom never much liked
seining on the beach: the constant bickering among men
who had their own stubborn ideas about almost everything—Tom is no exception—persuaded him that he'd
rather work alone. Stuart Vorpahl, Jr., another one-time
seiner who is now a trapper, feels the same way: he speaks
of "the peace of mind, and a real, real heavy sense of freedom. The only individuals I have to deal with are the gulls,
and I don't understand them, and they don't understand
me, and we get along fine."

"I'm Stuart Vorpahl, Jr., from Amagansett, and I'm bitter," this man said as he stood up. "How come you people
don't go after Dupont Chemical and General Electric and
Hercules? The mess down in the Chesapeake ain't our problem, but we're the ones payin for it."

Stuart's grandfather had come originally from Sayville,
on the Great South Bay; his maternal grandfather[4] was a
swordfisherman who in 1950 built the first charter boat
dock in Montauk harbor. Stuart Vorpahl, Sr., the founder
of Stuart's Seafood, was born, lived, and died on Oak Lane,
Amagansett, across the Montauk Highway from Poseyville.
He hauled seine in the spring and fall, hand-lined for sea
bass and set winkle pots in summer, and went codfishing

(and fur trapping), during the winter. In recent years, Stuart Jr. has built a big steel trap down at Napeague; he is also an East Hampton Town trustee.

Stuart Vorpahl said that small "summer weakfish" had been so thick back in '52 that their schools had extended all the way from Promised Land on the bay side around the Point and down the ocean beach to Fire Island, only to vanish almost entirely the next year. Not until 1974 did a few big weaks appear in his trap at Culloden Point. "Them weakfish tumbled, then the blowfish, and the next year there weren't none at all! Now they're comin back a little, and them bass will come back, too. It ain't man that takes care of that, it's Him up there!" Shouting, Stuart pointed at the ceiling, and the younger men in the audience grinned and looked down at their shoes. (Tom Lester admits with discomfort that his mother once begged him not to lift his eel-pots on Easter Sunday, and when he gave in to her, and lifted the next day instead, he was rewarded by a record haul of 1,100 pounds of eels that slithered out of his truck all the way home. For such rare blessings, the older generations in the fishing families can give credit to the Lord, but most of the younger people cannot do so.) "We can survive with Mother Nature's laws," Stuart Vorpahl continued. "We cannot survive with the laws of man, not laws like these!" This time the young fishermen cheered.

When I ran into Stuart two weeks later, he seemed less bitter than bewildered. "I just don't think those politicians realize what they have done," he said.

Doig acknowledged that the polluters of the Chesapeake had not been dealt with, and said that New York State's pressure on its own industries was apparently the cause of the strong resurgence of the Hudson River bass. He also said that his department was in hopes that regulations might be changed in a few years, once the Chesapeake spawning population was reestablished. This brought a new groan from the fishermen, for most of whom "a few years" would be too late. Anyway, everyone knew that the Chesapeake stripers would never return until these bureaucrats mustered enough guts to demand the restoration of the bay. Until then, the only enforceable law would be a moratorium on possession or sale of striped bass in any state at any time. When someone mentioned the Rhode Island moratorium, it brought a despairing cheer from the whole audience.

# 19.
# The Seine Crews:
# Autumn

For the next two days, the surface of the sea was calm, but big rollers came in from a distant ocean storm, and no dory could go off through the surf. On Sunday, November 6—the last day that small bass could be taken legally for local sale—the Havens crew went down before daylight to the easternmost set, known as Umbrella Stand, where a beach pavilion had once stood in Montauk's heyday. It was a beautiful clear windless morning, with autumn warmth in the early sun out of the ocean, and a deep red color in the beach plums on the cliffs, but the smooth rollers were too big for the dory, and the fishermen sat in their trucks and watched the surfcasters, shoulder to shoulder, drag big bluefish flopping from the sea. "Week ago today," Benny Havens said, "right here, we had the biggest haul of bass we made this year. Know what it was? Maybe eight boxes! And them fellas there"—he pointed at a knot of surfcasters—"them ones that's throwin back their bluefish cause they ain't no money in 'em, they come over and told us we was destroyin the striped bass, it was goin extinct, just like the buffalo!"

"Just like the buffalo!" Billy Havens said, disgusted. He

described the time, back in the seventies, when they had taken the rig south right after the bass season to haul seine at Cape Hatteras, North Carolina. "All the crews from up here went that first time, and we took over the whole stretch of beach; didn't know we was doin it, you know, but we put them local boys right out of business. We done so good that the fella that run the packin house come down and told us that he wasn't goin to take no more of our fish. Them Rebels had told him that if he did, they was goin to burn that packin house right to the ground, so we went home. But another year just this one crew went, us two and Lindy and Pete Kromer and our cousin John. And they kind of took to us at first, cause we helped 'em out, you know, and showed 'em things. But then we got 1,245 boxes in one set, and I guess that kind of changed their attitude."

Billy whistled, as if exhausted by the memory. "We was thirty-six hours nonstop on that one haul. A lot of them fish was eighty pounds or better, had to be, it took a man on both ends to heave 'em up into the truck. And they was full of roe; the roe was just runnin out of all them fish, I got sick of the smell of it. Them fish must be goin up into *all* them rivers! That is the home of bass down there, the home of bass! We landed two thousand boxes in three days. And not long after that them Rebels got the federal government to outlaw haul-seine rigs from out of state in the goddamn Carolina fishery."

We waited a couple of hours, watching the ocean, in the hope that the seas might diminish when the tide turned. "Had a lighter boat, now," William Havens said, pointing at a narrow break in the wave pattern, "we could go off right in that little place there, scoot right through quick." Though William does not complain except in a joking manner, one of his crewmen told me that he had been depressed all year by the poor fishing. The crew has made about one half of last year's earnings, which were already the lowest in recent memory. Both bass and weakfish have been scarce this autumn, and a few days before the crews were notified not to ship any more bluefish to the market.

Any day now, the small bass would start to show up in the nets, and no one knew just what would happen. William shook his head. "Brent Bennett told me yesterday that them small bass are just strikin in to his gill nets around Gardiners, but they ain't goin to be no good to nobody."

Doug Kuntz, who has fished with the Havens crew for many years, repeated Stuart Vorpahl's observation that the baymen were "walking around like dead men." Speaking quietly, Doug said, "It's true. The fishermen seem to have lost their spirit, all but Calvin; that guy is amazing. He just fishes hard day after day, just looks straight ahead, never lets it bother him, no matter what. Until two years ago, this crew was high hook on the beach, nobody near us, but it's Calvin now, and even Calvin's getting wired.

"It's not just the lack of fish, it's all the pressure. The sportsmen and tourists crowding them off the beach, and the cost of living. Used to be that the farmers and fishermen were this whole town; now the town doesn't care about 'em any more, all they care about is the goddamn resort economy. Benny has had to tell his kids that they're going to have to find some other way to make a living, or else there's no way they can even afford to live here. That's a hell of a sad thing to have to say in a fishing family. Because the Havens and the Lesters are the main fishing families left, and Benny thinks that in ten years they'll all be finished."

On Monday, November 7, the day the bass law went into effect, Pete Kromer's crew seined 5,800 pounds of large bass at Hither Plains, one of the best hauls recorded in these failing years, and the Havens crew had 3,300 pounds not far to the eastward, at Umbrella Stand. These landings did not include the undersize bass scattered among big flopping cows of forty pounds or better. The Havenses had 500 pounds on Tuesday, November 8, and 980 pounds the following day, and this first—and last—good week of the bass season was spiced by the Election Day defeat of the bass bill's sponsor, Patrick Halpin.

Most of the crews culled their large bass out of piles of giant bluefish. With thousands upon thousands of attendant gulls, the blues were ranging everywhere along the beach, and the surfcasters caught as many as they wanted. I had a twelve and a fifteen-pounder on Election Day, and took one still larger in a few minutes on the beach the following afternoon. In the market, the price on bluefish fell to ten cents a pound. As William Havens said, it was painful to see so many tons of bluefish dumped back into the surf when so many people in the country had to go hungry. "Ain't that somethin, now, bein a fisherman and not wantin to catch such a good fish?" Although some blues, freed fast enough, survived the shock and beating of the nets, this species is much more volatile and less well-armored than the bass, which is designed for rocks and surf, and many of those returned into the water washed up again farther down the beach.

Inevitably the sportsmen's magazines decried the callousness and waste of this "dirty fishery." Yet all American fisheries are dirty because so many edible species go to waste as trash fish—too bony or ugly to attract overprivileged consumers. Countless tons of fine protein are destroyed each year that would be precious anywhere else on earth, including Europe, and the waste is much more damaging to the commercial men than it is to the sportsmen, who rarely show much righteous indignation when dogfish and daylights and sea robins die in the nets.

Jens and Francis's crew was the only one that had not had at least one good catch of bass, and on Thursday morning it was first to arrive on the Montauk set in front of Gurney's Inn, where Calvin had had good fishing all that week. ("We're not competin," Danny King says, "but if one guy catches fish in one spot for a couple of days, another crew will say, 'Well, they're not goin to have that set tomorrow morning, *we're* gonna be there.'") Autumn fogs under the crescent moon of the night before had been a sign of a change in weather, and by dawn the wind had shifted to the eastward. The crews hurried to make a haul before the sea became too rough to set.

No crew that morning had more than a few bass in the nets, and Francis was discouraged. "No matter where we go," he said, "we can't seem to get it right." He started to pick blues from the net, wandered away, then picked briefly somewhere else, as if too disheartened to work systematically. There was no hurry anyway, since with blues everywhere, and the longshore current accumulating with the east wind, none of the crews would make a second set. He called to the younger men to save a few blues for local sale, to pay for gas, but they continued skittering the fish in the general direction of the sea, and Francis shrugged. "They're just sick and tired of havin these things chew hell out of the net, sick of havin to ice 'em and pack 'em up and ship 'em and not get nothin for it but more net-mendin. In all my life I never seen so many big bluefish, not as late as this, and looks like we're stuck with 'em, too, long as the ocean stays so warm."

Down the beach to the eastward another crew was finishing a haul, and driving past I recognized the man standing in the truck bed, on the ocean sky, as Lindy Havens. He had a gray mustache and long gray sideburns, but otherwise he was the same tall, rangy, and good-looking man with big hands and big ears who had once vowed to throw his congressman into the surf.

As I approached, Lindy's glance looked dim and guarded, without the humor I remembered, and when I said, "Don't guess you know me," he turned back to the winch, saying, "Don't guess I do." But when another man yelled across the wind, "Where *you* been, bub? Ain't seen *you* around in years!" Lindy turned back for a better look. Reminded of that disastrous haul back in 1954, when all those fish had poured out of Ted's bunt, he nodded somberly. "I remember that day, all right. Don't forget a thing like that. I seen one other bunch like that, fishin with Bill around '68, only that day we saved most of 'em, must have landed pretty close to four hundred boxes. They ain't beat *that* yet, not around here. And even that was nothin like we seen in '73, down in Carolina—thirty-eight truckloads! Thought we'd never get off the beach, it was a nightmare! Caught too many, that's what we done. Didn't mean to, but we caught too many. With all them fish, there was no price on 'em, and that one haul, more than anything else, got outside crews kept out of Carolina. All we done was teach them fellas how to fish. They never had no waders and no winches, not even a bag in the goddamn net! Used to run down into the water, try to gaff those fish up on the beach!"

The other crewman, Milton (Minny) George, was observing me carefully, trying to place where he had seen me a quarter century before. Finally he said, "Didn't you work one year over there t'the seine house at Promised Land?" When I shook my head, he said, "Could swear I seen you there. Ain't you the one had that old double-ender, that one still had the bark on the double hull?" Pleased to run into someone who recalled the *Vop-Vop,* I told him that sometimes while out scalloping, she had put into Promised Land for fuel. "*Thought* that was you," Minny said, very pleased, too; he is celebrated among the fishermen for his strong memory, and so is his mother, who was born around the turn of the century and still loves to eat bunkers ("Sweet but bony," as one fisherman says. "Takes quite a while to pick 'em bones out. That's why we say, when a feller is late, Where *you* been, bub? Home eatin bunkers?").

Another veteran, Don Eames, Sr., was on the far wing with Pete Kromer, who had bought Ted Lester's rig back in the sixties; this crew was the most experienced on the beach. A man loading the net looked familiar, too, and when Minny spoke to him, I recognized Lindy's old partner, Dominick Grace. Dom-Dom had lost some teeth and looked his age, but he yelled at Lindy as peevishly as ever as the bunt came into the surf—"Goddamn it, Lindy, pull her in, don't you see the other side? You're runnin 'at goddamn winch too slow again!" Minny George winked gleefully, and I laughed. Lindy and Dom had always hollered at each other, and as in the old days, the abuse served to ease the suspense of bunting up, and was ignored. But the bag held another haul of useless bluefish; there were seven or eight bass altogether. "That weather's got to change, clear out them bluefish, fore we do any good at all," Minny said.

On November 17, at the first monthly Baymen's Association meeting after the bass bill had been enforced, the fishermen stood with caps in hand and hands on hearts, pledging "allegiance to the flag and to one nation indivisible with liberty and justice for all." In an old-fashioned way, without waving the flag, the baymen are very patriotic, and many are conscientious citizens; they work in the volunteer fire department and maintain a volunteer lifeboat service—the Dory Rescue Squad—at their own expense. In recent weeks they had turned down an offer of financial help from an outside friend, fearing the money's allocation might cause trouble; not long thereafter they pitched in generously to help a bayman whose son required prolonged care in the hospital. In this time of hardship, the sight of these men lined up facing the flag gave me a funny tingling around the temples.

President Danny King was absent, and Vice-President Donnie Eames presided, with Secretary Arnold Leo doing most of the talking. A number of topics were discussed, including the news that the Hudson River bass were officially edible because of lower residues of PCBs found in the flesh; however, a commercial bass season in the Hudson, would not be opened for at least another year. Also dis-

cussed was the death the night before of the popular bay
constable, Jack Conklin (already constable when I was on
the beach); the associate membership of Jeff Eames, aged
fifteen ("Better fisherman than his father!" Calvin Lester
hooted as Herb Eames, Jr., grinned); the use by the Coast
Guard Auxiliary of docking space at the Commercial Dock
in Three Mile Harbor, which might interfere with sand eel
seining. "Goddamn it," Richard Lester shouted, "What is
this horseshit? What are you guys arguing about? Them
people is savin lives and property! You're broke down out
there on the bay, you ain't goin to be worryin none about
no dock space, nor sand eelin, neither!" As other people
shouted back ("You'd be the first to holler, Richard!") Richard nudged me comically, rolling his eyes. "Guess I've had
my say for tonight," he said.

These days Richard is "baitin" (seining silverside minnows, called spearing, or whitebait) in Georgica Pond, and
"gettin by all right, I guess; long as I get by, I'm happy."
But he hesitated—"Got to put bread on the table"—before
putting his dollar in the raffle, half of which goes for the
potato chips, soda pop, and beer after the meeting and the
other half to the winner. Richard won. "First thing that
come out right in months," he muttered, returning to his
seat with his twelve dollars. "My luck must be changin." A
few days later he injured his back while serving as a volunteer fireman and was laid up for the rest of the year.

Some proposed bass bill amendments were discussed,
and everyone got serious. A uniform eighteen-inch limit for
New York State was probably too sensible to be accepted,
and so was a summer moratorium on resident bass. The
prospects for a hundred-pound daily allowance of small
bass taken while netting other fish might be much better,
since the federal government had approved such "by-
catches" in other fisheries. But no one contested Tom Knobel's opinion that no amendment would work unless the
D.E.C. endorsed it, which for the moment seemed very un-

likely, and the meeting ended on a discouraged note. This fall, many part-time fishermen, such as Jarvie Wood's younger brothers Dick and John, had not even bothered to put traps in. Under the twenty-four-inch law, it did not seem worth it.

Drinking a beer after the meeting, a new man on one of the haul-seining crews had mentioned that someone had been calling up and bothering his wife. One of his fellow crewmen said, "Hell, I don't never bother to call, I just go over there to your house and let her have it." Another said, "Wish you'd fix that back step, bub; fella could hurt hisself," and somebody else said, "Yeah, that back door light, too." The new man had laughed easily, without protest; he understood that this teasing was a way of telling him he was accepted. And I had laughed, too, though the tone bothered me. There had always been rough teasing on the crews, but the teasing these days seemed much more aggressive, with an undertone of anger and frustration.

Perhaps because the increasing regulation of their life appears discriminatory, or because they accept no subsidy or welfare, or because they have fished here since the days when the only limits on a man were his own strength and ambition, many of these otherwise conservative, religious men feel entitled to ignore the laws imposed upon them by outsiders. Some take short lobsters or scrape the berries (roe) off female lobsters and toss them into the tank after the rest; some take bug scallops and short bass. Even in the days of the sixteen-inch limit, marked boxes of undersized fish were sometimes shipped to the Fulton Fish Market and shunted quickly into other trucks for illegal sale. Like their precious independence, their traditional freedom to come and go as they please and the traditional right to use anything in the natural world that they may need are hard to relinquish. "They ain't controlled *me* yet!" one man assured me.

When Mickey Miller mentioned how many bass he had

released from his Hicks Island trap in the last week alone, a Montauk man said, "Wish that was me, bub! *I'd* know what to do with them small fish!" Convinced that the sportsmen are ignoring their own law, certain baymen will not hesitate to convey small bass into the markets, where they cannot be distinguished from fish caught elsewhere. Others, in gestures of protest that they themselves recognize as futile, are stuffing a few into their boots, or filleting them for use at home.

Because these fish are now illegal, the fishing families are developing a new taste for bass, which most baymen dislike. Even before the passage of the bass bill, they ate it rarely, partly because of its high value, and Danny King's wife, Marsha, says she has never tasted a striped bass in all her life. "Sea robin is better'n bass or bluefish both," Calvin Lester says. "Striped bass is a big name, that's all it is: I wouldn't eat one of them goddamn things! I tried it several times, I just don't care for it." This prejudice against striped bass, with its flaky meat and delicate pale flavor, is partly accounted for by Bonac cookery. "They eat striped bass in these New York City restaurants a lot different than we cook it," Donnie Eames admits. "We flour it up, throw it on the frying pan with some salt. They got all kinds of sauce and herbs and all this other shit on top of it, can't taste the fish no more. A bluefish tastes like a fish. Them people don't want something that tastes like a fish, they want something that tastes like a recipe."

"I was kind of young when you was on the beach," Brent Bennett told me after the meeting. "About nine, I guess. But I was fishin even then. Soon's I come home from school, first truck that come along—pfft!—I was *gone!*" Brent, who is Walter's younger brother, is perhaps the most versatile fisherman out on the bay, and has taught his business to younger baymen such as Tom Knobel, one of numerous outsiders—Arnold Leo and Doug Kuntz are others—to whom the baymen have been hospitable since Ted Lester first welcomed outsiders to his crew back in the fifties. Brent said he had seen more small bass in his nets this year than at any other time in a decade, and that these fish would ordinarily account for more than half his income. "Weren't for that law here in the middle of the season, it would have been a banner year for me, maybe a thousand pounds a day in them four nets. Now I'm settin out lobster pots, tryin to keep goin."

Brent has rigged his twenty-two-foot fiberglass skiff with the console and pot hauler on the port side, leaving plenty of deck space; it is now an efficient lobsterman as well as net boat. This winter he will build more lobster pots and repower his boat with a larger motor that will permit dragging and power seining. In the spring he will set a whole series of gill nets of different mesh sizes for mackerel, weakfish, and blues. With a variety of fishing gear, kept in good shape, he intends to be ready for anything that comes along. He also maintains an efficient scallop opening house, which he rents to other baymen. Like Calvin, he says he will never give up fishing. He intends to move from one fishery to another until he is driven off the water, because fishing is the only thing he wants to do.

"The fisherman is very independent," Brent's brother Walter says. "If one of them left and went to work, he was never looked down upon because everybody knew he was goin to be back fishin eventually, it was just that he had had a bad spring or fall and he had to make ends meet and that's all there was to it. But they knew eventually that he would be back. And pret' near all the fishermen that were on the water came back.

"My father was a fisherman and he started Brent's Store. Up until then, he always worked on the water, and after that, when I bought the business from him, he went back to playin around the water. And I sold it in '75 cause *I* went back to the water.

"Fishin wasn't a job, it was your station in life, so to

speak. Though it was a lot of hard work, it was not a job, but somethin you were born with and brought up with. A job was somethin like drivin nails or rakin leaves. Like the old sayin goes, 'If you have saltwater in your blood, there ain't nothin you can do, you just gotta *do* it.'

"When Grandpop [Cap'n Frank] was young, now, he used to make up a crew, and there would be a lot of people from up-street that have businesses today. They didn't have saltwater in their blood, but they would fish for a while, cause fishin at that time was payin more than a carpenter would get. The fisherman and farmer were No. 1 and No. 2 on this end of the Island, and now they're at the bottom of the heap, and your carpenters are gettin twenty-five dollars an hour, some of 'em, and your plumbers and masons. Everythin is bypassin us, and we're still doin the same thing. It don't look too good. It was a way of life, you know, it's like the Indians handed it down to our ancestors and they handed it down through the generations, and all of a sudden we're findin that we're goin down the drain. It's what they call progress.

"My older son Wally, he's into it now, and it's a good life, no doubt, but there's so much pressure bein put on, losin boat landins, losin water rights. And the federal government, or even the state, never helped the fishermen because they never asked for anything. They were always independent, and they always made it through."

"Every year you're into fishin, you do better," says Stewart Lester, who is as stubborn about staying on the water as his cousins. "You learn where to be, what time of year to be, and what the tide is doin, how hard the wind's blowin, how much line to put out, and this and that; you just know the job, that's all. . . . You can't fight the water, you gotta learn to live with it. There's a lot of guys don't have no respect for it, try to fight it, and it only makes their work twice as hard." (Jarvie Wood agrees: "It's very unpredictable on the water. You think you know a lot but you don't know nothin.")

"You're your own boss, your own time, you go and come as you want—you're independent. And that's born and bred in me. I've tried about everythin there is—truck drivin, plowed snow, bulkhead work, carpenter's helper, electrician's helper, dug ditches and put in wells: when you're young you like to try things. You ain't makin too much money fishin, you got a bad year, so you go lookin around. But not no more. If I get jammed into a corner, I'll do 'em, but otherwise not. As I said, I wasn't my own boss, and it gets to be a grind, same thing every day. Fishin is never the same thing every day; you never know what's goin to happen or what to expect or what you're goin to find."

Like all baymen, Stewart is saddened by the change in quality that is overtaking the fishermen's way of life. "I trailer my boat home all the time. You got so much tied up in it, you don't want to leave it. I used to leave the drudges, the motors, and everything else in the boat, take the gas can out, the scallops out, and just anchor it off. Nobody ever touched it. Now they'll jump into it, put a tank on it, take the whole rig; they won't leave you nothin." In recent years, as straight young oaks and hickories become harder to find, even trap stakes are regularly stolen.

Another problem, since it often involves men they went to school with, is the competition with part-timers for lobsters and shellfish. "If a guy has the ambition, in one way I like to see him go down there and do it, cause I know he needs it," Stewart says. "But it kinda hurts us, too. I know seven or eight guys right now that's got jobs, makin a pretty good buck, and they go get their two–three bushels of clams a week, then when scallop season comes along, they're gonna take two weeks vacation if not three, go out scallopin. It hurts because there's so many of them. Used to be maybe sixty fishermen, commercial fishermen or baymen, in the first three weeks of scallopin, which is the best of it; there'd probably be sixty part-timers, too. But a couple years ago, I seen a hundred and sixty-eight boats in Napeague Harbor on openin day, and maybe a hundred and fifty guys with waders and tugs and baskets and scoop nets come over the beach banks.[1] I never seen nothin like it in my life! Never! They figured roughly 1,800 to 2,000 bushels of scallops went out of that little Napeague harbor in one day, and the second day was pretty close to that, too."

Considering his son's future as a fisherman, Stewart just shrugged. "It's really up to Teddy, you know, it's whatever he wants to do. The way fishin is goin around here, I just don't know. It could get tougher—could get more licenses, more this and that. It ain't like it was ten–fifteen years ago when for a thousand dollars, twelve hundred, a guy could come out and go clammin, go scallopin. If they live home, get their gear built up while they're younger, and have it to start out with, that's one thing; otherwise, you're talkin five thousand dollars—boat, motor, gear—just to start out." These costs do not include a truck, far less a heavy-duty truck for beach use, or a haul-seine rig. A good truck that is well maintained may be shot after five years on the beach, and even less if it is used to launch the dory; a full haul-seine rig—two beach trucks, trailer, net, and dory—would cost much more than any one fisherman could afford, and anyway, it would be a poor investment. Only in the best of years does the rig's share make any real money. Because of increasing restrictions and poor fishing, a worn-out rig will probably not be replaced, and ocean haul-seining may come to an end when a rig can no longer be patched together from other fishermen's backyards.

"You gotta be versatile, you gotta get into everythin at certain times, as the season changes. You've gotta be a clam digger for two–three months and a scalloper for three–four months, you go on a dragger or go trawlin codfish, settin winkle pots, pin-hookin porgies." The problem is that, to be versatile, at least twice as much gear is required, at an ever-increasing price.

"All those years ago we did a lot better than we do to-day," Jarvie Wood says. "It was more peaceful on the water. You'd go out there and go to work, and it was peaceful, got nobody botherin you. But nowadays you go out there, and if you're doin anythin, you got plenty of company. Watch out for boats, watch out for everythin, just like on the land. In order for a man to make a livin on the water now, he has got to keep goin every day, every minute, one thing to another."

# 20.
# The Trappers:
# Fort Pond Bay

O n Saturday, November 19, the gorged bluefish suddenly departed. The day before they had been everywhere along the beach, and the day after they were gone, leaving behind dark shadows of packed sand eels in the ocean. On the blowing sand, exhausted gulls blinked flat, hard eyes as they shifted position on the beach crest, feathers smoothed by the east wind. On Sunday the last charter boat quit for the season, and on Monday there was storm.

For most of Thanksgiving week there was no weather to haul. In their wives' old cars, to save a little gas, the men drove in groups to the beach landings and stared at the huge Atlantic, the wind spume and diminished flocks of gulls. Under those gray relentless seas, the bass companies that had congregated at Montauk from summer grounds along the New England coast would be moving southwest and offshore, taking the last hopes for the season with them.

Sunday morning, November 27, was clear, near windless, with black trees etched on the cold daybreak sun; the winds and rains of the days before had stripped the limbs of the last leaves of autumn. Sipping coffee at Brent's Store, Ben

Havens told me there was still no weather to go off; westerly
winds had knocked the seas down but now there was too
much current from the west. "We've made just four sets in
the last three weeks, and the wind's supposed to go southeast again tomorrow." He shrugged. "Guess we'll keep tryin
'em till the first snow. That's always been the last day of the
season." Most of the crews had already left the beach, discouraged not only by the weather but by swarms of dogfish,
which had replaced the bluefish as a plague.

That morning I went on down to Montauk with Jimmy
Lester and Sandy Vorpahl to lift their traps in Fort Pond
Bay, but the wind picked up before we cleared the dock,
bringing a hard chop to Block Island Sound, and we went
instead to Salivar's for coffee. Sandy is Danny King's sister,
married formerly to Billy Vorpahl, who runs Stuart's Seafood; her young son Wayne helps out sometimes on Danny's crew. The King family comes from an area of Springs
still known as Kingstown, near Copeces[1] Lane, which was
granted to it centuries ago when an ancestral King married
a Gardiner. "You can always tell them people by their wide
feet," Jimmy said, teasing her. "Need feet like that to get
around them Bonac swamps." The son of the late Billy Lester and grandson of Captain Bill, Jimmy lives on the north
side of the highway, behind the site of the old Lester homestead.

Jimmy had fished with his great-uncle Ted in Ted's last
years on the beach; he disliked haul-seining. "Never liked
that sand, you know, never liked the way it got into everything." For some years he went dragging with Captain Norman Edwards and with Lewis Lester, who ran the Edwards
boat when its owner was running bunker steamers out of
Virginia. "Lewis could navigate that boat just with the com-
pass, never mind the fog; he never come to trust all the
modern equipment, like radar and depth finders, automatic
pilot, never wanted to try it out or even look at it. Got by
all right without it, and a good fisherman, too. But he was

nervous, worse than Ted and worse than Francis, and them two could never sit still; Lewis wouldn't let *nobody* touch the wheel of that boat, not on a clear day in a dead calm."

On Monday the wind had gone to the southeast, and the bay calmed, but by daybreak, when we left Montauk Harbor on Jimmy's small blue dragger *Tern*, the weather was backing around to the northeast, with rain and cold. It looked and felt like the first day of winter. Small Bonaparte's gulls, which turn up at this season—"Call them ones crap gulls," Jimmy said, "I don't know why"—were dipping outside the Montauk breakwater. Long strings of the black sea ducks known as coot beat across Block Island Sound toward the high eastern cliffs of Gardiners Island, and the oak woods on Culloden Point were a dark somber brown beneath the restless skies. "First time in nine days there's been weather to lift," Jimmy said, picking up his trap skiff from a spile off the western shore of Fort Pond Bay. The old sharpie was low in the water, half-full of rain.

Big black-backed gulls, late cormorants, and a solitary loon abandoned the trap reluctantly as the *Tern* drew near. The square of dark water between the stakes was dark and silent, giving off an ominous suspense. Though most large creatures burst right through the trap, large sharks occasionally remain, and seals as well. Tom Lester, lifting the mesh, was once pulled overboard by a panicked sea turtle, and in the fifties his father, Randolph Lester, and Duane Miller took a drowned three-ton whale, sixteen feet long, from what was left of a trap out at Northwest. Hundreds of people came to see it, and Dr. Dave Edwards, who once attempted to harpoon a pair of porpoises that strayed into Three Mile Harbor, tried to put a tent around the whale and charge admission.

"Ever see so many strings and ropes?" Sandy Vorpahl said, as I tried to help without getting in the way. "Don't it make you wonder who thought up this rig in the first place? Jimmy says the design of these traps ain't hardly changed in hundreds and hundreds of years; there's only this one way that it fishes best." Nevertheless Jimmy was working on a new funnel design to deter crabs, which sometimes invaded in discouraging numbers.

"In 1983, we had a real good year on squid and butterfish, got clean hauls that year, could shovel 'em right up into the cartons," Jimmy said. "The last few years we haven't caught too many bass in Fort Pond Bay, but we always have caught bass here. In 1984, in fact, if we were allowed to keep bass over 16 inches, we would have had one of our best years."

The northeast wind held the *Tern* against the trap posts, and in the sharpie Jimmy circled the pound, lifting the netting as a few brown disks—small skates and daylights—rose to the surface. Through the water's roil moved the black dorsals of skipjack herring, the pale tail fins of the backward-scooting squid. A dogfish appeared and sank away again, then a small striped bass. "Another shortie," Jimmy said. "Ain't seen one money fish yet." As the net rose toward the surface, more and more fish appeared, until finally all poured together in a flapping, skittering brown-silver mass. Among the fish crawled a few lobsters, together with rock and spider crabs—both are good eating—and also hermit crabs, lodged tight in the big round silver shells of moon snails.

Jimmy bailed the catch onto the deck, using a long-poled wide-mouthed dip net that was hoisted over the *Tern's* side by winch and pulley. Most of the fish were herring of four species—skipjacks, alewives, blueback herring, a few coppery bunkers—none of which were worth the cost of shipping, though all are very good when cooked and pickled. The skates and daylights, the sea robins, angler fish, and "dogs" were not worth bothering with, and the butterfish, flounder, eel, blackfish, mackerel, and mullet were too few to ship. What was left was a carton of squid and some small striped bass, twenty-five or thirty of them, which a few weeks before would have been worth three hundred dollars; not a single bass was big enough to keep. Unlike some of the fish, they were fresh caught; bass rarely remain in a pound trap more than a few hours before finding their way out. Jimmy said, "Toss 'em," and I scooped them up and eased them over the side, hoping he did not feel obliged to be law-abiding just because I was there. The bass were quick and solid in my hands, and watching the beautiful silver creatures strike the surface and dart into the depths, I felt exhilarated, as if setting free the last bass in the world.

"How's that for a nine-day haul?" Jimmy Lester said cheerfully. He nodded his head as if answering his own question. "Let's take her out," he said in a different voice. He had freed the netting from the stakes, and using the trawler boom, we winched it up on deck. "It don't pay to fish no more this year," said Sandy Vorpahl, one of the few women who goes out on the water all year-round. "With weather like this, all you can do is sit on shore and watch your net get tore to pieces."

The cold wind had increased, and the cold rain, and the *Tern* pounded upwind across Fort Pond Bay to Culloden Point. At Pell's fish house, we iced and unloaded the carton of squid and hoisted the net into Jimmy's truck; the skipjacks would be left on the dock for a friend's lobster pots, and the odds and ends—eel, flounder, blackfish, a half bushel of squid—would be taken home.

It was close to noon, and we went back to Poseyville to try Sandy's pickled herring. While she made lunch, Jimmy showed me the fine sharpie he was building in the new shop by the old shed out back where his happy-go-lucky greatuncle, years ago, had hung himself, unable to bear the ringing in his head.

Toward the end of Thanksgiving week, I stopped by Lazy Point, at the mouth of Napeague Harbor. In a stiff wind, Mickey Miller hauled his skiff onto its trailer, as the coot shooters in off Cartwright Shoals roared in behind him, washing the hard shore with their wake. "That storm finished me off," he said. "Trap stakes layin around out there like matchsticks, and two of 'em broke clean off." He laughed an odd laugh with no trace of mirth in it. "Told my wife this mornin that what was in them traps today would be our Christmas money." He pointed at the pile of stakes and twisted net and laughed that laugh again. "Don't look like much of a Christmas, I don't guess." Mickey thought he might go have a look at the southeast corner of Napeague Harbor, where this hard blow should have washed scallops ashore. "Got to do somethin, don't I?" He yelled at his dog to get into the truck, then gazed at the broken stakes out of the window. "Well, I had some good years there," he said. "Don't want to go gettin spoiled or nothin."

Leaving the landing, he caught a length of Stuart Vorpahl's trap net on his fender, and some netting was dragged down the road a way before he noticed. The frustrating episode seemed to stand for his whole season, and he slammed out of his truck, too disgusted and depressed to speak. We rolled the net back onto the grass, and he kept on going.

On the day the bass law went into effect, Mickey had been so disheartened that he could not bring himself to lift his traps; his father had offered to do the job himself. "Must have been two thousand pounds of bass in that one trap," Milt told me, "and at least one thousand pounds of 'em would have been keepers under the old law. Just heartbreakin. The rest of 'em was real little fish—one thousand pounds! That's a lot of little fish! Billy Schultz, Brad Loewen, all the trappers have seen them fish, and the biologists go right on sayin they can't be there. It's like their information on bass numbers. Them people don't know that bass move in paths, so they measure the bottom, measure fish by the square foot, like they measure clams.

Why hell, they don't even know how to measure clams!
Maybe twenty years ago, used to take my dragger out of
Shinnecock to them big beds of surf clams in the ocean.
Used to set a buoy out in a good area and keep draggin
right back to that buoy, cause clams set in layers, you know,
the smallest ones deepest, and when the ground is softened
up, caved in, the dredge picks up more on the second and
third drag than it does the first time. Be up to your knees
in clams on deck, sixteen–seventeen bushels a twelve-minute
drag and up to three hundred bushels in a day. Sold 'em
off to Howard Johnson's and them places for fried clams,
got a dollar a bushel, sometimes fifty cents.

"Well, them biologists go out where I told 'em and they
make a set and they get two clams. They're off the set.
Maybe ten feet away they would have loaded up, that's the
way clams are. And so they come up with figures showin X
amount of clams per square foot, which don't mean nothin.
So I took 'em out there and showed 'em them clams, and
they couldn't believe it."

At his father's house in Three Mile Harbor a week later,
Mickey was trying to decide whether to mend and reset his
ravaged trap or wait until spring. Maybe he would build
and set some flatfish fykes. "Tom Lester and Francis always
set fykes, and they always talk poverty, too, but I notice they
keep right on doin it." Mickey managed a grin, jerking his
thumb at his father, who was mending a gill net in the corner of his yard. "I'm tryin to get him to tell me what to do,
so's I can blame it on him if I make the wrong choice."

Milt glanced at his son, saying nothing, and remained
silent a little while after Mickey had gone. Milt had moved
here to Olympic Heights because the place "came with a
little land. I like to spread out a little, too"—he gestured
toward the yard and hillside filled with nets and fishing gear
and decrepit boats—"but I ain't doin so much any more; it's
really for him. He ain't got room where he is now, and our
kind of people can't afford to buy no land around this town

no more." Milt reloaded his net needle from a spool of twine that he located under the chipped hull of a blue cabin boat. "Got this old boat here pretty cheap, but she needs a lot of work; guess I'll get after her this winter. Course I could set in a rockin chair instead, maybe be dead in about two weeks."

The day was cold, and to my relief Milt said, "Let's go inside." In the sunny rooms, very spare and empty, he introduced me to his wife, Etta, before we sat down at the kitchen table, which Milt, obsessed by all the questions about bass, was soon thumping urgently with a thick finger.

"The Chesapeake is the only place where striped bass have been really researched, and all the laws they recommend come out of that. The biologists claim the bass don't leave the Chesapeake until it's fourteen inches long. Well, my son's been trappin about ten years, and in that time I'd say two-thirds of the bass caught in them traps have been under fourteen inches, thousands and thousands of them; I seen some no more'n about four inches, don't go the length of my hand. Them little fellas never come up here from the Chesapeake, I'll tell you that. And how about all them big cows with roe, show up here in spring? And that's good roe, too, because [Dr. Robert] Valenti's hatchery in Napeague raises fingerlings from it. Now where do them great big fish spawn? You never hear about big fish like that spawnin in them Chesapeake tributaries, nor in the Hudson, neither. In my opinion, there's very few fish of that size *ever* goes back to the Chesapeake; I believe they winter off here in deep water.

"It's like that haul the Havenses made down in Carolina, biggest haul ever made anywhere on striped bass, far as we know. Saved 1,200 boxes, I think it was, and Carolina crews picked up another five–six hundred boxes from the same bunch, and practically all of 'em big fish, Benny says. And that dragger thirty-five–forty miles offshore on Diamond Shoal, picked up another record haul of them big ocean fish, forty thousand pounds. That's three hundred miles south of the Chesapeake! What are them fish doin down there in late winter if the Chesapeake is where they go to spawn? And think of all the places them fish *could* be spawnin that's never been properly researched—Rhode Island and Connecticut, up here in Peconic! In the old days there was bass in all them rivers, and they may be in some of 'em yet. But the main point is, the biologists don't really know, and that law was passed anyway, and it's unenforceable; anybody with a knife is going to take his striped bass fillets home. The only fair thing would be a federal law eliminating all taking and possession of bass anywhere. We can live with that if we have to; at least it's fair.

"When I was young, crews would haul all day and never get more than a couple hundred pounds of bass, and here in the bays we caught hardly any—just a straggler here and there. Back in the fifties, *you* remember, if we had one or two real big hauls in a season, we was doin good. By the late sixties, we was gettin seven to eight thousand pounds of keepers, sixteen inches or better, and at least that amount of smaller fish that we let go. You couldn't believe the amount of bass was around here in them years! The crews would go down day after day and bail 'em into the trucks. Why, them fellas never set at all unless they seen fish breakin out—we never had anythin like that!

"Everythin's changin on us, too fast to keep up with. Used to be you would watch the shadbush in the spring and know when the shad would come by when it bloomed; you can't go by that stuff, not no more. Weakfish don't go up bay no more the way they used to; there's too much pollution, in my opinion. Used to have loads of spawn bunkers goin up into the bays in spring, and just floods of little bunkers comin back in fall; you don't see them little bunkers no more, and I believe it was this damn pollution that put an end to the bunker fishery. Cherry Harbor used to be as clean as any place, cause we don't have no industry or open sewage around here, but for the last twenty years or so it's been gettin more and more condoms and plastics and crap, hung up all through the gill nets—well, that damned stuff's comin from a long way off.

"I've seen bluefish come and go in my lifetime, and striped bass, too. The bluefish is a wild fish and a hardy fish, and because he don't go up in them dirty rivers, he'll survive where the striped bass will go down. All the fish around here come and go in cycles, and years back, you could anticipate the cycles, but today, with the pollution the way it is, you can't be so sure that a fish that's gone will ever come back at all.

"Because of them surfcasters, there's too much attention bein paid to the haul-seiners and their effect on fish. Back in the late sixties, when the bass was at their height, Ted and Stewart had that nice Maine boat, called her the *Posey*, and Ted designed a trawl net for Stewart that would fish close inshore. Kenny Edwards had the same idea, and them fellas done good; nobody ever dragged so close before that time. Well, ever since, the draggers been takin more bass than the haul-seiners, and nobody never says a thing about it. By the time the draggers bring them bass ashore, they're all packed up, they're not layin in the back of a truck for them sports to see. And them big bass have always been out there, way offshore, in my opinion. Nobody talks about it because any fisherman is goin to keep somethin like that secret. I don't know if them big foreign ships were takin 'em, nor how many, but we do know they weren't throwin no fish away. All them boats that you see out there today, they're reapin the ocean dry."

# 21.

# The Winter Ocean

December 2 was a cold clear windless morning, with bright stars. For the first time this autumn, the temperature had fallen below freezing. With the last stretch of bad weather in late November, Jens Lester, Pete Kromer, and Danny King had left the beach; the Havens and Calvin Lester crews were the last ones left. At Brent's Store in Amagansett, Walter Bennett turned up at 6 A.M. for coffee, and Calvin, rolling up with the dory a few minutes later, told him that they would be heading west for Flying Point, in Water Mill, where a few medium bass had appeared the week before.

At William Havens's house, on Abraham's Path, Ann Havens was bandaging her husband's thumb, splayed to the bone while shucking chowder clams the previous day. "Told him to go to the doctor, but he wouldn't; just like a little boy!" Mrs. Havens was angered by the editorial in the *Long Island Fisherman*, which expressed disdain for haul-seining as a "dirty fishery." "Them people always get everythin wrong! Had a picture of *our* crew there, longside a picture of Calvin's dogfish on the beach! Anyways, why don't they know it don't do no good to throw most of them fish back? It ain't the haul-seiners' fault nobody wants 'em! Last week

my men here shipped 309 pounds of bluefish. Know what
we got back, after payin the shippin? Eleven-fifty! Eleven
dollars and fifty cents for three hundred and nine pounds
of good *bluefish!* Does that seem fair to you?"

I shook my head, feeling outraged myself. In a local
restaurant that week, a friend had ordered bluefish, paying
precisely eleven-fifty for less than a half pound, or more
than seven hundred times as much as the men who caught
it were receiving. The Havenses knew that those bluefish
that brought them three pennies a pound did not go to
waste, that the markets and restaurants did fine while the
men who supplied the fish went into debt, and this knowledge intensified their sense of futility and bitterness. Already the draggermen were anticipating the same treatment; they were getting a good price for early whiting, but
within a few weeks, when the whiting came in thick, the
price would drop quickly to three cents a pound, which
would scarcely be enough to pay for fuel.

We went down to Napeague just as the sun came up on
a calm wintry sea. In this season whales are sometimes seen
from shore, and the white flash of diving gannets, harassing
the fish schools heading south, but this morning the sea was
entirely empty, a gray waste extending without a mark to
the horizon. The clouds of bait had disappeared, and the
bird legions; the rush of storm seas had subsided to a soft
whisper in the shining shallows. On the tide line were thin
windrows of dead sand fleas, killed by the first frost of coming winter. (Whiting are sometimes gathered on the beach
as "frost fish" because they chase bait into the shallows and
are transfixed by the frozen air.)

The quiet men stared out at the dead ocean; its very
emptiness seemed somehow ominous. The autumn storms
had carved the beach away, making it narrow and difficult
to work. The rain-soaked sand no longer drained well or
packed down, and in the half-frozen mush, the trucks were

balky. "Don't know if we should set at all, with all them dogfish," William said after a while, still gazing off into the empty distance. "Goddamn dogs! You get a mess of *them* things gilled from one end of your net to the other, take you all day to get it straightened out!" Most fish move offshore as the sun rises, and Benny thought they ought to wait a little before setting, despite the risk that any bass would move off, too. Over the CB radio from Flying Point came word that Calvin's crew, for fear of dogs, was also waiting. For the past two weeks, the dogfish had plagued the draggers and net fishermen up and down the coast.

"Hell," Billy Havens said, in sudden restlessness. "This season's over. Let's make our set and get it done with, get off this damn beach." He backed the dory trailer down toward the water's edge, and Ben climbed up into the boat and started up the motor; Doug Kuntz, still half-asleep, would set the net. Through the cab window, Billy hollered, "Ready?" He backed the trailer fast into the water, then slammed on the brake, and the dory shot off the roller, coasting easily through the surf, and moved rapidly offshore as Doug tossed over a big coil of line that made a loud slap on the surface.

The dory turned away toward the southeastward. Soon it was silhouetted on the sun. Young Fred Havens hitched the line to William's truck, then got into Ben's old Dodge with Billy and headed eastward to where the dory would come ashore. "How come they tossed that whole coil into the water?" William complained. "No sense in that; could have left most of it ashore. And they turned off east too soon . . ." He stopped fretting and shook his head. "Gettin nervous, I guess. Everbody on the beach is nervous, noticed that? Guess we don't know what's to become of us. That one crew Old Bill had, I guess we was together near to fifteen years, and I don't recall no snappin and snarlin, not like this." When I reared back a little, raising my eyebrows,

William grinned. "Well, we done some yellin, buntin up, I guess, to let off steam. Remember Ted jumpin around like a jack rabbit when the bunt come in? Seems to me we had more fun in them years. The crews always helped each other out—now you can't count on it." He grumbled about this CB radio that had recently come into use; one time he had spotted fish and sent word back to Benny's truck, only to have another crew come flying in and make the set ahead of them. "Other day here, one gang got loaded up with dogs, and we helped pick 'em out, thought nothin about it; next day was us got loaded up, and they come along, looked at the mess that we was in, and took off to westward."

William laughed, remembering a day that Ted's old Model A had gotten sanded here at Napeague, and before he could dig it out again, his brother Bill had come along and took the set. "Course Ted got pretty good at that hisself, but that day he was hollerin some, yes, yes. Well, Bill went right ahead. He got one fish!" William shook his head. "Don't think I could do that—just ain't worth it. But there's a couple of 'em would do that yet today."

William climbed onto the truck bed as Doug Kuntz came back down the beach and took the jack line to the water's edge to tie on. Asked if he would be a fisherman if he had it to do all over again, William said quickly and bitterly, "Not if I knew how it was goin to be in these last years." He shrugged, looping the sandy rope around the winch and taking a strain. "Hell, I don't know, Pete. Probably too stupid to do anythin different."

All of the long-time fishermen say this in one way or another, and one way or another they believe it. But it's also a way of declaring something that, most of the time, they are too shy to say out loud: that they are fishermen because their fathers and their grandfathers were fishermen, it's "in their blood," there's nothing to be done about it; that this is not only their livelihood but their way of life—this is

where they belong—and that they will stay on the water as
long as they can put food on the family table. This year, for
the first time in their long memory, their independence has
been seriously threatened by a law rammed through by well-
organized outsiders who have lined up all the bureaucrats
and politicians, who have no true sense of this ocean land
or its fish and sea and weather, or any real need for the
extra money that they make on striped bass. "My brother
Orie," William was saying, "that lives over there by Hampton Bays, he's the only one had the brains to get out of
fishin, but he never done no better'n the rest of us."

A green pickup came along the beach from Amagansett,
and William said, "Here's Richard. That fella had him a
mess the other evenin." The night after Richard had
wrenched his back as a volunteer fireman, the rusted-out
axle on his trailer had given way, dropping his boat on the
road. Stuart Vorpahl and Tom Field had given him a hand,
and Stuart had jerry-rigged a new axle, but this one, too,
had busted under the heavy boat, and the men did not get
home until two in the morning.

Wearing thin street pants and street shoes, Richard
looked stiff as he got out; he held onto the truck door as
he watched the haul. Any other day he would be shouting
at the other fishermen, teasing them in his rough cheerful
way, but today he kept apart and remained silent. He was
behind two payments on his house, and his small dragger,
the *Rainbow,* was for sale.

Doug Kuntz was dealing with driftwood snarled up in
the net, and I took the line down to the water to tie on. My
hands remembered how to do it, but when I lifted one hand
in signal to William to take up on the winch, Richard hollered, "You forgot how to tie on there, bub? Got to face the
ocean, the way I do!" He was grinning, but he moved carefully, and his eyes looked red and tired. "Works better this
way," he said, showing me his style, then looked uncertain

as my own hitch, working just fine, bobbed past his street shoes. "For me, anyway," Richard said.

We watched the bunt just coming in to the soft breakers. There was no sign of fish at all, and the men were quiet. "Rough life, ain't it? What we gonna do this winter?" Richard threw his head and shoulders back and jerked his chin at me, just as Ted used to do when posing a question for which there was no answer. He cleared his throat. "Know something, Pete? This is the first time I been broke in twenty-eight years!" He said this in a bewildered way, as if still unable to believe it. "Always had a couple thousand dollars in the bank, a little money in my pocket; now I'm down to nothin and can't pay my bills!" He tried to laugh, as if this was just ridiculous, but others were as desperate as he was. Someone had said that Danny King had two bank accounts, one of which held twenty-eight dollars and the other seventeen. "Well, he's the president of the Baymen's Association," another said. "Guess we can't *all* be rich."

Now Donnie Eames had come up in his truck, and Richard called, "What's the matter with you fellas? Never hauled?" Donnie said that most of Calvin's crew had wanted to wait a little while before going off, for fear of dogfish, and that Calvin had yanked the dory off the beach and headed home. "He's been so wired up and nervous this past week, with nothin goin for us, nobody can talk to him!"

"Well, how come *you* ain't nervous?" Richard demanded. "Everybody else is!"

"Not me. I was takin it out on my wife, y'know, practically had a divorce! Everybody on the beach been doin that, snappin at each other right over the radio. And then I figured there ain't nothin I can do about no weather and no goddamn fish and no goddamn money and that goddamn law, nothin at all, I just got to take her one day at a time."

"Shit!" Richard said. "You got your bills paid, ain't you? Guess *I* could take her one day at a time, I had my bills paid. Somebody show me five hundred pounds of them short bass, I'd know what to do with them, by Jesus!"

"You ain't the only one." Donnie glanced at me. "Them people are makin criminals out of us," he remarked bitterly. ("Might as well go to jail, get somethin to eat," says Wally Bennett. "Give us somethin to do for the next five years.")

Now Jens Lester had arrived, and J.P. Fenelon came up in an old beach wagon, driving Bill Lester, who had come to see the last haul of the year. Cap'n Bill greeted me out of the window: "Don't like this cold weather much no more, do you?" Bill said he had fixed some caviar from a sturgeon taken recently by a Shinnecock dragger but otherwise had not been doing much. "Got eighteen pounds out of it, but kind of fatty, y'know. There's only so much you can do with it."

Someone had seen a striped bass in the bunt, and Richard, favoring his bad back, walked down slowly toward the water. "It's a great life if you don't weaken, ain't that right, Pete? Maybe you and me better get together, write up my story." He managed a short laugh, and Donnie Eames laughed, too. "He's got stories, all right! Can't even write his own name hardly, Richard can't, and here's he's talkin about writin books! Open up *that* book, find nothin but X's in there!" Donnie yelled with laughter, we all laughed, Richard, too. "People ain't gonna go for *that* shit, Richard!" The laughter died as the bag came up into the shallows.

"Have a daylight," Donnie muttered, stepping up onto the boat-sized bag and treading on the sliding creatures, balanced like a tightrope walker; the anger in the gesture was disturbing. The bag was solid full of dabs, two tons or more of worthless daylights, mixed in with a few skates and squid, a sculpin, some short bass: there were only eleven medium bass, less than one hundred pounds in all, that could be marketed under the new law. There was also the last bluefish of the autumn, and with it the first whiting of the winter. Ben Havens opened the puckering string, and the pile of brown fish poured away into the shallows.

The season was over and the long winter had begun, and Ben and Billy loaded the net in silence. Asked what they would do this winter, Billy Havens said, "Go on the draggers. With scallops the way they are, we got no choice." Ben Havens nodded, as Jens and Richard and Donnie and Old Bill walked up the beach to their cars.

# 22.

# South Fork Spring:
# Montauk, Georgica,
# and Hither Plains

O ne cold spring morning of 1984, I met Francis Lester at his house in Poseyville. The last time I drove into this yard, which lies just east of Ted Lester's former property, was an early winter evening, thirty years before, when Francis tossed those cod out of his boat that would disappear under the snow. The oldest son of Cap'n Frank, and Ted's contemporary, he is spry at the age of seventy-five, and continues to live a fisherman's life, though happy to have help with his boats and nets where he can find it. Francis is one of the few baymen who continues to set fykes for black-backed flounder and white perch as soon as the ice breaks and fish begin to stir in the late winter, just as his father and his Uncle Harry did for a half century.

"S'posed to blow fifteen–twenty southeast this mornin," Francis said, "so we'd better get started, ain't we?" In his rust-ridden red truck, dragging his scarred sharpie on a trailer, we drove over to Stuart's Seafood on Oak Lane to scavenge some old filleted fish from the big bins, then headed down across Napeague and Hither Hills to the Star Island boat landing on Montauk Lake, where we shoved his homemade boat into the water. I had chosen this morning to leave my own waders behind, and I cursed as a cold tongue of winter water came curling into Francis's knee boots, which he'd let me borrow. "Never told you, did I, bub," Francis said, mildly embarrassed. "That goddamn right boot's got a hole into it."

Like his father before him, and his son, Jens, too, Francis is famous for his loyalty to decrepit gear, and his fatalistic attitude about it. Tom Lester, who hauled seine with him for seven years, describes a day when, going down the beach, Francis lost the gas tank off his truck and never noticed, driving on until the truck coughed to a stop; the gas tank was way back down the beach, sitting in a hole. "Wonder what's the matter now?" Francis said. "Think I got fuel problems." The second truck, honking in vain, had retrieved the gas tank, but with all the fittings rotten with salt rust and the gas line broken, there was no way to mount it. Francis rigged a hose from the gas-oil mix in the dory's outboard motor tank to the truck carburetor and, blowing thick black smoke, kept right on going.

On Francis's skiff, the outboard clamps have worn holes through the transom, so that the motor must be set off center. "Had a piece of plywood crost there once; don't know what happened to it. Got to find me another." The motor itself appeared exhausted, coughing and shuddering as we lifted a few lobster pots along the west shore of the lake. Francis reviled it, concluding sadly, "After all the work I done on her, I could have swore she'd be runnin like a charm!" Switching the spark plugs (but not changing them), Francis urged the old motor on in a running tirade of perplexity and abuse, and observing this resourceful fisherman—the broken-down gear, the nervous hurry, the ceaseless improvising and worried chatter, the Posey nose, blue eyes, and sly innocent grin—I remembered that damned Ted and could not help smiling. "We want to get done out here today, we got to get more speed out of her than *that!*" Francis was saying, lifting the cap from his wind-burned face to scratch his pale wispy head.

Near the south end of the lake, Francis ran the boat ashore, disgusted, and replaced the motor with another that was lying in the bows. Like its companion, this motor was so old that its original identity lay hidden beneath the coats of gray surplus paint that held the rust together, and its own bad noises were mingled with the clatter of a loose screwdriver that Francis kept handy inside the motor housing. This motor, too, started up smartly with the first pull of the rope and puttered along, coughing too hard, thereafter. Despite the salt water that splashed onto the wiring as the wind increased, Francis ran both motors with their housings off, the better to tinker with them and keep their spirits up. "Got five or six of 'em, you know," he sighed, "and every damn one of 'em cantankerous; must be out of date or somethin. Fella tryin to put together a day's pay don't need this kind of aggravation. I make any money lobsterin this summer, first thing I'll do is get me a new one. Yis, yis, bub! Got her all picked out!"

The first pot we lifted held four lobsters, three of them big counters up to four pounds each; another big lobster came up in the next pot, together with some thick red rock crabs, which, like so many unmarketable sea creatures, are very good to eat. "Damn!" Francis said. "Never get lobsters big as this out in the bay, now ain't that funny? Think they'd be bigger out there but they ain't." Old reeking cod heads, white and colorless, were replaced by the fish carcasses we had scavenged earlier at Stuart's; each pot also contained a bright piece of metal or other shiny object to attract the lobster, which suffers from a fatal curiosity. We slid the pots back over the side, moving on south to the cove where two of Francis's three fykes had been set out close together, then across the lake to a third fyke on the eastern shore.

Fyke nets, rigged on a series of four hoops, each three to four feet in diameter, are pulled to their full length by a pair of anchors, creating a kind of miniature fish trap. A wing net leading out from shore turns the fish toward the fyke, and they enter the trap in attempting to go around the offshore end. Together the three fykes produced about sixty pounds of good-sized perch and almost the same amount of flounder; there were also a number of horseshoe crabs and bunkers that Francis tossed into the bow for his son Jens. "Big horsefoot like that, now, bait three–four eelpots with that. Eels runnin good this spring, nice big ones, too. Jens had three hundred pound in thirty pots the other day, up Georgica."

The pots on the east shore were empty, and we hauled them aboard and took them back to the west side to be set again. At the landing, we loaded the fish and lobsters into the truck and hauled the sharpie over the Montauk moors to Ford Pond Bay. From the beach, Francis honked at Jimmy Lester, who was out on a raft rigged with a water jet, sinking his trap stakes. The tarred and copper-painted stakes—usually oak sapling—are driven about four feet into the bottom, with perhaps six feet protruding at high water.

Jimmy waved without turning around and kept on working. Asked who owned the raft, Francis answered, "He does. Good raft, too. Every piece of gear that fella has is good, and he takes good care of it. Ain't like me." Francis laughed in his worried way, contemplating his old boat and old motors, the bilges awash in oily brine, bait, rusted tools, rubber bands for lobster claws, old bits of rope, gaffs, crabs, and buckets, unmatched oars, torn rain gear, rags, and a mislaid flounder half dissolved in black salt and gurry. "Some mess, ain't it? Good enough for niggers and Bonackers, that's what they used to say, niggers and Bonackers." Finishing his coffee, Francis tossed his white styrofoam cup onto the plastic beach litter along the tide line and picked up an old piece of plywood with brass fittings. "Fit this plywood crost that transom, maybe. Doin pretty good today, ain't we?"

We shoved the sharpie off the roller and went out along the eastern shore of Fort Pond Bay. Where the old fish companies once stood was the lately defunct Ocean Science Laboratory, which Perry Duryea and other Montauk speculators, it was said, were promoting as a site for condominiums.

Francis's two gill nets had been set in deep water southwest of Culloden Point, and one of the nets was missing its flag buoy. As a result, it had a big tear where a dragger or lobsterman had run right through it. "Hell, that don't hurt nothin," Francis said, hitching the cork line back together and setting the net again without mending the hole. "That's good enough. Been mendin this old rag for thirty years, seems like, just ain't worth mendin her no more." I wondered if this was the ancient net that Francis had scavenged years ago from William Havens's backyard, after William had abandoned it forever.

I took the lead line and we hauled the net, wrenching out dead mackerel and bunkers. The mackerel run, which begins every year between the twelfth and fourteenth of April, reaches its peak a fortnight later, and should be strong until mid-May, but this year the run was tapering off early. Because of the continuing bad weather, the nets had not been lifted in four days. A number of bunkers had been badly chewed by cormorants, and most were rotten, and the crimson gills of the night-blue sea-striped mackerel had already begun to lose their vivid color. "Struck in two days ago, looks like," Francis said. "But meat's still firm; this April water's better'n a ice house. Good price on mackerel last week, you know, Benny got 107 cartons one day on the beach, but now everybody's into 'em, all the way down to Jersey, so the price is dropped—that's fishin for you."

Francis lifted his cap and scratched his ear, then lit his pipe before we started for the shore. "Course you got to like this life or you wouldn't be stupid enough to do it. But if I had mine to live over again, what I'd do is make a lot of money before I come back to fool around the bay." Once a man started making money, I suggested, it was hard to return to a simpler life, even with a good wife who approved. Francis nodded. "Don't see too many millionaires out here, now do ya? Not *this* time of year, anyways." He squinted at the sky, which had turned dark gray. "Comin on cold. We'd better head back west to Devon, lift that other net I got off there, or that wind's goin to catch up with us." This was the first I had heard of that other net.

On the Napeague stretch, we turned off the highway, crossing the rail bed and cranberry bog and heading north on the road toward Lazy Point, where Francis's Grandfather Eames had settled when he came here from Connecticut. "Guess they called it Lazy Point because 90 percent of the people here drank heavy and laid around whenever there was money enough for rum. When the rum was gone, they'd just go clammin two–three days, cause in them days the clams was thick all over Napeague, and there was always a market for 'em. Boat would come over from Connecticut, load up clams maybe once a week, oysters and scallops, too; you just pushed a dip net through that eelgrass and come up clean scallops. When I was a kid, back in World War I, we used to go down and stay there at my grandfather's shack, so many people in there sometimes that the kids slept on the floor. Never bothered us none. Them was the good old days, and the livin was easy."

Francis headed the truck west toward Promised Land, turning off into the fish hatchery operation[1] that has leased some of the old Edwards Brothers property from Norman Edwards. Here he traded his four lobsters for fifty dollars while I peered at the twenty-pound striped bass in the tanks. These Chesapeake bass, bought from the watermen to be used for breeding, had swollen eyes turned a sick white, and later, I heard, produced a roe that was black and dead.

From Promised Land we went around the bay to Fresh Pond landing. The wind had backed into the east and was blowing harder, with cold rain; whitecaps were forming on the bay. Francis cursed at his balky motor, checking the plugs again, adjusting the needle valve, waiting her out when she got flooded, barking the knuckles of his tough old hand as he yanked futilely on the cord. There was no cough. "I'd get me an electric starter, but net's always gettin hung up, you know, when you keep batteries and all that shit in the damn boat!" Eventually the old outboard kicked over, and we went out on the bay and lifted the net as the waves slapped over the uncovered motor. There were only a few old gray-blue mackerel gilled in the mesh, and we took the net aboard with its buoys and anchors. "Never mind them few fish," Francis said, when I started to pick out the mackerel. "I'll clean 'em out later, in my yard." We returned ashore and winched the boat onto the trailer.

Back in the truck and out of the cold rain, he fished out his tobacco pouch. With the lobsters, mackerel, white perch, and flounder, he had a fair day's pay, and was content. "I'll light my pipe and we'll be under way," he said, looking and sounding just like Cap'n Frank, old Cap'n Smoker.

Francis did not think there was much future in fishing. In fact, he said, he had tried to talk Jens out of it. There were too few fish and too many regulations, too many "people from away"—scallopers, gill-netters, and draggermen from up-Island where the clam beds were already polluted and the fishing had gone all to hell. But he felt that the men who had been fishing longest would also be the last to quit. They'd been through scarcity before, and would always believe that something would turn up.

In the old days, when fishing was poor, there was usually a good clam set in Bonac or Napeague, and the baymen could all go clamming for the summer people. Now the clams were too thinned out to support more than a few baymen, scratching together a poor bushel here and there. Once the codfish, too, had been dependable; they turned up in the bass nets around Thanksgiving and would remain from a quarter mile to three miles off all winter. Francis had enjoyed codfishing ever since those boyhood days when he had gone with Ted, and he had persisted in it long after most others had given it up, sometimes with old Stuart Vorpahl and sometimes with his Uncle Bill. He and Bill codfished together for ten or fifteen years, Francis remembers. "We was the last ones to go. We was the last codfishermen on the beach here." Then the cod had dwindled, and those that were left had moved offshore, under pressure from the ever-increasing draggers. In the last few years, however, Calvin had set some of his father's tubs off Hither Plains, and had done better than he was letting on. It looked as if the cod might be coming back.

In early spring I had visited Bill Lester, who shook his head over the loss of four young draggermen in the wild storm of March 29 that had raised winds up to eighty miles an hour and ocean waves thirty feet in height. The whole community had responded to the tragedy. Almost everyone knew at least one of the families, just as a much smaller community a half century before had known the stricken family of young Nat Edwards. The dragger *Windblown*, long-lining for tilefish south of Block Island, "was a steel boat, y'know, she wasn't but four years old. But she had a plywood pilot house, and they found that pilot house way off to the westward. Must have blew off, or a big sea struck it, and once that happened, they was done. Them boys was on their way in from the east canyon,[2] and when I first heard about it, I reckoned that boat went down under the Light. But now they tell me a dragger[3] tore up his nets on a new fast that wasn't there before, off to the south'ard; the hull must have drifted some, but we think that's her." The *Windblown*'s last radio report had indicated a location about twelve miles southeast of the Point, and any boatman who has ever crossed that reach of ledge and current in rough weather could testify to its twisting rips and big freak seas. Discussing the *Windblown* after the April baymen's meeting, Stewart Lester rolled his eyes toward the ceiling, remembering his days of ocean lobstering, and describing how close he had once come to being overwhelmed by a huge following sea before he could spin his wheel and turn back into it.

By April 16, 1984, when the spring bass season opened, the wild weather of early spring had not abated; for several days after, it remained too rough to permit a haul. Of the six rigs on the beach last fall, only three were ready, and not one had the same crew as five months before. A woman had telephoned Calvin Lester to say she had heard that his crew was through with ocean haul-seining and that the rig might be for sale; Calvin and Donnie Eames, who own the rig, were still angry ten days later.

Jens Lester and Francis, discouraged by the fall season, were still fyking and eeling in the ponds and bays; they would not bother to scrape up a crew until a few fish came along. Danny King had lost his long-time partner, Bill Le-land, who was cutting cordwood with his brother, and Pete Kromer's crew of old-timers had dissolved. Lindy Havens and Don Eames, Sr., had joined the Havens crew in place of Billy and Young Fred, who had worked all winter on the draggers and figured that it made more sense to stay there. Doug Kuntz's place had also been filled. When I went to Amagansett toward the end of April to see how things were going, Lindy and Don were still trying to show the new man how to work efficiently. "Take it easy, bub, don't go learnin so fast!" Lindy was hollering. "Don't want to learn too much too fast, you know!"

This new crewman was Eddie Trufanoff, who had come to Bonac after high school from up-Island in the area of Massapequa. "E.T.," as he was popularly known, was a good carpenter and mechanic who liked to hang around the fish-ermen, shrugging off in an amiable way the abuse and hard teasing he sometimes received for his chronic incompetence on the beach. He was also one of Lindy's drinking partners, and he had been drunk that September day in Sagaponack

when he accompanied the fishermen to picket Assemblyman Halpin. I remembered him now as the skinny young
guy with untended straw hair, reddish stubble, and loose
grin who waved a beer can as he reeled down Bridge Lane,
hollering some anti-Semitic jibe against Halpin's hosts.
"Ain't even a fisherman," somebody said, knowing that this
episode, which appeared in the papers, would do nothing
to help the baymen's cause. Nevertheless, the fishermen accepted him. Lindy, especially, liked E.T., if only for the fun
that he provided. One day on the beach I asked E.T. how
he was doing, and he looked at me warily before he said,
"Not much."

Watching his new crewman wander around, William
Havens shook his head. "Ain't got his bearins yet, and don't
look like he will, do it? But can't get nobody else, and you
can't blame 'em. Get some fish along, men'll show up fast
enough, but so far it don't look so good, no, no."

William looped his line around the sand-shined winch,
taking a strain; the line shivered, and the first hank of net
bobbed up the beach. Picking up the free end of the line,
Benny went down to tie on again, as William said, "Just can't
get fellas you can count on no more, you know that, Pete?
Soon's the fishin falls off, they take off, too, and even while
they're here, they ain't much good. Bill and Ted, now, they
never would put up with crew like that. Course they knew
there were always men that could replace 'em. Remember
how Ted used to unload the bag? Firin them fish back up
onto the beach, usin both hands, like a dog diggin sand?
One day there he had a fella was usin just one hand to pick
up fish, had the other hand stuck in his pocket. And Ted
got so excited he said, 'Get your goddamn pants out of your
pocket!' Really tore into him, you know, and we never seen
that fella on the beach again."

Captain Joshua (Jack) Edwards, attended by his dog,
came down the beach using his cane. He is seventy-five and
has recently had open-heart surgery, but like all the Ed-

wards family, he is doughty. Casting off Benny's tie-on hitch when William slacked up on the line, he carried the bitter end down toward the surf. "Goin to tie on for us, Jack?" Benny Havens said, taking the line, and Cap'n Jack said shortly, "Sure. Why not?"

Jack's cousin Dick, younger brother of Nat, who drowned back in '33, runs one of the draggers in the fleet of twenty or more boats that were visible this morning off the ocean beach. His brother Kenneth, who was Nat's partner on that April day, was still sailing his dragger out of Montauk in 1976, when he died of a heart attack while working as winter caretaker on Gardiners Island. The youngest brother, Norman, now sailing out of Cameron, Louisiana, was working his last season as a bunker captain. After nearly a century, the era of Edwards bunker captains was near its end.

Leaving the beach, I ran into Cap'n Bill, who had driven his old green pickup down to the beach landing. "How'd them boys make out this morning?" He shook his head at the bad news that Danny had three bass and Benny none. It seemed to me that one problem was all those draggers; in addition to the local fleet, Massachusetts boats drawn to the freezer ships had been joined by others from Virginia and the Carolinas, and so many boats roiling the bottom might drive the fish offshore. "No, no," said Cap'n Bill. "I don't believe it. Cold spring, y'know, kept them fish off; one of these days they'll be comin in thick as they ever was." Bill gets more optimistic every day. Haul-seining with Calvin a few years ago, he used to say, "Ought to be seein one or two by now!" almost as soon as the jacks were in the surf.

# 23.

# Bluefish Summer

In the first days of May came changing weather, with big gray-green silver seas breaking in a misty sunlight on the bar and dark rain squalls and thunderheads in every quarter. I drove my pickup down the beach to Georgica, where Jens Lester had fykes and eelpots in the pond. Georgica (named originally for Jeorg-kee, an Indian whaler employed by Jacob Schellinger "to go to sea and kill whales"[1]) is one of the long coastal ponds behind the beach—Sagaponack and Mecox are others—where the seaward flow of a freshwater stream had been sealed off by sand built up by the westerly set of the ocean current. In the fifties, shooting ducks on Georgica's eastern shore, our favored method was to slip quietly up its long creeks in a canoe and pass-shoot the teal, wood duck, black duck, and mallard that would swim up to the head of the dreen before jumping up and flying back out over the canoe toward the open water.

Greater yellowlegs whistled from across the pond, migrant sandpipers flew restlessly along the margins, and strings of spring cormorant, arrived from the south, were hurrying offshore to unseen fish sign in the ocean. The ocean beach had been scoured clean of litter by the fierce

line storm on March 29 that had drowned the four young
fishermen off Montauk, and the violent erosion of the
dunes had exposed the small Wainscott beach club to the
sea. The ill-conceived jetty east of the gut, jammed in by
the Army Corps of Engineers, had been overwhelmed by
sand within a few years of its construction, while the ocean
had cut away the dunes behind it.

We launched an old boat from the west shore of the
pond, and Jens tended the outboard while John Beckwith
hoisted the keg-sized pots and dumped the eels into a garbage can, baited each pot with a chunk of horsefoot—"Females catch three times better than males; eels like them
eggs"—and slid the pot back over the side. The horsefoot
or horseshoe crab, an ancient creature—not a crab at all—
occurs today on the west side of the Atlantic and also in the
East Indies, halfway around the world, and nowhere in between; it has blue blood with important medicinal proper-
ties, black roe like caviar, and vulnerability to pollution of
the wetlands, to judge from the fact that in recent years it
is much diminished.

Jens' boat—an abandoned gunning punt—leaked very
freely, and as our cargo increased, I was bailing steadily to
keep the operation afloat. Some of the large pots, almost
full, were rolling with live eels, while others, far back up in
the coves where the water was warmer and spring algae
were coating the wire mesh, had but two or three. One
perch fyke contained an immense snapping turtle, and another turtle surfaced not far off, its dark head poking from
the water like a rotten stick. These "torrops"—a local delicacy in the old days, stored live in slops barrels—are trapped
and sent to market live in oil drums, but only a few baymen
such as·Tom Lester care to handle them. "You want to fish
for them goddamn things, you let me know the day before,
so I can be doin somethin else," says John Beckwith, a draggerman who goes trapping in winter for muskrat, raccoon,
and fox. His grandfather, Gene Beckwith, a well-known

draggerman out of Montauk,[2] died of a ruptured appendix suffered offshore while harpooning a swordfish, and his father, Paul, like so many fishermen in the region, had gone ocean haul-seining briefly with Ted Lester.

Jens himself had fished with Ted in the early sixties, and laughed in recollection of the time that Stewart had come back to the beach to fill in for a missing crewman, then argued so violently with his father that he finally abandoned the whole set and drove one of the trucks away over the dunes. "He come back, though," Jens remembered. After his apprenticeship with Ted, Jens went lobstering for three years. Eventually he joined his father's beach crew, in an informal family fishing partnership that has lasted to the present day.

Jens's thirty pots produced at least three hundred pounds of slimy bronze-yellow fish, which writhed to the top of two big plastic garbage cans, in a strange white foam. Three fykes in the cove off Baiting Hollow Road[3] produced a hundred pounds of big white perch, with a few alewives. "We're doin pretty good in Georgica, so we don't talk about it," Jens said. "My Uncle Harry has some pots up at the other end, he's the only one eelin besides me, and he don't talk too much about it neither."

Late in the year, I ran into Harry Lester at the Marine Museum in Amagansett, where he was celebrating the Baymen's Association Christmas party with his cousin Johnnie Erickson. Harry did not recall me from thirty years before, and when Johnnie said that I now lived in Sagaponack, he expressed vague resentment of outside people taking all the land. "How many generations *you* been here, bub?" Harry demanded, losing interest in his own question before I could answer. Although he had done all right this year, he talked poor out of old instinct, and congratulated me on my escape from fishing.

"Ol' Ding-Ding!" said another cousin, Donnie Eames, slapping Harry on the back. "Got to strap it to his leg, *he* does! Sonofabitch got enough there for all of us!" Harry is easy-going and good-natured, but he may be weary of his nickname after all these years; contemplating Donnie, the blue Posey eyes under the cap focused briefly in the ruddy unshaven face.

Waving his beer can, Harry Lester gestured around the room. "Somethin's the matter with us people," he muttered. "Too many damn cousins. Weren't enough women to go around back then; families got too close." Twirling a finger at his temple, he laughed a sudden raucous laugh that reminded me of his brother Richard.

In Easter week, the price on mackerel was already falling, due to heavy landings offshore and in New Jersey, and the crews were barely getting by with a few cartons of weakfish and shad picked out from the sea robins that were snarling up the nets of all three crews ("When the rob, rob, robin comes bob, bob, bobbin along," Jimmy Reutershan would sing sourly at times like these). Bill Lester came down and retrieved some small brown robins, which he prefers to the big reddish species[4] (and to bass and bluefish, too), but few nonfishermen care to fool with the spines of either breed. And seeing the tons of tasty robins dumped, pitchforked, hurled, and booted back into the sea, I regretted anew the great chance lost with the closing of the fish flour factory over in Greenport.

Among the robins were some tiny silver bass, a small remnant of the many more that had sprinkled through the mesh, and the men speculated that the little fish might have come from local ponds such as Georgica and Sagaponack, where the gutways had opened up with the spring flooding, dumping the salt ponds' life into the sea. Good numbers of small bass, six to twenty-one inches, were also entering the traps. In April and May, Stewart Lester told me, he had taken just one legal bass, and Calvin, Donnie, and Wally, with their four traps to the east and west of him, had done no better. Jimmy Lester had more small bass in his traps at

Fort Pond Bay than he had ever seen in all his life. "For a while there we got nothing but short bass and trash fish, not a damn thing to take home!" Sandy Vorpahl told me later in the summer. "I was so upset that I just stood there yelling." (The short bass has become a trash fish, her former brother-in-law Stuart Vorpahl observes bitterly.)

On May 15, Danny King released about three hundred pounds of illegal fish. "When it's clear bass, it's okay," Danny says, "because they can be dumped quickly, and most live. But where there is a load of trash fish, many bass are killed, or die before they can be returned to water. Bass are the last to enter the bag, they stay up in the throat, and we just don't get to them in time."

Not all of the crews (nor all of the trappers, draggermen, and sportsmen) were returning all small bass into the sea. Beach trucks are vulnerable to inspection, and very few illegal bass were being shipped to market by the crews, but a lot of short bass were being filleted off for use at home. I was offered small fish more than once, and felt uncomfortable when I refused them. One day I tossed some back into the surf before I realized it was not up to me to do this, and I got in the habit of departing the beach soon after the haul, not caring to know who was stowing short bass under the tarps and who was not. (In early September some short bass and short fluke would be found in a routine D.E.C. check at Stuart's Seafood, and it was common knowledge that good numbers of such bass were turning up one way or another at the Fulton Market, where they brought half the price of legal fish of the same size from Maryland and Virginia.)

All spring, only the King and Havens crews attempted to make the daybreak haul each day. Though they kept a close eye on the beach, and hauled occasionally, Calvin, Donnie, and Wally were still trapping at Napeague, while Jens was tending traps at Fort Pond Bay. On May 8, when I went over to Two Mile Hollow on a day of rain squalls and increasing southeast wind, the Havens crew, on the Eagle Boat set, was the only one on the whole length of the beach. "One legal fish this mornin," Benny Havens said. "Makes twelve altogether in three weeks of haulin." The ocean fishing had just started to improve a little when an easterly storm that carried over into early June kept the crews idle for more than a week, in the worst season on the beach in memory.

In this cold spring, the weakfish were late in arriving, and so were the small bluefish, which brought a good price at this time of year. Unable to put together a day's pay, the men would leave the beach after the daybreak haul and go over to the bay. Benny was setting winkle pots, while Danny King, trying in vain to fill a contract to supply bait to a fishing station, was hunting for sand eels everywhere from Northwest Creek to Accabonac. Brent Bennett and Milt Miller did well after late May, gill-netting blues in Cherry Harbor and Bostwick Bay. Because so few were being taken, the price for blues was ninety cents a pound.

A scattering of large bass appeared in early June, but the Havens crew never caught more than three or four in the dawn haul, and Danny King's crew did no better. In unseasonal weather, the ocean remained cold, and blues, weaks, butters, porgies, and fluke were scarce; with no money for fuel, the silent crews could not try their luck farther westward. On June 15 the winch broke on Danny's truck, and Benny's was already out of action. ("Can't get parts for it. Got some goddamn kind of mishmash or morphadite axle part, I guess," his father said.) Both crews had to operate with borrowed trucks, and still the men tried to remain cheerful. "Goin to give you a fish to eat," Danny laughed, "just soon's we catch one!" But later he said seriously, "No fish along at all. And when them fish come back, won't make no difference, cause the tourists'll holler till they throw us off the beach." By November, Danny was predicting, the last beach rigs would be up for sale for next to nothing. "Call the bass endangered! You seen all them little bass? They ain't near so endangered as we are!"

The trappers were trying to make the most of a good spring run of loligo, or long-finned squid. (Fresh squid, though delicious, is treated in this country with as much suspicion as scallops and mussels, blowfish and monkfish used to be, and is mostly in demand as bait.) Those doing best were Stewart and Calvin Lester, whose traps were in the Water Fence stretch between Hicks Island and Hither Hills. In a single day, Stewart had bailed 6,700 pounds of squid from his two traps, together with a few weaks, butterfish, and porgies; Calvin and his partners had taken 7,000 pounds in one day, 5,500 the next. The price remained high because much of the squid being taken offshore by the draggers was being sold to Japanese processing ships for export, leaving a strong market for the local catch. However, Massachusetts boats that had sold formerly to a Spanish ship were dumping their catch on the New York market, and the price, as usual, was falling.

Down at Lazy Point, Stewart Lester shoved his yellow skiff into the harbor channel between Lazy Point and Hicks Island, and we headed east into the dawn. "That's Mickey's trap there," Stewart said, pointing at a trap hard by the chimney ruin of the old bunker factory on Hicks Island, "and that's Herbie Eames, and Stuart Vorpahl—steel trap, y'know, built that himself—and that next one's Donnie Eames, then me, then Calvin, then me again—hell, there's traps all the way along to Jimmy Lester, in Fort Pond Bay, and on down to Gin Beach. But most of the big squid run this spring was right in here off Water Fence, Calvin and me; them guys to the west of us didn't do much."

Off Water Fence, where a road comes down through Hither Hills to Gardiners Bay, Stewart worked his way around the pound, or box—twenty by thirty-two feet in dimension—lifting the netting toward the surface and hitching it to the hickory and oak stakes before bailing the catch into the boat. Most of the haul was loligo squid of a strong reddish color, and the water in the trap was black with ink, but the thousands of pounds taken earlier this season had diminished now to a few hundred, in addition to a half-carton of porgies, a few fluke and blowfish, a single small weakfish, and a big tautog. A dozen horsefoots were saved for his son's winkle pots; the crabs, sea robins, skates, daylights, and short bass we tossed over the side.

Earlier this spring Stewart had had seven or eight salmon in his traps, and Calvin had caught some salmon, too. "They can't get into them polluted rivers over there"— he pointed north between the islands toward the gray-blue shadow of New England—"so they're comin back over here to our clean water."

Flying down the coast in his fast sharpie, Calvin pulled alongside to see how we were doing. He had already lifted his two traps, and had twice as many squid as we had, but it was clear that the spring run was near its end. In the last fortnight he has gone back to the beach, where a few big bass and blues were turning up, but with this stiff wind from the southwest it was too rough on the Backside; it looked as if he would have to tong for clams. Calvin wiped the salt spray from his glasses and took off again, long blond hair flying, pounding west across the chop toward Napeague Harbor. ("He's *always* going somewhere," says his wife, Diane, who has resigned herself to Calvin's intense ways.)

According to Stewart, the younger fishermen have grown lazy ("If my dad could see how they fished today, he'd have a fit."). He made an exception of his cousin Calvin, who was still "grindin it" in the old way. "Got to, if you're gonna make it full-time, got to go from this to that. But most of the fellas fishin now are just makin a few extra bucks in their spare time. Ain't but twenty, twenty-five of us full-timers left that know where to go accordin to the tide, and most all of 'em's Lesters and Havens.

"When I get done packin these few fish, I'll go on home,

rest a little, and around noon I'll be out in this old boat again, tongin clams in Three Mile Harbor, maybe pin-hookin for porgies, whichever looks best. People think them things is easy cause anybody can *do* it, but you got to know where to go and when. There's a world of difference between a good clammer and a fella who's just out there clammin, and pin-hookin porgies fast enough so you're makin a day's pay, the way them older fellas like Uncle Bill and Johnnie Erickson do it, that's a kind of art."

The day before, I'd run into his cousin Lewis, who had pin-hooked thirty-five dollars worth of porgies early that morning and was complaining that he had had to quit to go to work. Complaining, with Lewis, has always been a half-humorous nervous habit, and Stewart rolled his eyes—"He don't never stop!" I mentioned the day nearly thirty years before when Lewis had asked me to join his new haul-seine crew, saying he needed a good, experienced man. "Must have been desperate," I said, to hide my pride in it, and Stewart stopped bailing fish long enough to squint at me. "You *was* experienced, by Jesus, after three years with my old man! You graduated from Cap'n Ted's School of Hard Knocks, and you done it in them years when you had to *row!*"

Stewart skittered a daylight over the side. "The captain's captain! Remember how he hollered that day down Hither Plains when we both broke an oar on the same side, goin off? You was on bow oars, me in the middle and him settin net—he wouldn't let Richard go in the dory because Richard wouldn't put his back into it, the Captain said. Weren't no weather to go anyways, no good slatches at all. And next thing I know I hear ol' Pete catch his breath behind me—*Jees*-us!—and I look back, and then I look *up*, because *up* was where that goddamn sea was, over your head! Talk about puttin our back into them oars! We stood up and heaved, but that damn sea must've sucked all the wash right out from beneath us, dropped the boat, and them old oars of his struck into the sand, busted right off with the boat's weight comin back, and that sea rolled the dory broadside, filled her up, and net all over the place—oh, that was some hell of a mess, bub, *that* was!

"So the old man was runnin in every direction, gettin things back together, damned if he weren't goin to try her again, remember? Yellin at us and me yellin at him; used to get so mad sometimes, I'd drive right off the beach! Trouble was, he was always right, that's what bothered me the most!" Stewart laughed. "Just like me and Teddy! But that was one day he was wrong. Shoved us off at the wrong time, and on a day when we should never have gone off in the first place."

On the way in, we met Mickey Miller at the landing. "Can't change my luck," Mickey said, looking over Stewart's catch. When Stewart reminded him of the five good years he had had earlier, he did his best to grin, without much success. "Can't put those years on the table, can I?" Mickey said. Not long thereafter, Mickey took his trap nets out, and he did not bother to put them back in the late summer, preferring to scallop rather than deal with the fall run of short bass.

Rough weather persisted through the soft June season of white potato blossoms and ocean fogs shrouding the fields. The sea winds continued through a fortnight of July; Danny King's crew[5] made just three hauls in two weeks. In the mid-seventies, Danny had built a pleasant house with a small swimming pool, but these days, sand eeling and clamming, he felt lucky to make enough to pay for groceries. His seven-year-old son, Danny Junior, has cerebral palsy, and was soon to be hospitalized with complications; Danny, already broke, looked haunted. "We'll just have to grind it a little harder, is all," he said. Yet when I left the beach, Danny yelled after me, "Where you goin, bub? Better take home a couple fish to eat!" When I yelled back that he'd better catch some first, Danny held his open hands out wide, then grinned and waved.

In late July, Calvin's crew landed 180 cartons of bluefish, weaks, and a few bass. Although the bluefish had already fallen from ninety to twenty-five cents a pound, it was the best haul made so far this year. Richard had picked that day not to show up, and was so disgusted that he announced his retirement from fishing. "Meant to do it last year, by the Jesus, make better money doin somethin else! I'm gettin sick of all this aggravation!" Next time I saw him, in the fall, he was back on the old family crew with Jens and Francis.

August 1 was a soft, humid day, and the Havens crew, making a set in front of Gurney's Inn, was sweating hard as the men picked up the sand crabs after the haul. "Bad place to leave 'em!" William grunted, glancing up at the early risers on the sun decks. "Gets them tourists hollerin. Them people got us comin and goin. Don't like it if a fish gets left on the beach and don't like it if we throw 'em back and they wash up. Don't like comin out here and settin their ass down on a sea robin, is what it is."

The CB radio was crackling in the truck, and William listened a moment, nodding his head. "Calvin done good again this mornin! Never misses, that fella. He's lucky, he's got the Posey smell, and he don't never stop." But this crew, too, had done all right, with twenty-two cartons of blues at eighteen cents, and two hundred pounds of bass at three dollars a pound.

Striped bass were now worth fifteen times as much as bluefish, and the price of bluefish kept on falling. By late August, huge schools ranged everywhere along the beach, herding the bait against the shore and rolling in the breakers as they surged and chopped, chasing packed sand eels right up onto the sand. "Most fish my dad ever seen along this beach in his whole lifetime," Benny Havens said.

"Thirty-one solid miles of 'em right on shore, Montauk to Shinnecock! Why, we was *kickin* 'em out of the surf; never seen anything like *that!* Surfcasters as far as you could see, and every damn one of 'em with his rod bendin."

The markets were already refusing bluefish, and the crews did their best to unload the bag into the surf and throw back stranded fish that were still alive, but the new man on the Havens crew was too fed up to bother, slinging the blues any old way despite angry warnings from Billy Havens. Finally E.T. threw a fish at Billy, who went after him ("Look up t'other end and damned if I don't see them two skirmishin around," grinned Billy's father, much amused). That day, E.T. quit the beach for good.

Despite the crews' efforts, the shore was littered with thousands of bluefish killed in the nets; in the calm hot weather they were there day after day. The swarming gulls could not keep up with them, and disgusted anglers and sunbathers cursed the netters. "Most horrifying thing I ever saw!" one surfcaster told me angrily, refusing to hear out my explanation that there was no way to return so many slammers, choppers, alligators, and gorillas—as the sportsmen call them—into the sea. Finally the crews quit the beach. "Them big blues chew up your nets so bad, wouldn't have nothin left for fall," Ben Havens said. "Market don't want 'em, and ain't nothin else comes in the nets. Ain't *nothin* wants to mix with all them bluefish."

The bluefish moved in and out for three straight months, into November, the snapper blues attacking the spearing and sand eels, the bigger fish seizing everything in sight, snappers included, and grabbing at lures even when bursting with bait fish, swallowed whole. One big blue, before taking my plug, had been laid open by a fresh bite wound that must have been made by a frenzied fish of its own size. On many days there was a strike on every cast, until finally the anglers, sick of cleaning and eating bluefish, no longer able to give any away, went over to light tackle and barbless hooks, and even fly rods.

To all the hue and cry about extinction, the bass itself had paid little or no mind. With Indian summer, striped bass appeared in greater numbers than the crews had seen in seven years. Throughout October, in warm steady weather, hauls up to several thousand pounds were common, and although these catches could scarcely be compared with the huge landings of the early seventies, the high market price made up much of the difference. At the Baymen's Association meeting in October, a shouting and smiling atmosphere prevailed for the first time in two years, not only because of the unexpected bass run but also because the scallops, well spread out from Lake Montauk to Peconic Bay, would probably see most of the men through the long winter.

On November 6—Election Day—the beach crews made their biggest hauls since 1978, according to Billy Havens, "the year most of these rigs last got new trucks." That day the Havens crew was entirely composed of Havenses—William's brother Lindy, his nephew Fred, and his three sons. Nick Havens, who had recently lost a fingertip on the dragger *Tide Three,* had filled in for his father, who was out with a bad back; the best William could do was drive down to the beach landing and watch the trucks and dory in the distance. "Knew that was a charge o' bass soon as the bag come in, even from a good ways off. Don't know how I knew it, but I did."

On the east end of Long Island, in the fall of 1984, there were more bass caught by anglers and commercial men than in any year since 1978, with steady and profitable hauls of legal fish throughout October. On November 6, there were landings of nearly sixty thousand pounds by five crews making one or two sets each—considerably more in a single morning than was taken in most of 1983. Since the crews were spread out along eight miles of beach, the thirty tons of legal fish caught in the nets must have been but a fraction of the huge body of striped bass congregating that day off the south shore. Many of these fish were big—much too big to have been spawned in the last good Chesapeake spawning of six years ago. Where had these fish come from? For years biologists have been saying that 90 percent of the striped bass in this region originated in the Chesapeake, but in May 1984, the D.E.C.'s Byron Young acknowledged that at least half of these fish came from the Hudson, and much higher estimates have been made since.[6] Increasingly, so it appeared, striped bass from northern estuaries were moving into the ecological niche emptied out by the decline of the southern migrants.[7]

Or perhaps they have been here all along. Bill Lester says that in "open winters when warm water comes in from the Gulf Stream, brings some bait, we have fished bass practically all winter." In March 1984, the ocean draggers were taking large nonmigratory bass on the continental shelf, six or seven miles offshore, at fourteen fathoms, while other big bass were reported overwintering in deep channels near the mouths of Connecticut rivers. These signs, together with the shoals of little bass in the traps and nets, all point to regional populations of unknown size and distribution. The one thing that can be said for sure is what the baymen have been saying all along, that the information on bass distribution on which most legislation has been based is woefully incomplete, therefore inadequate.

Possibly the big fish that turned up this year are old Chesapeake cows that for some reason convened off the South Fork, but the same cannot be said of all these small ones. One day this year the Havens crew released myriads of these little fish—more than fifteen hundred pounds—from a single haul, and many more bass even smaller must be passing through the mesh. Since all the evidence suggests that "stripers do not travel far until they are two years old,"[8] what is the source of these little bass, some of them no larger than big minnows? Could bass be spawning in the Peconic River, or in our tidal creeks, or the coastal ponds that are opened periodically to the sea? Are many of these little bass devoured by the hordes of bluefish, as Bill Lester suggests? (A boat angler[9] who works the north rip at Gardiners Island told me recently that he has found small bass in his gutted blues.) If so, then the inevitable end of the bluefish cycle might permit the return of the striped bass that the baymen so wistfully predict.

On November 7, the wind backed around to the northwest, knocking the seas down, and the air turned cold. Some school bass would move along the beach until mid-December, but "the heighth of the bass" was already over. Flocks of black scoters, down out of the north, hurried across the wind in tight black bunches, and bone-white gannets with their big brown young moved in off the Atlantic to fish with the loons and cormorants along the bar.

The dories went off in silhouette on the cold pewter sea. The first day after the big haul, Calvin's net got sanded twice on the way in, and the most bass taken that day (by Danny King) was two hundred pounds. "Never get bass two days in a row." "Never get bass with them big rock crabs." "Never get bass when you see them shitepokes"—the men laughed, mimicking these old sayings, knowing that, whatever happened, they would survive to fish another year. "Hell, we don't know nothin," Lindy sighed. "And we never did."

# EPILOGUE

I n the winter of 1985, beginning in mid-February, the East End draggers made small but regular catches of striped bass, which were widely interpreted as good evidence of a local and increasing bass population independent of Hudson and Chesapeake stocks. In the spring, small bass showed up early and in good numbers in the traps and seines.[1] (On April 27, in Calvin Lester's bunt, I saw a 12-inch bass with a bright yellow Maryland tag on it. This fish and another that showed up a few days earlier in the Havens nets were the first products of the twenty-year Chesapeake tagging program that these men had ever seen.)

One morning in early May, Danny King's crew took an estimated ten thousand pounds of bass, all of which were returned into the surf. Farther east on the same day, the Havens and Calvin Lester crews released another ton of bass between them. But because of the disputed data on bass numbers and the disputed data on PCBs and the tangle of restrictive legislation that had resulted, even the large fish had to be let go, and this at a season, after the hard winter, when the men were broke. By May 8, when the bass season began, the weather was fitful and the fish so scattered that

Danny King took his crew off the beach, by no means certain he would come back in the fall. Two crews were left where once there had been seven to ten, and both were to suffer the loss of a key man.

At a Baymen's Association meeting in late April, Donnie Eames announced that he was giving up fishing for a caretaker's job at the Amagansett School, and no one doubted that there would be others. "I was just beatin my head against the wall," he told me a week later on the Flag Set at Amagansett, where he was making his last haul as a regular on Calvin Lester's crew. "Calvin's still kinda stiff about it, but when you have young kids you got to have some kind of security." He shook his head. "That decision was the hardest of my life."

I asked Calvin's son Danny, who was helping load the net, if he intended to be a fisherman, and without hesitation this twelve-year-old boy said, "No." He shook his head firmly. "No," Danny Lester said again. "Won't be nothing to fish for." And Donnie Eames said, "Kind of sad to hear that from a Posey, ain't it? When I was his age, the one thing that I wanted to do, that was go fishin."

On Sunday afternoon, May 12, Lindy Havens and Eddie Trufanoff went out on Gardiners Bay in Lindy's sharpie to try out Lindy's new outboard motor and perhaps pick out some locations for his gill-nets. Lindy wore knee boots, and E.T. wore the heavy black waders he had used on the beach the previous spring. A southeast wind was blowing, and the day was cold, but in the lee of Hedges Bank, between Cedar Point and Sammis Beach, where the Northwest Woods overlooks the water, the bay was calm.

Lindy must have been teasing E.T. as usual, for the two were heard shouting and laughing by people in the housing development above. The motor, which had apparently cut out, now started up again, and a few moments later, a man standing on the stair that leads down to the rocky beach heard the sharpie suddenly accelerate. Glancing over, he saw both men floundering in the boat's wake.

The man on shore was casually acquainted with Ed Trufanoff, and reported that E.T. had gone over first, since he saw his reddish head twenty or more yards farther back in the boat's wake than Lindy's dark one. Though Lindy was a veteran boatman, it appeared that he had lost his balance and gone over the side when he spun the boat hard to retrieve the other man. Since the two were less than two hundred yards offshore, the onlooker considered swimming out to help them—he told me he had once been a lifeguard—but he knew from recent experience, out clamming, that he would go numb in this cold water once he was in over his waist and would never reach them.

The man with the dark hair was treading high in the water with his shoulders out, dodging the sharpie, which was making tight circles. A few seconds later, when the witness ran to telephone for help, Lindy seemed to be making his way toward E.T., who was flailing desperately without making a sound. Glancing back just once, the witness thought he saw them both, but he wonders now if what he thought was E.T.'s head, low in the water, was actually a pot buoy, and if E.T. went under before Lindy reached him. Perhaps Lindy never got there at all, for when the witness got back to the stair less than three minutes later, both heads were gone. (Later Lindy's old friend Dominick Grace would ask him mildly, Why didn't you go in after them? DomDom nodded his head understandingly when the man explained.)

During those three minutes, a second witness who had come to the cliff edge saw one man—almost certainly Lindy— waving his arms and crying out for help. Then the bay was still but for the empty sharpie, which spun in tight circles until she ran aground, an hour later.

Apparently the balky motor had been started up in gear and at full throttle, kicking the skiff out from beneath the upright Eddie. Apparently E.T. knew how to swim, but even a strong swimmer would have trouble staying afloat in heavy waders, which are difficult to take off in deep water. He appears to have surfaced only briefly, whereas Lindy seems to have been in good control. Perhaps Lindy hollered when he felt himself growing paralyzed in the cold May water, and very likely his heart stopped, since if his lungs had filled in drowning, it seems unlikely that he would have floated. Yet he went under at least briefly, since both men on the cliff edge say he disappeared. By the time his body was recovered about twenty-five minutes after the accident (by a private boat out of Three Mile Harbor that answered a "May Day" emergency call on its ship-to-shore radio), the southeast wind had drifted him several hundred yards to the northwest, off Tom Lester's fish trap.

"Salt water and drinkin just don't mix," said a bayman on the Dory Rescue Squad, which tried to coordinate the search for E.T.'s body. The police divers worked mainly in the offshore stretch where the drifting body was recovered, despite the first witness's strong feeling, relayed over the baymen's radio, that Trufanoff must still be on the bottom at the inshore spot right off the cliff stair where he disappeared. "I clam there all the time, and there's no current, not inshore," the unhappy man told me a few days later, still upset by the thought that there was some way he might have helped. "I feel sure he's right there now. I liked E.T.; you couldn't help but like him. He didn't have anything much to say but he was always smiling. It gives me a funny feeling about going clamming, knowing he's out there." Eddie Trufanoff's body washed up on Sammis Beach two Sundays later.

A memorial service for Sidney Lindbergh Havens, one of the best fishermen on the East End, was held in a funeral home on Newtown Lane in the late morning of May 16, an hour which permitted most baymen to attend. There were copious flowers and floral wreaths, some in the shapes of fish and anchors, and the room was crowded. The Amagansett Fire Department, of which Lindy was a member, carried his flag-draped casket to the Oakwood Cemetery, where he was buried toward mid-day of a soft spring morning. Three old friends from the haul-seine crews, Don Eames, Sr., Pete Kromer, and Milt Miller, were among his pall-bearers, and Milt was chewing on his lip as the casket was lowered into the Bonac earth.

Leaving the cemetery, Milt put his arm around my shoulder, and we walked along a little. "Kind of a sad day," I said. "Old Lindy had a lot of spirit." But Milt had grieved and made his peace with his friend's death and was on his way back to the bay, which is just what Lindy would have wanted. He nodded politely at my glum remark before cocking his head to look at me with that wry squint. "Well, I don't guess *none* of us are goin to get away with it, now are we, Pete? Try as we might." I laughed quietly, and he laughed, too, shaking his head. It was what Lindy might have said at Milt Miller's funeral, and we both felt better.

# NOTES

PREFACE

1 Henry B. Bigelow and William C. Schroeder, *Fishes of the Gulf of Maine*, United States Fish and Wildlife Service, Washington, D. C., 1953.

2 Clam seeding and planting programs funded by East Hampton Town also benefit the numerous noncommercial clammers.

3 The finback, largest whale on earth except the blue whale, attains a length of seventy to eighty feet.

CHAPTER 1

1 Lion Gardiner's son David, born at Saybrook in 1636, was the first white child born in the Connecticut colony; his daughter Elizabeth, born on the Isle of Wight, was the first child of English parents born in what is now called New York State.

2 Like North Sea and like Riverhead (at the head of the Great River), Maidstone was a Kentish name; the original Maidstone is a seaport ten miles up the River Medway from the North Sea.

3 Originally Easthampton; Southampton remains one word.

4 Jason Epstein and Elizabeth Barlow, *East Hampton: A History and Guide*, Medway, Sag Harbor, 1975; rev. ed., Vintage Books, 1985.

5 Daniel Denton, *A Brief Description of New York*, 1670.

6 William Wallace Tooker, *The Indian Place-Names on Long Island*, Putnam, 1911.

7 The *Panama*, out of Sag Harbor.

8 Within a century of the first landings from Great River, there were only four hundred Indians left in all Long Island. In 1759

the Indians were pleading for the right to cut winter firewood, and in 1778 the New York State Superintendent of Indian Affairs felt obliged to request the citizens of Montauk to honor Indian fishing rights established in the early covenants, which were being ignored to the same degree as the Indians themselves. In 1791 Thomas Jefferson, making a study of Long Island's disappearing Indians, recorded a few Montauk words, but by now, as John Lion Gardiner would write a few years later (1798), the Montauk tribe was "small and of mixed breed, few speaking the language."

As for the remnant Shinnecocks, they were widely exploited as slave labor and many would marry African slaves, who had arrived with the first settlers.

In early days, the Indians' land was seized because they were "savages" who were letting it go to waste; it was subsequently said that because they had "lost their culture" (which was untrue), there was no legal basis for aboriginal claims. Stephen "Talkhouse" Pharaoh, a whaler, Civil War soldier, and one of the last of the Montauks, passed away in 1879. "I was quite disappointed to find only two families of Indians," wrote Emily Strong, whose father became keeper of the Montauk Light in 1885. "And they had white wives, so they didn't interest us much." The last of the Montauks had assumed that the rights to Indian Field, near Montauk Point, guaranteed them in the terms of the 1660 sale, had not been compromised in 1879, when Talkhouse died and Arthur Benson, a real estate developer, acquired all Montauk for $151,000. In 1895 suit was brought against the Bensons by the last stubborn families referred to by Mrs. Strong, and for some years afterward the Fowlers and Pharaohs continued to use ancestral lands of which they felt themselves to be a part, despite relentless rulings against them; in 1910 the courts decreed that all property claims by Montauk Indians were invalid, on the grounds that they no longer existed as a tribe. Maria (pronounced mo-RYE-ah) Fowler Pharaoh Banks, widow of Stephen Pharaoh and last "queen" of the Montaukets, born at Indian Fields about 1848, was promised eighty dollars a year by Benson's son for forfeiting her claim upon the land; she moved off Montauk when her husband died, only to have her house burned down and the payments stopped. ("Plenty of law but very little justice," wrote Wyandank Pharaoh, in a letter of 1916 to the East Hampton *Star;* he died five years later.) "Those were the happy days and how I have longed to be back home and live the same life over again, but it is too late now, those days will never return," she said, not long before her death in the late thirties.

9  Also called trot lines, or long lines.
10  Now called Devon, a summer haven for small yachts.
11  Settled by John Osborn in 1668. (The "up-street" members of the clan have added an "e" to their name.)
12  The Bennetts, in fact, are the Gardiners' only peers among the first families of the South Fork. The first of this clan, a Dorset man from the Channel coast, arrived as a servant to Lion Gardiner in 1639; in 1723 a Samuel Bennett was acquitted of charges of murdering a Gardiner while the two were hunting deer at Three Mile Harbor. Among local families, this one is perhaps most insular; in the nineteen fifties, certain Bonac Bennetts had never been as far west as New York City, which has been regarded with suspicion by the local community since the reign of the damn Dutch and perfidious British.
13  G. Brown Goode, *The Fisheries and Fishery Industries of the United States*, Washington, D. C., 1887.
14  Today the Atlantic right whale, reduced to an estimated three hundred individuals, may be the rarest whale on earth. The mother and calf reported off the ocean beach in early January 1985 were the first seen off the South Fork in many years.

CHAPTER 2
1  Probably bearberry.
2  For an account of shore whaling, see *Whale Off*, by Everett Edwards, Jr., and Jeannette Edwards Rattray, Stokes, 1933.
3  See interview with Milton Miller by John Eilertsen for the Town Marine Museum Archives; also Eilertsen's interview with Milt Miller and Peter Matthiessen.
4  Boxes made of sugar pine holding six hundred pounds.
5  The tough long clams, or skimmers (the big ocean form of the same species is called the surf clam) held onto the hook better than soft clams, or steamers, which were used only when skimmers were hard to find.
6  Captain Clint Edwards's dory, built in 1910 by Tom Bennett of Amagansett, may still be seen behind Stuart's Seafood off Oak Lane in Amagansett.

CHAPTER 3
1  Jeannette Edwards Rattray, *East Hampton History and Genealogies*, Country Life Press, 1953.
2  Like the sturgeon, the local blue crab is no longer numerous enough to constitute a commercial fishery. For a fine account of Chesapeake crabbing, see *The Beautiful Swimmers* by William Warner, Penguin, 1976.

3  Seapoose (from Narragansett Indian *sepoese*, or "little river") refers to the cut, or gut, periodically opened to the sea from
   ponds—such as Sagaponack and Georgica—that build up back
   of the beach where sand has blocked a freshwater stream; sea-
   puss, or poose, which derives from this term, is a strong rotating
   eddy alongshore.

CHAPTER 4

1  In the beam trawl, the dragger net was held open by cables from
   the ends of a long spar, or beam; in the otter trawl, water pressure against heavy wood "doors" at the ends of the cables holds
   the mouth of the net wide.
2  No fisherman seems to know the derivation of this ancient term,
   which signifies intense or extreme behavior, good or bad.

CHAPTER 5

1  Ralph Gabriel, *The Evolution of Long Island*, Yale University Press,
   New Haven, 1921.
2  The free-swimming larvae "set" after eight days—or up to three
   weeks if the water remains cold—on the hard surface of a loose
   cultch such as dumped jingle shells. Shell cultch, unlike rocks, is
   readily spread on underwater beds for efficient harvesting.
3  Good clam rakes, like scallop dredges, are mostly handmade by
   craftsmen in this region, with certain distinguishing character-
   istics: the Port Jeff clammer, for example, has straight long teeth;
   the Greenport sloop dredge has a long shank with a crossbar.
4  Sometimes called Sammy's Beach.
5  In state waters, it is ten per man, twenty per boat.
6  Codium was introduced accidentally in Greenport harbor in the
   twenties or thirties apparently from Japan, and is now widespread on the East End; it was called Sputnik weed because it
   seemed (and looked) as if it might have dropped from outer
   space.
7  Lighthouses were installed on Little Gull Island in 1806 and on
   Plum Island in 1827; both of these lights are still in operation,
   though no longer manned.
8  The construction of this problematic chain, out of date so long
   before its own completion, eliminated an obscure species of
   mouse called the Gull Island vole, but an uncommon bird called
   the roseate tern still nests in the crumbling ruin of the gun emplacements on Gull Island, which is now owned and administered
   by the American Museum of Natural History.
9  It is sometimes said that Fishers Island was named after a certain

Vischer, who served the Dutch navigator Adriaen Block as a cartographer, but more likely it refers to an isle of fishers, or fishing Indians, who called the island Munnatawket (very likely these Indians were the sea-going Montauks).

10  Like most of the beach lifeboat stations—there were twenty-eight on the Long Island shore in 1929—Georgica had been closed down after World War II, when depth finders, radar, and loran became standard equipment on oceanic vessels, and kept them from going aground in snow or fog.

CHAPTER 6

1  Jeannette Edwards Rattray, *Ship Ashore*, Coward-McCann, 1955.
2  C. F. Waterman, *Fishing in America.*
3  In this same place, twelve years before, three spies were put ashore by a German submarine that managed to strand itself for a few hours on the bar before grinding free again. The spies, reported by a young Coast Guardsman on beach patrol, were tracked to New York and Washington, and eventually executed.

CHAPTER 7

1  By this time the East Hampton *Star* was owned and edited by Arnold Rattray, who had married Captain Evvie Edwards's daughter, but it had been sympathetic to the commercial men before this time and maintains interest and sympathy to this day, under the successive editorships of Jeannette, Everett, and Helen Rattray.
2  Named for U.S. Submarine Chaser #17 of the Eagle Boat class, which went aground and sank west of Two Mile Hollow in 1922.
3  Anthony Taormina, director of the Marine Fisheries Division of the New York State Department of Environmental Conservation.
4  Bigelow and Schroeder, *Fishes of the Gulf of Maine.*
5  Until recent years, Hudson River fish were thought to confine their coastal movements to Long Island Sound east of Stratford Shoal and the south shore of Long Island west to Moriches Inlet; the bass at the east end of the Sound, entering from the east, were assumed to be Chesapeake fish. This is no longer true, if indeed it ever was.
6  Most quotations of this passage leave out the words "pass out of a pounde" (a fish trap), which alters the sense of it considerably.
7  Quoted in D.S. Jordan and B.W. Evermann, *American Food and Game Fishes*, Doubleday, Page, New York, 1903.
8  Bigelow and Schroeder, *Fishes of the Gulf of Maine.*
9  Goode, *Fisheries and Fishery Industries of the United States.*
10  Jordan and Evermann, *American Food and Game Fishes.*

11   Paul Bailey, *Long Island: A History of Two Counties*, Lewis Historical
     Publishing Company, 1949.

CHAPTER 8

1   Old-timers pronounce Montauk with an accented second syllable.
2   From the Algonkian *Wapaneunk*, "to the east."
3   The iron pier had a fish trap at the end.
4   During World War I, the Long Island Rail Road laid a cinder
    track parallel to its own roadbed, south of the old sand track,
    and this cinder track was paved in the late nineteen twenties.
5   In 1984 there were fifty-three traps in East Hampton Town,
    from Culloden Point to Northwest Harbor, and about ten on the
    shores of Gardiners Island.
6   A rock needle twenty-four feet below the surface, discovered the
    hard way by the iron ship *Great Eastern* that later laid the first
    trans-Atlantic cable.
7   In 1781 the 161-foot British gunboat *Culloden,* after striking on
    Shagwong Reef, sank under the bluffs of Fort Pond Bay.
8   Off this Napeague shore, the slave ship *Amistad,* in 1839, com-
    mandeered by its cargo under the leadership of an extraordinary
    African named Cinque, was taken in custody by the revenue brig
    *Washington,* thereby precipitating a political crisis and an epochal
    decision by the U.S. Supreme Court in the national conflict over
    abolition that would lead in a few years to civil war.
9   In Australia, all bluefish are called tailors, pronounced "tie-lers,"
    apparently an old English term, still used locally for two- to three-
    pound bluefish.

CHAPTER 9

1   Milt Miller and Don Eames, Jr., and probably others, question
    antiblack prejudice among the fishermen, although, in fact, it is
    quite widespread among the local people.
2   Clarence and Joe Midgett, respectively.

CHAPTER 10

1   A nervous jerking motion of the rod tip, to attract the attention
    of the fish.
2   John Yost.

CHAPTER 11

1   Built with overlapping planks (also called clinker-built) rather
    than smoothsided (carvel-built).
2   Invented by Captain Benjamin Tallman of Portsmouth, Rhode
    Island.

3  The first local bunker steamer—and the prototype—was the *Eugene F. Price,* built in 1874. The *Price* fished menhaden for nearly a century until she was scuttled about 1965. See "The Booming Bunker Fishery," by E. L. Sherrill, the East Hampton *Star,* January 31, 1985.

CHAPTER 12

1  The ground nut, *Apios tuberosa.*
2  Called Bull's Head in early days.
3  In 1662 Smith was convicted of illegally cutting down trees, which once extended down to the back of the dunes, but presumably there were other offenses.
4  A fast-moving storm front that appears as a visible "line" low in the sky; such a storm, when brief, is sometimes called a line squall.
5  Source: Stuart Vorpahl, Jr.
6  In Civil War times, one Josiah Kirk had sued the town for exclusive rights to this excellent marine mulch.
7  Everett T. Rattray, *The South Fork,* Random House, 1979.
8  An Algonkian word meaning "snowshoe wood"; tamarack or larch wood.

CHAPTER 13

1  See "Speakin' Bonac: Echoes of Dorset?", a two-part article by Isabel Norton, the East Hampton *Star,* April 1977.
2  The opposite of up-street was "b'low the bridge," a vague terrain beginning at Freetown and Lily Hill, on the north side of the railroad bridge, all the way out through the Springs District, which extends from the east side of Three Mile Harbor through Accabonac. While "Accabonac" signifies that creek community, "Bonac" may include a much larger area, spreading south and east to eastern Amagansett.
3  Clammers were not equated with the folks of Little Hollywood, at the head of Three Mile Harbor, who were, Sally says, "a pretty wild bunch, free love and everything." Jenny agrees: "If you socialized with anyone from Little Hollywood, your name was mud." And in fact the sisters have rarely laid eyes on one of their own aunts who married at thirteen and offended the family when she moved there.
4  Since then, Ditch Plains had been given up anyway, since the set was too small to be hauled by the much larger seine that came into use a few years later.
5  The summer flounder (as opposed to the winter or black-backed flounder, yellowtail, halibut, and others) is "left-handed," with its

eyes on its left-hand side, and right side on the bottom—hence the name "fluke."

6  Lobsters less than 3³⁄₁₆ inches from eye socket to end of carapace.

7  A good bushel of scallops will produce five to five and a quarter pounds of eyes, and there are nine pounds in a gallon.

CHAPTER 14

1  Billy Schultz, Brad Loewen, and others.

2  The clam raft program was set up by Arnold Leo, Tom Field, and Larry Cantwell, who was then bay constable.

CHAPTER 15

1  Only the phytoplankton seem to survive.

2  "The Venerable Striped Bass" by Dick Russell, *Amicus Journal*, Fall 1982. "They measure the food content and say, 'Well, there's not enough food around so they're starving to death.' Then the chemical company or the agricultural company isn't responsible because it's 'mass starvation.' But you've got to go back to the eggs and larvae stage and see, are the fish active? . . . They just don't move, they're paralyzed. Hell, they can have all the food in the world but no ability to move and catch it. I have a strong feeling that the chemical and farm industry has simply put a 'no' on looking into this."

3  "Striped Bass Management in New York," unpublished manuscript.

4  *New York Fish & Game Journal*, Vol. 15, No. 1, January 1968.

5  Dr. G.C. Matthiessen, marine biologist, concludes: "There is nothing about the decline of the striped bass that is really *clear*. . . . Some of the most polluted estuaries in New England we found to have the greatest abundance and diversity of fish populations, although some of the migratory species such as bass were not necessarily reproducing there. I think it is probably safe to say that a combination of factors are at work, overfishing being one of them. Certainly no one will argue about the impact of intensive and efficient fishing upon the stocks of haddock, yellowtail, blackback, and other species that are now in trouble."

6  Drs. R. Mansueti and Edgar Hollis, "Striped Bass in Maryland Tidewater," Natural Resources Institute, University of Maryland, Educational series No. 61.

7  Dr. Ted S.Y. Koo, Chesapeake Science, Vol. II, No. 2, June 1970.

8  Benjamin Florence and Joseph Boone, *Maryland Conservationist*, May/June 1978.

9  Judith Hope.

10  New York's pound trap fishermen and gill netters catch small

school bass up to twenty inches almost exclusively, and this is true also in Rhode Island, where in 1981, 92 percent of the bass taken were between sixteen and twenty-four inches; a Rhode Island gill netter reports that small bass bring in 80 percent of his income. As in New York, the netters believe that the striped bass wax and wane in cycles, and are not endangered. In the fall of 1981, Tallman and Mack, the Newport ocean pound trap firm that years ago bought their ocean traps and anchors from the Edwards Brothers, landed 130,000 pounds of bass—the third highest figure since the firm was established in 1910.

11  On the keypost set or flag set, east of Kuzmier's.

12  Emergency Striped Bass Research Study, an amendment to the Anadromous Fish Conservation Act, 1979, sponsored by Senator John Chafee (R) of Rhode Island.

13  *New York Times*, August 10, 1983.

14  Dr. John Boreman of National Marine Fisheries Services and Dr. Philip Goodyear of United States Fish and Wildlife Service.

15  Charter boat Captain Jim Price, quoted in "A Rain of Death on the Striper?" by Robert H. Boyle, *Sports Illustrated*, April 23, 1984.

16  The Potomac River is relatively unaffected, for the same reason.

17  See "Fisheries Management on the Chesapeake," by Dick Russell, *Amicus Journal*, Fall 1984.

18  Dr. Gene Cronin, the *New York Times*, September 30, 1984.

CHAPTER 16

1  A small whale-spotting hole under the eaves.

2  Laughing gulls.

3  Terns.

4  Calvin Lester, Harry Lester, Mickey Miller, Stuart Vorpahl, and others ship from the Seafood Shop in Wainscott.

5  See Rattray, *Ship Ashore*.

6  Interview by Susan Pollock in the East Hampton *Star*, 1978.

7  E.L. Sherrill, the East Hampton *Star*, January 31, 1985.

CHAPTER 17

1  Carol Havens, in interview with John Eilertsen.

2  Hammerhead.

3  Little northern porpoise.

4  Cutlass fish or ribbandfish.

CHAPTER 18

1  This committee, which became "the Governor's Task Force on Striped Bass," and included Arnold Leo among its members, supplied Cuomo with a factual basis for his eventual support of

the beleaguered commercial men in 1985, and won them strong allies in the governor's office and various critical departments, offsetting the seeming prejudice in favor of the sportsmen demonstrated in almost all decisions of the D.E.C. In this critical period, 1983–1985, the Baymen's Association officers—Dan King, Don Eames, Jr., and Leo—traveled repeatedly to Albany, where the association had become an effective lobby.

2 General Electric dumped its PCBs into the Hudson for over a quarter of a century, 1950–1976. The pollution was discovered in 1975, by which time the Hudson could claim the worst PCB pollution in the country.

3 Recently the tagging program has been intensified. On April 27, 1985, in Calvin Lester's seine, I saw a twelve-inch bass with a yellow strip tag on it; another that day and a third caught the previous week by the Havens crew were the first tagged Chesapeake bass haul-seiners had ever seen.

4 Arthur Bengston.

CHAPTER 19

1 In 1984 the town of East Hampton sold approximately 150 commercial shellfish permits, as opposed to well over ten times that number of noncommercial licenses.

CHAPTER 20

1 Copeces—pronounced locally "co-pex"—is an Indian word for "little cove," an apparent reference to the head of Three Mile Harbor, according to Tom Lester.

CHAPTER 22

1 Multi-Aquaculture Systems, run by Dr. Robert Valenti.

2 Eastern stretch of the Block Island Canyon.

3 The *Captain Johnny.*

CHAPTER 23

1 Journal of the Trustees and Commonalty at East Hampton Town.

2 See "Our Fishing Heritage," by S. Kip Farrington, Jr., the East Hampton *Star,* October 24, 1935.

3 Here, in the old days, cattle were "baited," or fed, before being driven down to summer pasture on Montauk.

4 The striped robin; the smaller species is the common robin.

5 Joe Olzewski, Fred Havens, Walter Bennett, Danny, and Danny's former brother-in-law, John Haviland.

6   See Striped Bass Task Force report to Governor Cuomo, June 1, 1984.

7   Ironically, a resurgence of the bass was no guarantee that a fishery would be permitted. On August 20, 1984, the Food and Drug Administration had lowered the acceptable PCB level in fish from five parts per million to two, which laid the basis for a closure of the fishery by the D.E.C. On March 13 of 1985, the D.E.C. reported that a sample of bass taken in New York State exceeded the new PCB limit, and the commercial men, already reeling from a threat—later withdrawn—to forbid the sale of raw clams in New York restaurants, braced themselves for the D.E.C. closure that they had expected all along.

Meanwhile the Governor's Task Force on Striped Bass, which tended to offset the D.E.C.'s clear bias in favor of the sportsmen, had accumulated evidence (see "PCBs: Is the Cure Worth the Cost?," January, 1985, The American Council on Science and Health; see also (untitled paper) by Dr. Joseph O'Connor of N.Y.U., due summer of 1985) that of the 209 chemical components of PCBs (a stabilizing element used in transformers and other electrical equipment to reduce fire risk, etc.) only 16 were known to interact with living organisms, and none of these 16 had been found in Hudson fish; that unrelated dangerous chemicals were involved in the industrial accident in Japan that caused the PCB scare in the first place; that two studies of fish eaters by Michigan and Connecticut public health services revealed no known ill effects from PCBs; that many authorities agreed, in any case, that Hudson fish lost most of the PCB concentration in their fatty tissue by the time they reached the east end of Long Island. In short, the data on PCBs was as incomplete as the data on bass distribution, and on March 31, 1985, the Cuomo administration, citing the fact that the bass sample from local waters had been inadequate, exempted the east end of Long Island—those waters east of an imaginary line from Wading River on Long Island South to Mastic on the ocean shore—from a new ban on commercial fishing of striped bass in New York State. Also—pending more conclusive PCB tests—it would continue to permit recreational fishing rather than destroy a five million dollar industry. It also imposed a recreational bag limit of two fish (twenty-four inches or over) per day. This decision infuriated not only the sports fishermen but the charter boatmen, who claimed it would do serious damage to their business, especially in June, October, and November, when the striped bass was the fish most sought after by their clients. In short, nobody was happy, and nobody thought that the bureaucrats were finished with them yet. The publicity over the controversy, fueled by the politicians (Mayor Koch of New York City considered a total ban on the sale of bass, and Assemblyman Halpin demanded one), had affected the popularity of bass so severely that some markets announced they would not handle bass at all.

8 Bigelow and Schroeder, *Fishes of the Gulf of Maine.*
9 Harry Cullum.

EPILOGUE

1 In the autumn of 1985, the numbers of striped bass on the ocean beach had increased markedly over the previous year, and a number of large hauls were made; wherever they came from, the bass were coming back. Yet in mid-October, the Atlantic States Marine Fisheries Commission recommended a new minimum size limit of 33 inches, to be implemented as of 1987, and the D.E.C. indicated that it would endorse it. The fishermen could scarcely believe it. They discussed defiance of this latest ruling, in order to force a test case into court, although they had small hope that they would win. "That's it," the men said. "That's the death knell."

In the spring of 1986, despite the disputed data on PCBs and the strong resurgence of the bass, the taking, possession, or sale of this species, by any method, was indefinitely prohibited in New York State, and the seine crews vanished from the ocean beach. That fall, the "endangered" bass were more common along the beach than they had been in years, and the surfcasters took all they wanted; neither the PCB scare nor the ban was taken seriously. In effect, just as the seiners had predicted, the D.E.C. had established a recreational bass fishery while forcing the commercial men out of business, and the D.E.C. made it official, in the spring of 1987, by permitting the anglers one bass a day over thirty-three inches. Since these larger fish are more important in the reproduction of the species and have a higher PCB concentration than the smaller ones (which are much better to eat), the logic of the D.E.C. seemed as murky as ever.

Meanwhile, a brown algae of unknown origin, filling the bays from Riverhead east to Napeague, had damaged the trap and gill net fisheries and entirely destroyed the scallop harvest. With the simultaneous loss of scallops and striped bass, it was all but impossible for even the most stubborn fishermen to make a full-time living, and many resigned themselves to the loss of a family tradition of hundreds of years.

# ABOUT THE AUTHOR

Peter Matthiessen was born in New York City in 1927 and had already begun his writing career by the time he graduated from Yale University in 1950. The following year, he was a founder of *The Paris Review.* Besides *At Play in the Fields of the Lord,* which was nominated for the National Book Award, he has published four other novels, including *Far Tortuga.* Mr. Matthiessen's unique career as a naturalist and explorer has resulted in numerous and widely acclaimed books of nonfiction, among them *The Tree Where Man Was Born* (with Eliot Porter), which was nominated for the National Book Award, and *The Snow Leopard,* which won it. His other works of nonfiction include *The Cloud Forest* and *Under the Mountain Wall* (which together received an Award of Merit from the National Institute of Arts and Letters), *The Wind Birds, Blue Meridian, Sand Rivers, In the Spirit of Crazy Horse, Indian Country,* and, most recently, *Men's Lives.* His novel-in-progress and a collection of his short stories will be published by Random House.